INSTRUCTOR'S MANUAL, VOLUME I

CASES IN MANAGEMENT AND ORGANIZATIONAL BEHAVIOR

Teri C. Tompkins
University of Redlands

Prentice
Hall

Upper Saddle River, New Jersey 07458

Acquisitions Editor: *David Shafer*
Associate editor: *Michele Foresta*
Project editor: *Theresa Festa*
Manufacturer: *Technical Communication Services*

©2001 by Prentice Hall, Inc.
Upper Saddle River, New Jersey 07458

All rights reserved. No part of this book may be
reproduced, in any form or by any means,
without permission in writing from the publisher.

Printed in the United States of America

10 9 8 7 6 5 4 3 2 1

ISBN 0-13-086897-3

Prentice-Hall International (UK) Limited, *London*
Prentice-Hall of Australia Pty. Limited, *Sydney*
Prentice-Hall Canada Inc., *Toronto*
Prentice-Hall Hispanoamericana, S.A., *Mexico*
Prentice-Hall of India Private Limited, *New Delhi*
Prentice-Hall of Japan, Inc., *Tokyo*
Prentice-Hall (Singapore) Pte Ltd
Editora Prentice-Hall do Brasil, Ltda., *Rio de Janeiro*

TABLE OF CONTENTS

PART I

CASES IN MANAGEMENT AND ORGANIZATIONAL BEHAVIOR

PART III

PART IV

PART I

INTRODUCTION

Why Was This Book Written?

If you are like me, you value cases as a teaching tool. You may, however, be frustrated with end-of-the-chapter cases in textbooks that lack emotional tone or storyline and where the answers are blatantly obvious. Alternatively, you may have tried the more developed cases available from case catalogues, such as Harvard and IVY. These cases often require extensive preparation for you and your students and are time-consuming to teach. How can you include interesting and challenging cases in your teaching, yet still leave time for other teaching techniques, such as lectures, student presentations, and classroom exercises? The need for cases that are challenging, engaging, and not too long led to the writing of *Cases in Organizational Behavior and Management* and this instructor's manual.

Like me, you may have relied on teaching notes in textbook instructor's manuals that were little more than a few questions followed by a short answer. Would you prefer more detailed analysis and an idea of how much time to allow when teaching the case? Do you want teaching notes that have a consistent format allowing you greater efficiency when preparing your courses? This instructor's manual has been designed to meet those needs and with two types of instructors in mind:

1. Busy instructors, who need a faster way to prepare for class.
2. New or inexperienced case teachers, who would benefit from explicit teaching plans and detailed answers.

In the following pages, I'll tell you a bit about the manual and why I think you'll find it supportive of your teaching. Let me begin by explaining how the book and teaching notes are organized.

Organization of the Instructor's Manual

If the instructor's manual is going to be a useful tool, it has to be more than merely twenty-one individual teaching notes. It needs integration. It must provide some logical framework that connects cases with other cases and key topics.

The Instructor's Manual is organized in four parts. In Part I, the introduction, I created a matrix table suggesting cases for key sections of several textbooks. The matrix helps when the casebook is used as a supplement with Organizational Behavior or Management texts. The teaching notes in Part II come next and are described in greater detail shortly. In Part III, I suggest hints to use the Critical Incident Case Assignment described in the casebook. I also include potential homework questions that you may copy and distribute to students. In Part IV, I indexed key topics from the teaching notes so you can quickly find an appropriate case for your teaching. I rarely see an Instructor's Manual that has been indexed, yet I've often wished they were because they help you quickly build your teaching plan.

The Teaching Note

The cases in the Casebook are rich and can be taught numerous ways. If you are an experienced case teacher, you may only glance at the teaching notes in this manual and then teach the case as you see fit. The teaching notes in this manual are for those who desire a little more support or who find they lack sufficient time to adequately prepare their own teaching plan.

Each teaching note begins with a list of topics. The topics were chosen because one or more answers to the discussion questions addressed the subject. Topics with an asterisk (*) are subjects that are covered in the teaching plan timetable and are clearly important to the case.

An explicit case overview explains most of the case facts and key players. If you don't have time to read the case or if you need a refresher, you can become somewhat familiar with the key players' circumstances and the organization. The case overview is also useful when you are designing the course.

For instructors who organize their teaching by industry, the company is described, including its size, if known.

Case objectives were written based on the answers to case questions and the primary topics. Not all objectives need to be covered when you teach the case, but they give an overview of what to expect from the rest of the teaching note.

Introduction

Each case is referenced to <u>other related cases in Volume 1</u>. You can use this feature to connect cases to each other, especially if you do cases on a week-to-week basis.

There is also a reference to <u>other related cases in Volume 2</u>. The 21 cases in Volume 2 are also organizational behavior and management cases. If you are concerned with students sharing the outcomes of the cases with students who take your course next term, you may find it convenient to switch back and forth between volumes. Alternatively, if you have a heavy emphasis on case teaching, you may want to have your students order both volumes, since the combined price of *Cases in Organizational Behavior and Management, Volumes 1 and 2,* is so low. You will have an ample variety of cases from which to choose.

To find cases that are more appropriate for undergraduate, graduate, or executive students, the section on <u>intended courses and levels</u> may be useful.

Some teaching notes have a detailed <u>analysis</u> section if the case warrants it. Most analyses are imbedded in the question and answer section.

I think it is important for the instructor to know how a case was researched. The <u>research methodology</u> briefly describes how the author got the data to write the case. Every case in the casebook is real.

The <u>teaching plan</u> is the heart of the note. I designed the table because I find it a useful tool when I teach. In it, we provide a timetable to manage a 60-minute teaching session. We also provide a 25-minute timetable for instructors who want to use cases, but don't want to use them exclusively during a teaching session. The activity and expected student outcomes are described in detail. New case teachers will find the student outcomes column especially useful as it often discusses what kind of answer you might expect from the activity.

I have always been bothered by answers to discussion questions that hardly begin to probe the case. I usually find these in Instructor Manuals where cases aren't the primary concern. In the <u>discussion questions and answers</u> section, you will find detailed answers and references. Often, the answer might include a quick overview of a topic along with the specific application to the case. My hope is that you might bring organizational behavior and management topics to life by illustrating the theory with real-life case examples. In some teaching notes, I provide a bullet point summary to help you quickly scan the page for the answers when you are teaching. The detailed answers in this section also make it an ideal grading reference guide when you assign homework questions for write-up outside of class.

Please also note that each question is labeled based on Bloom's taxonomy. In days when outcome assessments are a top priority in teaching, these labels will help you evaluate your students' learning. In addition, the labels help you distinguish between undergraduate- and graduate-level teaching. Undergraduate questions typically include knowledge, comprehension, application, and analysis questions. Graduate questions typically include application, analysis, synthesis, and evaluation questions.

Most cases include <u>references</u>. We tried to include a variety of organizational behavior and management textbooks to support those of you teaching from a particular text.

Finally, nearly every case has an <u>epilogue</u>. Very often students, after they have discussed the case, want to know what happened afterward. Some of the epilogues are particularly poignant. I've suggested saving time to discuss the epilogue in several of the teaching plans.

A Final Note

In case teaching, there has always been a bias toward decision-focused cases. Personally, I enjoy teaching cases that require a decision. But I think that it is also appropriate to use cases to illustrate theory. In *Cases in Organizational Behavior and Management*, I have selected a variety of cases, some decision-focused, some illustrating theory, and some that do both. I hope you enjoy the variety.

One last point. I'm always looking for suggestions on how I can improve the case and the teaching note or suggestions for topics not currently in the books. If you have any ideas and would like to share them with me, please drop me a line. My address is University of Redlands, Management and Business Department, PO Box 3080, Redlands, CA 92373. Or you can send me an e-mail at <u>tompkins@uor.edu</u>.

Acknowledgements

Thanks to Rasool Azari, Amber Borden, Lori Dick, Mittie Dick, Terri Egan, Ann Feyerherm, Dan Gilbert, Karen Hruby, Nathan Meckley, Kate Rogers, David Ruble, Jim Spee, and Jonnetta Thomas-Chambers for their support in completing this manual. I could never have made the deadline without you!

Regarding Copying Cases

We have tried to price *Cases in Organizational Behavior and Management* so that you can use only a few cases and still get value. A case or teaching note from Harvard Business School Publishing runs around $5.50. This book cost less than three cases from HBS Publishing, and we don't charge for the teaching notes. If you decide to use this book after adoption decisions have passed at your university bookstore, I hope that you will have your students order the casebook themselves rather than making illegal copies of the cases. Universities and publishing companies take very seriously professors' disregard for copyright laws. Students can order the book on-line, from sources such as Amazon.com and get it in a few days. Thank you for supporting intellectual property rights.

MATRIX OF CASES AND TEXTBOOKS

The tables below are sample organizational behavior and management texts where cases might supplement the sections. Instructors using other organizational behavior textbooks will find cases developed around the three levels: individual, group, and system. You should be able to readily adapt to your textbook based on the four samples given here. The management texts are organized around the four functions of management: planning, organizing, leading, and controlling. Some include management processes, global, ethics, quality, and other contemporary issues. The five samples of management texts should be illustrative if you use a different textbook than those listed. A very popular book on organizational theory and design rounds out the list of textbooks.

Sample Organizational Behavior Texts

Kreitner and Kinicki, *Organizational Behavior*	Volume 1 Cases	Topic
Part One: The World of Organizational Behavior	Problems at Wukmier Home Electronics Warehouse	Cultural Diversity and Hofstede's Research
	La Cabaret	Culture, Values, and Ethics
	Donor Services Department in Guatemala	Managing across Cultures
Part Two: Individual Behavior in Organizations	Costume Bank	Attitudes and Personality
	The Day They Announced the Buyout	Perception
	Your Uncle Wants You!	Motivation and Job Satisfaction
	A New Magazine in Nigeria	Equity, Expectancy, and Goal-Setting
	Handling Differences at Japan Auto	Feedback
Part Three: Groups and Social Processes	A Team Divided or a Team United?	Group Dynamics
	Temporary Employees: Car Show Turned Ugly	Power, Conflict, and Negotiation
	Shaking the Bird Cage	Group Decision Making
	Julie's Call: Empowerment at Taco Bell	Empowerment

Kreitner and Kinicki, *Organizational Behavior*	Volume 1 Cases	Topic
Part Four: Organizational Processes	Questions Matter	Communication
	Problems at Wukmier Home Electronics Warehouse	Performance Appraisal
	No, Sir, Sergeant!	Leadership
	No, Sir, Sergeant!	Occupational Stress
Part Five: The Evolving Organization	Shaking the Bird Cage	Structure
	Donor Services Department in Guatemala	Organizational Design
	Unmovable Team	Organizational Systems

Robbins, *Essentials of Organizational Behavior*	Volume 1 Cases	Topic
Prologue	Moon over E.R.	Current Topic
Part II: The Individual in the Organization	Costume Bank	Attractions and Abilities
	Problems at Wukmier Home Electronics Warehouse	Personality and Socialization
	Fired!	Basic Motivation Concepts
	Temporary Employees: Car Show Turned Ugly	Individual Decision Making
Parts III: Groups in the Organization	A Team Divided or a Team United?	Group Dynamics and Development
	The Day They Announced the Buyout	Communication
	Julie's Call: Empowerment at Taco Bell	Leadership and Trust
	Pearl Jam's Dispute with Ticketmaster	Power and Dependency
	Split Operations at Sky and Arrow Airlines	Intergroup Conflict
Part IV: The Organization System	Donor Services Department in Guatemala	Organizational Structure and Work Design
	Problems at Wukmier Home Electronics Warehouse	Performance Appraisal
	Split Operations at Sky and Arrow Airlines	Organizational Culture
	A New Magazine in Nigeria	Organizational Change in a Global Context

Robbins, *Organizational Behavior*	Volume 1 Cases	Topic
Part One: Introduction	Fired!	Career Choice and Job Fit
Part Two: The Individual	Moon over E.R.	Emotional Intelligence
	A Team Divided or a Team United?	Individual Perception
	Your Uncle Wants You!	Job Satisfaction
	A New Magazine in Nigeria	Expectancy and Goal-Setting Theory
	Julie's Call: Empowerment at Taco Bell	Empowerment

Robbins, *Organizational Behavior*	Volume 1 Cases	Topic
Part Three: The Group	Problems at Wukmier Home Electronics Warehouse	Group Development and Socialization
	Unmovable Team	Developing a Team
	Handling Differences at Toyota Parts Distributors	Communication
	A New Magazine in Nigeria	Charismatic Leadership; Power
	Pearl Jam's Dispute with Ticketmaster	Dependency
	Temporary Employees: Car Show Turned Ugly	Negotiation and Positional Bargaining
Part Four: The Organization System	Shaking the Bird Cage	Organizational Structure
	Donor Services Department in Guatemala	Work Design
	Problems at Wukmier Home Electronics Warehouse	Performance Appraisal
	Split Operations at Sky and Arrow Airlines	Organizational Culture
Part Five: Organizational Dynamics	Unmovable Team	Resistance to Change
	Split Operations at Sky and Arrow Airlines	Organizational Change

Schermerhorn, Osborn, and Hunt, *Organizational Behavior*	Volume 1 Cases	Topic
Environment	Split Operations at Sky and Arrow Airlines	High Performance Workplace
	A New Magazine in Nigeria	Global Dimensions of Organizational Behavior
Managing Individuals	La Cabaret	Diversity and Individual Differences
	A Team Divided or a Team United?	Attribution and Perception
	Fired!	Motivation and Rewards
	Problems at Wukmier Home Electronics Warehouse	Human Resources Management
	Donor Services Department in Guatemala	Job Design
Managing Groups	A Team Divided or a Team United?	Organizational Development
	Split Operations at Sky and Arrow Airlines	High Performance to Poor Performance
Managing Organizations	Costume Bank	Basic Attributes of Organizations
	Donor Services Department in Guatemala	Organizational Design
	Problems at Wukmier Home Electronics Warehouse	Organizational Culture and Socialization
Managing Processes	A New Magazine in Nigeria	Leadership Styles
	No, Sir, Sergeant!	Power and Authority
	The Day They Announced the Buyout	Communication
	Julie's Call: Empowerment at Taco Bell	Constrained Decision Making
	Pearl Jam's Dispute with Ticketmaster	Conflict
	Unmovable Team	Change, Innovation, and Stress

Sample Management Texts

Certo, *Modern Management*	Volume 1 Cases	Topic
I. Introduction to Management	Fired!	Career Fit
	Moon over E.R.	Workplace Violence and Social Responsibility
II. Planning	Donor Services Department in Guatemala	Chart to show progress on objectives improves production
	Costume Bank	Planning
	Pearl Jam's Dispute with Ticketmaster	Strategic Planning and Resource Dependency
	Jenna's Kitchens, Inc.	Constrained Decision Making
III. Organizing	Donors Services Department in Guatemala	Work Design and Global Environment
	A New Magazine in Nigeria	Authority
	Your Uncle Wants You!	Recruitment
	Split Operations at Sky and Arrow Airlines	Organizational Change
IV. Influencing: Foundations for Leading	Handling Differences at Japan Auto	Interpersonal Communications
	No, Sir, Sergeant!	Leadership
	Unmovable Team	Motivating Employees
	Temporary Employees: Car Show Turned Ugly	Informal Groups
	Problems at Wukmier Home Electronics Warehouse	Attitudes and Perceptions
V. Controlling	Questions Matter	Behavioral Control
	Donor Services Department in Guatemala	Production Management
VI. Topics for Special Emphasis	Julie's Call: Empowerment at Taco Bell	Quality and Empowerment
	La Cabaret	Diversity and Conformity

Daft, *Management*	Volume 1 Cases	Topic
Part One: Introduction to Management	Julie's Call: Empowerment at Taco Bell	Changes in Management Practice
Part Two: The Environment of Management	Problems at Wukmier Home Electronics Warehouse	Corporate Culture
	A New Magazine in Nigeria	Managing in a Global Environment
	Moon Over E.R.	Workplace Violence and Corporate Social Responsibility
	Costume Bank	Entrepreneurship and Small Business Management
Part Three: Planning	A New Magazine in Nigeria	Planning and Goal Setting
	Costume Bank	Strategic Planning
	Jenna's Kitchens, Inc.	Constrained Decision Making
Part Four: Organizing	Donor's Services Department in Guatemala	Work Design
	Split Operations at Sky and Arrow Airlines	Departmental Interdependence
	Unmovable Team	Resistance to Change
	Temporary Employees: Car Show Turned Ugly	Human Resources Management
	Problems at Wukmier Home Electronics Warehouse	Managing Diverse Employees

Daft, *Management*	Volume 1 Cases	Topic
Part Five: Leading	A New Magazine in Nigeria	Charismatic Leaders
	Questions Matter	Motivation
	Pearl Jam's Dispute with Ticketmaster	Communication
	Handling Differences at Toyota Parts Distributors	Communicating in Teams
Part Six: Controlling	Costume Bank	Budgetary Control
	Split Operations at Sky and Arrow Airlines	Operations and Service Management

Dessler, *Management*	Volume 1 Cases	Topic
Part 1: Introduction to Managing	Fired!	Managing Your Career
	A New Magazine in Nigeria	Managing in a Third-World Country
	Heart Attack	Ethical Challenge at Work
Part 2: Planning	Shaking the Bird Cage	Making Decisions
	Donor Services Department in Guatemala	Planning and Objectives
	Costume Bank	Strategic Planning
Part 3: Organizing	Donor Services Department in Guatemala	Work Design
	Unmovable Team	Building Team-Based Structures
	Shaking the Bird Cage	Reorganizing
	Your Uncle Wants You!	Recruitment
Part 4: Leading	No, Sir, Sergeant!	Leadership and Authority
	Split Operations at Sky and Arrow Airlines	Changing Organizational Cultures
	Donor Services Department in Guatemala	Motivating Employees
	Handling Differences at Japan Auto	Interpersonal Communications
	Temporary Employees: Car Show Turned Ugly	Leading Groups and Teams
	Julie's Call: Empowerment at Taco Bell	Leading Organizational Change
Part 5: Controlling	Questions Matter	Human Response to Behavioral Control

Robbins, *Managing Today*	Volume 1 Cases	Topic
Part One: Introduction	Temporary Employees: Car Show Turned Ugly	The New Organization
	A New Magazine in Nigeria	What Managers Do
Part Two: Decision and Monitoring Systems	Jenna's Kitchens, Inc.	Organizational Constraints and Decision Making
	Problems at Wukmier Home Electronics	Adjusting to Different Ethnic Cultures
	The Costume Bank	Entrepreneurship
	Questions Matter	Controlling Human Behavior
Part Three: Organizing Tasks and Shaping the Organization's Culture	Shaking the Bird Cage	Reorganizing
	Donor's Services Department in Guatemala	Work Design
	Your Uncle Wants You!	Recruitment
	Split Operations at Sky and Arrow Airlines	Former High Performance Team
	Problems at Wukmier Home Electronics Warehouse	Organizational Culture and Socialization

Robbins, *Managing Today*	Volume 1 Cases	Topic
Part Four: Leading and Empowering People	The Day They Announced the Buyout	Interpreting the World around Us
	Fired!	Motivation and Rewards
	Unmovable Team	Followers and Leaders
	A New Magazine in Nigeria	Limited and Visionary Leadership
	Handling Differences at Japan Auto	Interpersonal Communication and Conflict
Part Five: Organizational Renewal	Split Operations at Sky and Arrow Airlines	Changing Organizational Cultures

Robbins and Coulter, *Management*	Volume 1 Cases	Topic
Part One: Introduction	Fired!	Managing Your Career
	Julie's Call: Empowerment at Taco Bell	Current Trends and Issues
Part Two: Defining the Manager's Terrain	Split Operations at Sky and Arrow Airlines	Culture
	A New Magazine in Nigeria	Managing in a Foreign Environment
	Pearl Jam's Dispute with Ticketmaster	How ethical is it for the ticketing agency to keep one band from offering cheaper tickets?
	Jenna's Kitchens, Inc.	Organizational Constraints and Decision Making
Part Three: Planning	A New Magazine in Nigeria	Planning
	Costume Bank	Strategy and the Entrepreneur
	Fired!	How well did Tony plan and manage time? What could he have done?
Part Four: Organizing	Donor's Services Department in Guatemala	Work Design
	Your Uncle Wants You!	Recruitment
	Unmovable Team	Resistance to Change
Part Five: Leading	Problems at Wukmier Home Electronics Warehouse	Attitudes and Personality
	Shaking the Bird Cage	Characteristics of Teams
	Donor Services Department in Guatemala	Motivation
	No, Sir, Sergeant!	Authority
Part Six: Controlling	Costume Bank	Budgetary Controls
	Split Operations at Sky and Arrow Airlines	Operations Management
	Questions Matter	Information Controls and Supervision

Sample Organizational Theory and Design Text

Daft, *Organizational Theory and Design and Essentials of Organizational Theory and Design*	Volume 1 Cases	Topic
Part Two: The Open System	Julie's Call: Empowerment at Taco Bell	Contingency Thinking, Routines of Task Technology
	A New Magazine in Nigeria	Goal Setting
	Donor Services Department in Guatemala	Goal Setting
	Costume Bank	Stakeholders
	Pearl Jam's Dispute with Ticketmaster	Resource Dependency; Goals and Effectiveness
Part Three: Organization Structure and Design	Split Operations at Sky and Arrow Airlines	Service Firm
	Donor Services Department in Guatemala	Department Design Workflow Interdependence Contemporary Designs for Global Competition
Part Four: Organization Design Process	Shaking the Bird Cage	Change
	Unmovable Team	New Products and Change

Cases That Generate Strong Emotional Impact

A New Magazine in Nigeria	The death of the key character, Charlotte, which is described in the epilogue, drives home the challenges of management in a third-world country.
La Cabaret	An African American is accused by an African American comedian of not being "black" because he is dating a white (Persian) woman. What is racial reasoning and oppression? What is conformity?
No, Sir, Sergeant!	The new sergeant goes against direct orders to protect his men from a punitive superior. Lively discussion about authority.
Pearl Jam's Dispute with Ticketmaster	Pearl Jam, a popular rock band, wanted to offer cheaper tickets for its cash-strapped fans, but Ticketmaster's exclusive contracts with most large venues in the country allowed them to control the venue and service fee. Will Pearl Jam and Ticketmaster reach an agreement? How ethical and legal are Ticketmaster's contracts?
Problems at Wukmier Home Electronics Warehouse	A fight almost breaks out at the warehouse, and the human resources internal consultant suspects drug abuse. How do you handle the situation?

PART II
TEACHING NOTES

Teaching Note[*]
A NEW MAGAZINE IN NIGERIA

Topics (* = Primary topic with teaching plan)

    *Decision case
    *Power (sources, tactics, conflicts, and coalition)
    *Conflict, handling
    *Motivation (equity theory, expectancy theory, goal setting theory)
    Pioneering-innovations motive
    Commitment
    Motivation, behavioral requirements
    Job characteristics, Hackman-Oldham model
    Cohesiveness
    Control, managerial
    Organizational change
    Restructuring
    Entrepreneurship
    International, Nigeria
    Authority, acceptance of
    Small business context

Case overview

In 1986, Charlotte Demuren sold the idea of a weekly magazine to some wealthy journalists, turned businessmen, with whom she worked. They encouraged her to come up with a proposal and promised to provide financing for the project. She assembled a group of reporters, subeditors, advertisement representatives, and a handful of technical staff. Working together as a team, they produced a draft of the magazine for the financiers, who were so impressed, they enthusiastically provided money to start the magazine. It was called *Excellence* and it lived up to its name.

Everyone who worked for *Excellence* was just out of college and in their twenties. Led by Charlotte, the editor, and Ifeoma, her deputy editor, they were a hard-working, committed group, determined to change the "staid face" of journalism in Nigeria.

A board of directors to whom the editor reported headed the magazine. The chairman of the board was the publisher. The board met twice a year to review the general activities of the magazine. Initially, it did not interfere with the day-to-day running of the magazine. However, the more successful the magazine became, the more the publisher began to meddle in its content. If a story did not sit well with friends or business partners, he made the staff remove the article from the magazine before it was printed. He ordered that all articles and pictures be sent to his office for approval before publication. He became increasingly critical of Charlotte and her staff.

After a meeting of the board of directors, the publisher and his assistants decided to fire Charlotte and promote Ifeoma to replace her. However in case B, much to their surprise, Ifeoma did not accept the promotion.

Charlotte and Ifeoma tried to decide what their next steps should be. They were encouraged by the tremendous positive response from their readers who had grown to be fans. Shortly, a group of businessmen invested with Charlotte and Ifeoma in a new magazine. The two women made sure they had

[*]Source: Adapted from case prepared by Fola Doherty, Amber Borden, and Teri C. Tompkins, University of Redlands. The case and teaching note were prepared as a basis for classroom discussion rather than to illustrate either effective or ineffective handling of an administrative situation. Suggestions for improvement of this note should be sent to tompkins@uor.edu. Credit will be given in the next revision.

enough shares to let them have a free hand with the day-to-day running of the magazine and its content. The name of the magazine was *Eminence*.

Industry

Magazine publication in a third-world country. Entrepreneurial.

Teaching objectives

1. To analyze and evaluate the clash between Mba and Charlotte.
2. To decide the best course of action based on the analysis of objective 1.
3. To discuss management in a third-world country, especially the political and economic realities that affect business decisions.
4. To investigate concepts of power, authority, motivation, and handling conflict in another country.
5. To provide an international example of motivation theory.

Other related cases in Volume 1

Costume Bank (entrepreneurship); *Donor Services Department in Guatemala* (equity theory); *Heart Attack* (small business); *No, Sir, Sergeant!* (power); *Pearl Jam's Dispute with Ticketmaster* (goal setting); *Shaking the Bird Cage* (power).

Other related cases in Volume 2

A Selfish Request in Japan (management of conflict, power); *Cafe Latte* (conflict, entrepreneurship, small business); *Preferential Treatment* (equity theory, power); *Reputation in Jeopardy* (interpersonal conflict); *Richard Prichard and the Federal Triad Program* (expectancy theory, goal setting); *Then There Was One* (Hackman-Oldham model).

Intended courses and levels

Teaching objectives 1 and 2 work well for upper division graduate students, graduate and executive students in organizational behavior and management courses. Teaching objective 3 is appropriate for all levels. This case fits for all four functions of management and all three levels of organizational behavior; therefore, it can be positioned anytime during the term.

Analysis

All related analysis and references are embedded in the answers to the questions.

Research methodology

This case reflects the recollection of Ifeoma, the deputy editor in the case. The case is a true incident. Names and the organization have been disguised.

Teaching plan

This case can be used as an illustration of power, handling conflict, motivation, commitment, and job characteristics. The questions and answers are particularly insightful in this case and useful for examining course concepts. Instructors may want to start by teaching the theoretical concept appropriate to the topic, such as Hackman and Oldham's job characteristics model. After the lecture, ask the students to find examples of task identity or task significance in the case.

The case can also be used to launch a cultural and political assessment of Nigeria or the African region. Rich sources of sites are web pages, an e-mail to an AOL address in Nigeria, or texts. After gathering data, students could then compare their findings to the facts in the case. The answers to the motivation and power questions in this teaching note assume an American-centric culture (even though a Nigerian wrote the answers to the questions). Interesting analysis could be gathered about motivation or power as seen through Nigerian culture.

The case has been divided into parts and can be used as a <u>decision case</u>. Ask the students to stop reading before Part B and ask them to respond to the questions:

1. *What happened that caused the clash between Mba and Charlotte?* (Explores the case facts and helps students identify the most important cause and effects. Students should examine the clash from the various stakeholders' perspective/needs/motivations including the readers, financiers, employees, and management).
2. *What should Ifeoma do? Why?* (Students must make a decision and defend their reasons. Some students might say she should leave on principle; others might say that Ifeoma should stay because the readers deserve a decent magazine and Ifeoma would provide continuity to the publication).
3. *What should Charlotte do? Why?* (A variety of answers is possible, ranging from human resources issues [point out the laws are different in other countries] to starting a new magazine, to going into politics.)
4. *After reading Part B, what were the turning points or factors in this case that gave Charlotte the ability to recover from her dismissal?* (Students will note that Charlotte's popularity with readers gave her referent power, which was more enduring than Mba's legitimate/coercive/reward power.) Ifeoma's decision to leave was critical because it weakened *Excellence*'s management structure (at least temporarily) and gave Charlotte an emotional boost. *Excellence*'s ROI (return on investment) was evidently good, which would appeal to would-be *Eminence* investors. The relatively young age of the magazine employees and editors also helped because they were able to take greater risks (quitting their jobs and starting over) that employees with family responsibilities might find more difficult).

Charlotte's death, Ifeoma's flight from Nigeria and the demise of the magazines, described in the epilogue, can create an impactful discussion for students. You may want to allow at least 10 minutes to discuss their reactions.

Teaching plan topic: Power and Conflict
60-minute teaching plan

Preassignment: None

	Timing	Activity	Organization	Student Outcomes
I	0–15 minutes (15)	Read cases A and B.	Individual	Familiarity with case facts.
II	15–30 minutes (15)	*Q1: For an enterprise that requires a measure of autonomy to be successful, how do you explain the actions of the publisher in terms of power? Did Charlotte possess any counterpower? Explain.*	Small group or case method	Mba: Legitimate, coercive, and reward power. Charlotte: Referent power Charlotte was able to counter Mba's power through referent power, which is more enduring.
III	30–40 minutes (10)	*Q2: What if Ifeoma had let her professional commitment to* Excellence *override her instinct and moral commitment to Charlotte and her profession?*	Small group or case method	Ifeoma's actions powerfully influenced the outcome in this case and helped launch *Eminence*. It was pivotal because it left the publisher without an experienced editor, gave Charlotte and Ifeoma the chance to launch their own magazine, and caused the staff to resign and apply to *Eminence* for jobs.
IV	40–50 minutes (10)	*Q3: Using K. Thomas' conflict handling modes, discuss what approach(es) could have been useful in resolving the conflict between George Mba and Charlotte Demuren?*	Small group or case method	Mba was competing (assertive, uncooperative). It would have served him better to use collaboration. He assumed by firing her that he'd gain control of the magazine, not anticipating her ability to launch a

	Timing	Activity	Organization	Student Outcomes
				competing magazine (and the willingness of other financiers to back her due to ROI, which was most important to them.).
V	50–60 minutes (10)	Read the Epilogue to students. *Any reactions?*	Entire class	Upon hearing about Charlotte's death and Ifeoma's flight from Nigeria, students may feel sad, disappointed, or surprised. Political stability cannot be taken for granted. Violent or dramatic power struggles occur much more often in unstable environments.

25-minute teaching plan on power.

Preassignment: Students should read the case before coming to class (15 minutes reading time).
Do activities II (10 minutes), III (10 minutes), and V (5 minutes) in preceding 60-minute plan.

Teaching plan topic: Motivation
60-minute teaching plan

Preassignment: None

	Timing	Activity	Organization	Student Outcomes
I	0–15 minutes (15)	Read cases A and B.	Individually	Familiarity with case facts.
II	15–30 minutes (15)	*Q5: Explain why* Excellence *magazine was successful, and illustrate motivation theory (from your text) with case examples.*	Individually or in small groups	Answers will vary. See answer in Q5: There are a number of examples of motivation theory in the case, especially goal-setting theory.
III	30–45 minutes (15)	*Q6: Describe how Richard Hackman and Greg Oldham's job characteristics model explain the success of* Eminence.	Small groups or case method	Answers vary: see Q and A section. These elements were present at *Excellence* (before editorial challenges) and at *Eminence* Experienced meaningfulness of work Experienced responsibility for work outcomes Knowledge of results Students should observe and illustrate the following: Skill variety Task identity Task significance Autonomy Feedback
IV	45–55 minutes (10)	Read the epilogue to students. *Any reactions?*	Entire class	Upon hearing about Charlotte's death and Ifeoma's flight from Nigeria, students may feel sad, disappointed, surprised, etc. Students may wonder how meaningful the work can be in a politically unstable environment.
V	55–60 minutes	Do Muddiest Point assessment (For complete	A simple, remarkably	Instructions. Ask students to jot down a quick response to: "What

	Timing	Activity	Organization	Student Outcomes
	(5)	description, see Angelo, T.A. and K. P. Cross (1993). *Classroom Assessment Techniques: A Handbook for College Teachers*, 2nd ed. SF: Jossey-Bass, pp. 154–158.	efficient technique for discovering the most confusing part of the topic. Students jot down on a piece of paper with or without their names. Instructor collects them.	was the muddiest point on work design or motivation?" Purpose: Provides information on what students find least clear or most confusing. In response to this, learners must quickly identify what they do not understand and articulate the muddy points. Helps identify what needs review in next session.

25-minute teaching plan on group dynamics.

Preassignment: Students should read the case before coming to class (15 minutes reading time).
Do activities II (10 minutes), III (10 minutes), and IV (5 minutes) in preceding 60-minute plan.

Discussion questions and answers

Question 1

For an enterprise that requires a measure of autonomy to be successful, how do you explain the actions of the publisher in terms of power? Did Charlotte possess any counterpower? Explain.

Action question (calls for a conclusion or action).

Answer

It is undeniable that Charlotte Demuren had the responsibility to harmonize the interest of the board of directors with the goals of the organization. This she did by ensuring the bottom line, which is the return on investment (ROI) and the primary concern of the investors. She was able to motivate the staff of *Excellence* magazine and create a good working environment for them. This in turn was evident in the success of *Excellence* within such a short period of time.

Charlotte exploited avenues open to her for the harmonization of Mba's goals with her vision for the magazine. She tried to allay his fears and explain the motives behind her decisions about the magazine. There was, however, no reciprocation from the publisher. Perhaps as he saw her fame grow with the magazine, he saw her as some form of competitor.

Unfortunately, there was a clash, exacerbated by an imbalance of power in favor of George Mba, the publisher. He possessed "coercive power" described by French and Raven as "power utilized through the distribution of something negative or the removal of something positive" (Tosi, 1985, p. 150). To influence subordinates' behaviors, managers with coercive power "may resort to punishments such as public scolding, assignment of undesirable tasks or dismissals" (Wagner and Hollenbeck, 1998, p. 248).

Charlotte saw no resolution to the problem and had no choice but to carry on, hoping that the more objective members of the board would prevail over Mba. This however did not happen, and Mba evoked the power of his position to punish Charlotte.

It may be that the publisher was beginning to see Charlotte's fame as a source of erosion of his power. He felt that as a result of the staff's high profile, *Excellence* was now synonymous with them, rather than with him and the other investors. He felt a need to re-affirm who had the power. Charlotte disregarded his directives also, because she derived power, through fame, from being the editor of such a successful magazine. She felt as long as there was ROI she was untouchable.

The structure of the magazine at the top provided the power base for Mba's actions. He saw himself as a powerful superior dealing with a much less powerful subordinate. He provided patronage in the form of finance. He also possessed three of the five bases of power identified by French and Raven (1959): 1) He could exert his legitimate power or authority, 2) he could employ his coercive power, referred to as punishment power, or 3) he could apply reward power if she complied with his demands (1975, pp. 163–164).

The less powerful Charlotte was supposed to reciprocate his patronage by being submissive and dependent. She was expected to show deference and seek out his guidance. There would neither be resistance or conflict. But when power is exercised, employees have several ways in which to respond. She had the option to be compliant, to commit, or to resist (Steers, 1991, p. 487). The response is usually based on the subordinate's values. In this case, Charlotte was defiant. She resisted Mba's attempt to dictate what the contents of the magazine should be. She exercised her power as editor and proceeded with what she felt were her duties.

Another factor to consider in this case is counterpower. This concept focuses on the extent to which Charlotte, as the dependent, had other sources of power to buffer the effects of Mba's power. Charlotte was popular and knew she had an excellent relationship with her staff. She, however, did not know the extent of her counterpower and neither did Mba. Thus, when Charlotte's appointment was terminated, the resentment among the staff came as a surprise to both. To the extent that Ifeoma was willing to refuse the offer of promotion and expose herself to the vagaries of unemployment, one can safely say that her power strategy was "self-sacrificing" (Kanungo and Mendoca, 1994, p. 218). She used this strategy to manipulate the outcome of the aftermath of the conflict. The power tactic of forming an alliance or a coalition employed by the staff was used effectively. Such collaboration of power between the staff and Charlotte most likely occurs when parties are of roughly equal power. They used this through their willingness to abandon an already established organization for the uncertainties of a new one that might be fraught with problems. This was done to drive home their position on the conflict. It can be argued that although Mba had authoritative power and dismissing Charlotte was a reaffirmation of his power and status, Charlotte possessed referent power, a more enduring power manifested in her ability to attract the staff of *Excellence* to *Eminence*.

Question 2

What if Ifeoma had let her professional commitment to* Excellence *override her instinct and moral commitment to Charlotte and her profession?

Hypothetical question (poses a change in the facts or issues).

Answer

Ifeoma's professional commitment to the success of *Excellence* could override her instinct and moral commitment to Charlotte. She could argue that the public had already identified with the magazine and a gap would be created if she left. A case could be made that she and other members of *Excellence* had a responsibility to their readers by continuing as members of the staff and making sure that the magazine was on the street every Monday. It is pertinent to keep in mind that, at this time, there was no knowledge that *Eminence* would come into existence, although Charlotte and Ifeoma always talked about starting a magazine of their own. So nobody knew that a gap created by the demise or poor editorial content of *Excellence* would be filled by another magazine. Ifeoma also knew that she could not work in an environment where creativity was stifled by a continuous process of intervention in the workings of the magazine. There was also the fact that Charlotte's departure would compromise the very aspects of the magazine that made the public identify with it.

Besides this, Ifeoma knew she was in a position to influence the growing trend of interference by publishers who knew nothing about editorial matters but wanted to control journalists in their employ. Journalists were unjustly dismissed for not kowtowing to their financiers' demands about the contents of the journals, which they edited. Ifeoma realized that if she surprised the publisher by refusing such an opportunity, other financiers who were watching the power play at *Excellence* might be forced to take stock and evaluate their actions.

Some journalists in Ifeoma's position swallowed their professionalism and did whatever was required of them by the publishers. They rationalized their actions by explaining that they needed to put food on the table for their families. Ifeoma had no such responsibilities except to herself, of course, so she felt she could afford to make the sacrifice.

Question 3

Using K. Thomas' conflict handling modes, discuss what approach(es) could have been useful in resolving the conflict between George Mba and Charlotte Demuren.

Application skills (using information in a new context to solve a problem, answer a question, or perform a task).

Answer

Thomas (1997, p. 891) proposed that "Conflict is the process which begins when one party perceives that the other has frustrated, or is about to frustrate, some concern of his." He classified intentions in a given conflict situation under two underlying dimensions. First, cooperativeness, or attempting to satisfy the other party's concerns, and second, assertiveness, which is attempting to satisfy one's own concerns.

Thomas plotted five conflict-handling modes on these two dimensions. Competing (assertive, uncooperative) is an attempt to attain one's own concerns at the other party's expense, usually by overpowering the other, for example, through authority. This is the method employed by Mba. By contrast, accommodating (unassertive, cooperative) satisfies the other's concern at the neglect of one's own. Avoiding (unassertive, uncooperative) neglects both one's own and the other's concerns by sidestepping the issue or postponing the raising of the conflict. Compromising seeks partial satisfaction for both parties. It is an intermediate between competing and accommodating and seeks more joint satisfaction than avoiding but less complete mutual satisfaction afforded during collaboration.

Collaboration would have been an attractive alternative to competing, the method used by Mba in solving the conflict. Collaboration involves confronting the issue, which in this case is the increased interference in the editorial content of the magazine and Mba's attempt to control the staff outside official hours. Secondly, identifying the underlying concerns of both Charlotte and Mba in the conflict. Charlotte's concern was the excessive interference of Mba in the day-to-day running of the magazine, and Mba's concern was the erosion of his power. Posing each party's concern as the problem and finding out a way in which both parties concerns can be satisfied may have helped to resolve the conflict. Thirdly, finding alternatives to Mba's insistence on proofreading the magazine and Charlotte's refusal to cut down on her public profile and selecting the most jointly satisfactory alternative could have settled the conflict. A combination of "third parties" such as the board of directors and heads of departments would have been the appropriate body to intervene in the conflict. However, the board showed very little interest, and the heads of departments were not given the opportunity to intervene.

Question 4

***What premises of the pioneering-innovating (PI) motive, and Maslow's self-actualization need are present in the founding of* Eminence?**

Relational question (asks for comparisons of themes, ideas, or issues).

Answer

The PI motive—pioneering innovating motive—is the need for a unique accomplishment. *Eminence* was the first magazine to be established by women, and it was the idea of Charlotte Demuren who had always dreamed of owning her own magazine. Among the various groups in Nigeria, professionals can be particularly important agents of social change. Sometimes from impoverished backgrounds, living in a deprived society, their exposure to western technologies and ideas is likely to strengthen their modernity orientation. Maslow's self actualization need shares the same concern for growth and change with the PI motive, but while the self actualization motive is concerned with actualizing one's potential, the PI motive is concerned with unique innovative and path-breaking achievements. "The achievement motive is concerned with task achievement as is the PI motive, but while the achievement motive is concerned with achievement of all types of tasks the PI motive is concerned with transformational task" (Kanungo and Mendoca, 1994, p. 116).

Thus Charlotte satisfied her PI motive by establishing a magazine, the first by female entrepreneurs in the country. She also wanted to give back to a society that had come to her aid when she needed to go to school. She wanted to make a change with the proceeds from the magazine, so she established a home for the elderly. She also satisfied her need to make *Eminence* the largest selling magazine in the country.

A New Magazine in Nigeria

Question 5

Explain why* Excellence *magazine was successful, and illustrate motivation theory (from your text) with case examples.

Application skills (using information in a new context to solve a problem, answer a question, or perform a task).

Answer

The collective motivation and mutual cooperation that existed in *Excellence* magazine ultimately led to its success. The staff worked together as a team, and the employees looked on themselves as belonging to a family whose aspirations and objectives they felt committed to strive for. This cohesion was fostered by Charlotte and reinforced by the line editors. Consequently, every employee recognized that the family must succeed and could only do so by superior performance. Other factors were also crucial.

The success of the magazine can be explained using three theories of employee motivation: equity theory, goal-setting theory, and expectancy theory. Equity theory, a social comparison theory, focuses on individuals' feelings about perceptions of how fairly they are being treated compared to others (Weick, 1966, pp. 414–418). The staff of *Excellence* was highly paid compared to journalists in other magazines and more was expected of them. They also had a sense of being fairly treated by the management until the meddling of Mba in editorial matters.

The second theory of motivation, goal setting, propounded by Locke and Latham (Steers, 1991, p. 156–162) was also present. Right from the onset, the goal of *Excellence* was to fill the void created by the nonexistence of its type of publication and consolidate this goal by being the largest selling magazine in the country. The staff knew what the country lacked in terms of what the readers wanted, and they provided it. This led the staff to focus on both the desired and the attainable goals. It also enhanced their persistence and made them more creative in developing new strategies and action plans.

The staff of *Excellence* knew that if they worked hard, they would be rewarded, and the harder they worked, the greater the reward. Thus, the number of by-lines and story ideas one had was what determined the reward one got. The reward ranged from public recognition to cash awards and sponsored vacations. So there was the financial motivation to make the magazine successful. This correlates with Vroom's expectancy and valence theory, which is a belief that a particular behavioral act (such as working hard) will lead to a particular outcome (such as pay). This proved another factor that contributed to the success of the journal.

Organizations need three things from their employees in order to succeed, and these are referred to as the three behavioral requirements (Steers, 1991, p. 172). They are: commitment to remaining with the organization, dependable role performance, and spontaneous and innovative behavior—all of which the staff possessed. The staff of *Excellence* possessed the abilities, traits, will and desire to work. There was role clarity and acceptance and the opportunity to perform in order to achieve success.

Question 6

Describe how Richard Hackman and Greg Oldham's job characteristics model explain the success of* Eminence.

Application skills (using information in a new context to solve a problem, answer a question, or perform a task).

Answer

The Hackman and Oldham model postulates that internal rewards are obtained by an individual when he learns that he personally has performed well on a task that he cares about (Steers, 1991, p. 263). According to the model, employees' motivation and satisfaction are influenced by three psychological states:

- Experienced meaningfulness of work. Employees must feel that the work is important, worthwhile, and valuable. Coming from a background where they knew their work was important helped *Eminence*. The staff carried this feeling from *Excellence*, and this contributed to the success of the magazine.
- Experienced responsibility for work outcomes. Employees must feel personally responsible for the results of the work they perform.
- Knowledge of results. Employees must receive regular feedback concerning the quality of their performance. The staff of *Eminence* received feedback not only from their editors, but readers also

commended the staff when they felt their stories were good and did not hesitate to say so when they felt otherwise.

Hackman postulates what activates these psychological states:

- Skill variety, or the degree to which a job requires a number of different skills and talents. Journalism requires one to have such skills as writing, gathering news and stories, and being able to predict which would arouse readers' interests sufficiently to buy the magazine time and again.

- Task identity is the degree to which the job requires completion of a whole and identifiable piece of work. The only part of their job that the staff of *Eminence* did not have to engage in was done by machines, which in turn were staffed by technical personnel. The job began with story suggestions, then moved to gathering the information, writing the stories, proofreading, and laying out the pages of the magazine. This pattern of involvement bred a distinct sense of identification with both process and end product.

- Task significance is the degree to which a job has an impact on the lives or work of other people in the immediate organization and or in the external environment. Evidence of their job's impact on the external environment can be deduced from public feedback and the sales of the magazine. It became the highest circulating magazine within a few months of its existence. The turnout at Charlotte's funeral was a pointer to the impact of the magazine on the lives of many.

- Autonomy is the degree to which a job provides substantial freedom, independence, and discretion to an individual for purposes of scheduling work and determining the procedures to be used in carrying it out. Due to the very nature of the work itself, reporters could not be told when to report to the office or choice of expression to be used in writing the stories. So reporters had a lot of autonomy and were required to attend a conference only once a week to discuss their story ideas, strategies for gathering information for the stories, and deadlines for submitting them. They were left on their own to carry out their responsibilities.

- Feedback is the degree to which carrying out work activities required by the job results in individuals obtaining direct and clear information about the effectiveness of their performance. Staff did get feedback not only from readers as indicated earlier, but also there were awards and recognition nights when excellent contributions were acknowledged.

Finally, the model indicates that several personal and work-related outcomes result from the interaction of psychological states. Specifically, when people experience the psychological states described, one would expect them to exhibit high levels of internal work motivation, high quality of performance, high job satisfaction, and low turnover and absenteeism. Although the psychological states are not the only variables to affect outcomes, they are however believed to be important influences (Steers, 1991, p. 265). The staff of *Eminence* possessed these core job dimensions, and these in no small measure led to the success of the magazine.

References

Angelo, T.A. and Cross, P. (1993). *Classroom assessment techniques: A handbook for college teachers*, 2nd ed. San Francisco: Jossey-Bass.

French, J.R.P., Jr., and Raven, B. (1959). "The Bases of Social Power" in D. Cartwright (ed.), *Studies in social power*. Ann Arbor, University of Michigan, Institute for Social Research.

Hackman, J.R., and Oldham, G.R. (April 1975). "Development of the job diagnostic survey," *Journal of Applied Psychology*, pp. 159–170.

Kanungo, Rabindara, N., and Mendonca, M. (1994). *Work motivation: models for developing countries*. Thousand Oaks, CA: Sage.

Locke, E.A. and Latham, G.P. (1990). *A theory of goal setting and task performance*. Upper Saddle River, NJ: Prentice Hall.

Steers, R. M. (1991). *Introduction to organizational behavior*, 4th ed. NY: HarperCollins.

Thomas, K.W. (1997). *Toward multi-dimensional values in teaching: The example of conflict behaviors.* Thousand Oaks, CA: Sage.

Tosi, H. L., and Hamner, C. W. (1985). *Organizational behavior and management*, 4th ed., Grid, Inc.

Wagner, J.A. and Hollenbeck, R.J. (1998). *Organizational behavior: seeking competitive advantage*, 3rd ed. Upper Saddle River, NJ: Prentice Hall.

Weick, K. (1966). *The concept of equity in the perception of pay*. New York Academy Press.

Epilogue

In 1995, Ifeoma had to flee the country when the military regime of Nigeria became too repressive, threatening her family and locking up journalists whom the new dictator accused of plotting against him. The others continued to work on improving the magazine and fulfilling its goals.

Charlotte died in 1996, from complications from surgery; she was thirty-seven years old. Even in death, the publicity for which she was fired from *Excellence* trailed her. She was mourned by the national press and those lives she had touched, from her readers to the old people who had benefited so much from the proceeds of the magazine. Those who could not afford the bus fare walked for miles to her residence to pay their respects and bid her their final farewell.

Excellence and *Eminence* are no longer in existence nor are many other Nigerian magazines, thanks to the last military dictator. Importing or even buying raw materials such as newsprint, became such a problem that the magazines had to close down their operations.

A TEAM DIVIDED OR A TEAM UNITED?

Topics (* = Primary topic with teaching plan)
* * Synthesis case
* * Cohesiveness
* *Group dynamics
* *Interpersonal relationships
* *Leadership, autocratic
* *Leadership of groups
* Job satisfaction
* Conformity
* Control, managerial
* Empowerment or participative decision making
* Communication
* Termination

Case overview

Dan, Madeline, and Mark considered themselves lucky. They worked for Marketing Research Int'l, a great international marketing company, and in the short time they had worked together, they had become not only work friends, but social friends.

Now Madeline and Dan waited for a meeting to be called by their boss, Claire. They already knew the purpose of the meeting, and they angrily waited to see how she would communicate the fact that she had fired their friend Mark.

Claire was the sales/marketing manager, about 35 years old, with a master of international business from Thunderbird International School of Business. She had worked for the company for two years. She had three direct reports, Dan, Mark and Madeline . This was her first experience directly managing people.

In the first year, each team member had achieved his or her revenue target. However, Claire suspected that there was some dissatisfaction in the team, and she thought Mark instigated most of it. Claire thought that he created a disruptive atmosphere and that the team was being led astray. He called her "boss lady" behind her back, which infuriated her. Whenever there was a complaint about policy or how the team was managed, it usually came from Mark. He continually played the devil's advocate. A group decision was always a drawn-out process because of his interruptions and barrage of questions.

By mid-1994, it appeared that Mark would not reach his year-end revenue targets.

Mark was 30 years old with a master of international business from Thunderbird, as well. Mark felt that Claire said she wanted group decisions, but really wanted the team to agree with her. "I wouldn't kiss up to her and be a 'yes' person like she wanted, and she couldn't take it."

Dan was 27 years old, working on his master of marketing at Kellogg School of Business. As the only two men, Dan and Mark bonded quickly. Dan encouraged Mark to try another angle with Claire, but Mark wouldn't listen to his advice. Although he believed that Mark dug his own grave, he also believed that Claire was a poor manager and made her differences with Mark personal.

Madeline was 25 years old with an MBA from Drucker Graduate Management Center. In her opinion, Mark was the most qualified member of the team. She felt that Mark had smaller, less developed clients, and he had one client that required extra attention, leaving him little opportunity to develop sales opportunities with other clients.

The group's mission was to bring integrated multi-country databases into the corporate headquarters of fast-moving consumer goods manufacturers. On a work level, the three sales representatives were a cohesive team.

Back in the conference room, Claire entered and cheerfully greeted everyone in the room. "Mark's not here today because we had to let him go. He's wasn't making has revenue numbers and things weren't

---

*Source: Adapted from case prepared by Marlene Lowe, Amber Borden, and Teri C. Tompkins University of Redlands. The case and teaching note were prepared as a basis for class discussion rather than to illustrate either effective or ineffective handling of administrative situations. Suggestions for improvement of this note should be sent to tompkins@uor.edu. Credit will be given in the next revision.

working out. It's best for everybody. I do have some good news. We've hired a new person, Sharon Marello, and she will be starting on Monday."

Industry

Marketing Research Int'l is one of the largest marketing research firms in the world.

Teaching objectives

1. To explore factors that contribute to job satisfaction and group cohesiveness.
2. To analyze interpersonal relationships and to decide how interpersonal relationships affect leader behavior.
3. To evaluate the strengths and weaknesses of a leader in helping a team develop.
4. To recommend a course of action to improve team productivity.
5. To decide whether termination should occur, and if so, how it should be conducted.

Other related cases in Volume 1

Problems at Wukmier Home Electronics Warehouse (termination); *Temporary Employees: Car Show Turned Ugly* (cohesiveness).

Other related cases in Volume 2

Angry Branch Manager (termination); *Cost and Schedule Team at AVIONICS* (cohesiveness; interpersonal relations); *Heart Attack* (termination).

Intended courses and levels

This case works well for all levels: undergraduate (explore job satisfaction and group cohesiveness), graduate (objectives 2 and 3), and executive (objectives 4 and 5). It can be positioned at any time during the course, especially during group level OB course, or decision making or productivity in management courses.

Analysis

All related analysis and references are embedded in the answers to the questions.

Research methodology

The author interviewed Madeleine, Dan, and Mark to write this case. She did not contact Claire, the other members of the team, or Marketing Research Int'l company for alternative views of the case. The company is disguised, and the names of the characters have been changed.

Teaching plan

Teaching plan topic: Cohesiveness, Interpersonal Relationships, and Leadership
60-minute teaching plan

Preassignment: Students read case before class (15 minutes)

	Timing	Activity	Organization	Student Outcomes
I	0–15 minutes (15)	Read case.	Individually	Familiarity with case facts.
II	15–25 minutes (10)	*Q1: What factors contributed to Madeleine, Dan, and Mark's job satisfaction before Mark's firing?*	If used as a synthesis case, use small group or as a take-home case. Otherwise, case discussion format. Alternative: to allow	Students discover that they were three cohesive members of a noncohesive team who valued each other, worked hard, and had a common nemesis—Claire.

	Timing	Activity	Organization	Student Outcomes
			more time for each section, assign one question per group.	
III	25–35 minutes (10)	*Q2: Contrast Dan and Mark's interpersonal relationships with Claire. Why did Claire respond to each one differently when they both felt the same way about her? What conclusions do you draw?*	Same as II	Dan and Mark both disliked Claire. Dan tried to "get along" with Claire and cover up his feelings. Mark's personal characteristic didn't allow him to hide his feelings, and he was confrontational with Claire. Consequently Claire treated Dan as the favored member and Mark as the enemy.
IV	35–45 minutes (10)	*Q3: What were Claire's strengths and weaknesses as a leader?*	Same as II	Strengths: Ability to network and offer advice. Weaknesses: Poor listening skills, autocratic style.
V	45–55 minutes (10)	*Q4: Suppose you were a consultant to Claire; what advice would you give her to help her achieve the goals set for her department?*	Same as II	• Increase interactions or contact with team members in order to decrease isolation. • Create an open, safe environment that is free of retribution. • Open communications.
VI	55–60 minutes (5)	Summarize.	Full class discussion.	Students see how this case relates to the topic. You may want to tie it to other related cases.

25-minute teaching plan on cohesiveness, interpersonal relationships, and leadership.
Preassignment: Students should read the case before coming to class (15 minutes reading time).
Divide the class into four groups. Each group answers one question from II, III, IV, and V (10 minutes) in preceding 60-minute plan. Report out answers to full class (15 minutes).

Discussion questions and answers

Question 1
What factors contributed to Madeleine, Dan, and Mark's job satisfaction before Mark's firing?
<u>Exploratory question</u> (probes facts and basic knowledge).
Answer
- Common attitudes, interests, and goals
- Frequent interactions or contact
- Small size of group

Based on Wagner and Hollenbeck's analysis of group cohesiveness, there were four factors that encouraged group cohesiveness and resulted in job satisfaction for Madeleine, Dan, and Mark.

First, Madeleine, Dan, and Mark share many common personal attitudes and interests ranging from their dislike of Claire's management style to volleyball and their love for Chicago.

Second, there was strong agreement and dedication to their work goal—sales. Their competitiveness helped them achieve their sales target.

Third, their frequency of interaction—they worked closely both in the office as well as in social settings.

Finally the size of the team increased the group's cohesiveness. Because there were only three of them, each individual had many opportunities to interact with the other two and get to know each other better.

Question 2

Contrast Dan and Mark's interpersonal relationships with Claire. Why did Claire respond to each one differently when they both felt the same way about her? What conclusions do you draw from this analysis?

Analysis skills (breaking a concept into its parts and explaining their interrelationships, distinguishing relevant from extraneous material).

Answer

- In-group or out-group perceptions
- Perceived similarity
- Performing tasks beyond the formal job description

Dan and Mark took dramatically different approaches to Claire. Mark's headstrong personality compelled him to relate to Claire in a brutally honest manner. Dan chose to be subtler and manage his relationship to Claire. These approaches elicited dramatically different responses from Claire.

Claire's responses can be explained by George Grain's vertical dyad linkage theory of leadership. According to this theory a vertical dyad consists of two persons who are linked hierarchically. Because each person is an individual, each dyad relationship is unique. Because Claire viewed her relationship with Dan as amiable, she was more considerate and tolerant of him as compared to Mark.

Vertical dyad linkage theory also suggests that leaders tend to classify subordinates into in-group members and out-group members. Often, a leader will use arbitrary selection criteria to choose members for each group. The in-group members are willing and able to do more than the tasks outlined in a formal job description. Once they have been identified, the leader gives these people more latitude, authority, and consideration. This may be what Dan referred to when he explained that if he managed Claire properly, she would grant him autonomy. Dan encouraged Mark to become an in-group member by not challenging Claire, but Mark did not take Dan's advice and soon found himself in the out-group. The out-group members either cannot or will not expand their roles beyond formal requirements. Leaders assign these individuals more routine tasks, give them less consideration, and communicate less often with them. This could explain why Mark received the less desirable clients. Being assigned to the out-group was also detrimental to the communication between Claire and Mark.

Question 3

What were Claire's strengths and weaknesses as a leader?

Evaluation skills (using a set of criteria to arrive at a reasoned judgment of the value of something).

Answer

- Strengths: ability to network, set a clear agenda, and follow through
- Weaknesses: poor leadership skills, poor communications skills, and inability to empower team

Claire's strength as a leader was her ability to network, set a clear agenda, and follow through with it. Her weaknesses included poor communication skills and an inability to empower her team. Claire's leadership style stifled free communication from Dan and Madeleine. Dan and Madeleine shared Mark's opinion of Claire; however, because of fears of retribution by Claire, neither was willing to vocalize his or her point of view. Claire lost the valuable input of her team members. Thus decisions were based on the solutions that she dictated to the team. Mark, Dan, and Madeleine's knowledge and creativity were missing, and therefore the solutions were likely to be less comprehensive and certainly less accepted.

Question 4

Suppose you were a consultant to Claire, what advice would you give her to help her achieve the production goals set for her department?

Evaluation skills (using a set of criteria to arrive at a reasoned judgment of the value of something).

Answer

- Increase interactions or contact with team members in order to decrease isolation.
- Create an open, safe environment that is free of retribution.
- Open communications.

Efforts should be made to increase Claire's team interaction to decrease the sense of isolation from the team and to foster an environment of openness.

Claire needs to make a greater effort at the group level as well as at the individual level to improve her relationship with her team. One way to improve the relationship with the team would be to increase her frequency of positive interactions with the team, such as working on projects with individuals, traveling to client meetings with team members, and so forth. This would allow Claire the opportunity to interact with members of her team, show them her competency, allow her the opportunity for her to see each member's abilities at work and to build a personal relationship with team members. This may help Claire reduce her isolation from the team and become less of an "out-group" member of her team.

Another way to bridge her isolation from the team and improve communication is to provide an environment of openness. According to Wagner and Hollenbeck (1995, p. 422) one of the key values underlying organizational development is openness. Openness is essential to working together effectively. Claire needs to foster an environment free of criticism and fear of retribution. This might encourage the other team members to voice their opinions and allow Mark to relinquish the role of team spokesperson. This would also foster more trust and rapport between Claire and the entire team. In order for this to be successful, Claire would have to learn to actively learn from others and appreciate their comments and insights.

Question 5

Was termination the proper course of action for Mark? Assuming that termination was the proper action by Claire, how should she have terminated Mark to reduce Marketing Research Int'l's liability and to support Mark as a person?

Evaluation skills (using a set of criteria to arrive at a reasoned judgment of the value of something).

Answer

- Given Claire's management skills at that time, it was probably her only solution.
- Progressive discipline should have been used. Progressive discipline should include a warning that performance is not acceptable and a plan to improve performance. The employee should be made aware of the consequences resulting from failure to improve performance, and sufficient time should be given to improve performance. An employee should not be surprised that he or she is being terminated due to nonperformance.

Given Claire's management skills at that time, it was probably her only solution. If she had been able to increase her interaction with the team, thus decreasing her isolation from the team and fostering an environment of openness, it may have been possible to keep the team intact.

If the reason for termination was poor performance, Claire should have documented this over a period of time. By not doing so, she called into question whether performance was the *real* reason for dismissal and left the company susceptible to legal action.

She should have used progressive discipline:

First, Mark should have been notified in writing that his performance was below expectations. This notice should have detailed how Mark's performance was unacceptable and outlined steps for improvement. Claire should have met with Mark to discuss the letter and the plans.

Second, if Mark's performance did not improve in a timely manner, Claire should have met with Mark again to discuss his performance. She should then outline ways for him to improve within a specific time period (i.e., 30 days). She would follow up with a warning that if his performance did not improve, he would be terminated. Although Claire did notify Mark of his poor performance, she terminated him only four days later. This was insufficient time for Mark to improve his performance and indicated that the real goal was to fire Mark, not to improve his performance.

Finally, if Mark's performance was not up to par after the agreed-upon period of time, the third step for Claire would have been to terminate him.

Instead of following progressive discipline, Claire ordered Mark to improve and then precipitously, only several days later, gave him the option to quit or be fired. If Mark had chosen to seek legal counsel for a wrongful termination suit, he could have argued that he felt unlawfully pressured into resigning.

Finally, Mark should not have been offered a severance package. Termination for nonperformance should not include a severance package. This gives a mixed message to the employee. If the company is willing to pay the employee severance when terminated for nonperformance, the implication is that the company bears some responsibility for the separation. In this case, severance pay gives the impression of inducing Mark to leave for reasons other than poor performance. The severance pay could have been construed as "silence money" or coercion (to quit) if a wrongful termination suit had been pursued. If his leaving was really performance-based, then he did not deserve a severance package.

Progressive measures would have made Mark aware that his performance was not up to standards and that he needed to either improve his performance or consider employment elsewhere. This would provide him notice of what the expectations of him were and the outcome should he not improve his performance. Then he would not have been surprised by the subsequent events.

References

Wagner, J. and Hollenbeck, J. (1995). *Management of organizational behavior*. Upper Saddle River, New Jersey: Prentice Hall.

Epilogue

Mark's departure marked a turning point for the team. Sharon joined the team the following Monday and received an icy reception from Dan and Madeleine. It was a difficult transition time—the team was short-staffed and still recovering from the loss of Mark. Dan and Madeleine remained aloof to Claire and maintained their distance from her. Three months later, Dan left Global Services division (GS) to finish up the last semester of his master's degree as a full-time student. Shortly thereafter, Madeleine left the client service/sales team to head up a product development team for GS in Paris, France, and Claire accepted a promotion within GS to Director of Marketing. Within four months of Mark's departure, there was a new four-person client service team headed by a new sales manager. The many changes in personnel caused disruption in sales, and as a result sales for 1994 were below target.

None of the original GS client service/sales team is with Marketing Research Int'l today. As a result, the controversy behind Mark's departure is an unknown piece of history to the current GS client service/sales team. For those involved, life has gone on, and the experience of Mark's "separation" from Marketing Research Int'l is no longer the painful memory it once was.

Claire's career took a dramatic change when in 1996 she left Marketing Research Int'l to join a large management recruiting company. She thoroughly enjoys recruiting because it utilizes her strongest skill—networking—and does not require her to manage people.

Shortly after his departure, Mark opened his own one-person consulting company. He enjoys the perks of being his own boss—setting his own hours, pursuing business as he chooses, and most importantly being accountable only to himself.

Dan stuck to his career plans and took a position as the Director of Marketing for a startup internet company in Silicon Valley.

Although Madeleine eventually left GS, she stayed with the Marketing Research Int'l organization for another four years before returning to graduate school.

Teaching Note©
COSTUME BANK

Topics (* = Primary topics in teaching plan)
*Strategic planning
*Distinctive competence
*Job design and compensation
*Board governance
*Entrepreneurial process and vision
Control, budgetary
Nonprofit organizations
Management skills
Career choice
Organizational change

Case overview

This case chronicles the launch and rapid growth of a nonprofit business called The Costume Bank and the governance crisis that gripped the organization eight years later. The case focuses on the actions of Karen Simon who, after five years of education and apprenticeship in theatrical costuming, founded The Costume Bank and then served for eight years as the organization's only executive director and costumer.

The Costume Bank was organized as a nonprofit business, as a way to attract donations and grants and as a way to strengthen ties with the nonprofit theater groups that rented Costume Bank costumes. Karen Simon recruited a local, volunteer governing board. Membership on the five-seat board changed frequently. Except for the services of a bookkeeper and an office manager, Karen Simon performed all the activities of the business, from costume production to finance to fundraising.

The Costume Bank business had a predictable, seasonal flow. Each year, Karen designed and produced costumes that local theater groups rented for their new productions. Those rental costumes were then added to The Costume Bank's inventory, from which costumes were rented for other occasions. The pace of business tended to slow down each mid-winter. As word spread about Karen's expertise and her commitment to the local theatrical community, she found herself swamped with new clients.

Finances were always cause for worry at The Costume Bank. Under the organization's nonprofit status, rentals were priced below cost. Donations and grant monies were sporadic. Karen Simon never received a cent in salary for her work. During the early lean years, she supplied cash from her own resources.

After years of running the business by herself, Karen's was exhausted. By 1997, a longstanding health problem had worsened. Karen Simon submitted her resignation to the board. Around this same time, the board took steps to tighten control over The Costume Bank finances. It was time for the first confrontation between founder and board.

Industry

Custom production and rental of durable theatrical costumes. Nonprofit and for profit.

Teaching objectives

1. To illustrate the passage from entrepreneurial stage to a going concern.
2. To analyze the role of a governing board.
3. To provide a comprehensive framework for strategic planning.
4. To emphasize how any business is embedded in a pattern of relationships.

---

*This teaching note was prepared by Armand Gilinsky, Small Business Institute at Sonoma State University, and Karen Simon. The case and teaching note were prepared as a basis for class discussion rather than to illustrate either effective or ineffective handling of administrative situations. Suggestions for improvement of this note should be sent to tompkins@uor.edu. Credit will be given in the next revision.

5. To inspire empathy for an entrepreneur's zeal and talents.
6. To illustrate the contingency of job design and compensation.
7. To examine the limits of a board's power.
8. To frame the challenge of dealing with a "star player" in an organization.

Other related cases in Volume 1

A New Magazine in Nigeria (entrepreneurship); *Unmovable Team* (career choice, control).

Cases about nonprofit and community-minded for-profit ventures throughout D. Bollier (Ed.), *Aiming Higher* (New York: AMACOM, 1996). This book contains the cases written about winners of the Business Enterprise Trust awards for corporate social responsibility. The case about Gun Denhart and her children's catalog business (called *Gun Denhart and Hanna Andersson: Recycling Clothes While Building Customer Loyalty*) is particularly pertinent.

Other related case in Volume 2

Cafe Latte (group dynamics); *The Volunteer* (nonprofit organizations); *Unprofessional Conduct* (career choice).

Intended courses and levels

This case fits well in courses about small business, corporate strategy, general management, nonprofit organizations, and corporate governance.

Undergraduate students will appreciate investigating how a person's skills can be matched to a career, as well as how management constitutes a distinct function of an organization. Advanced undergraduates will benefit from the opportunity to locate a business in a pattern of relationships with stakeholders, as an aid in understanding strategic planning and strategic behavior.

Graduate and executive students will especially benefit from the issues of strategic planning, compensation, managerial control, and managing a "star player."

Analysis

All analysis is imbedded in the discussion questions and answers.

Research methodology

This case study was prepared by Karen Simon, under the direction of Armand Gilinsky, Director of the Small Business Institute at Sonoma State University. The authors relied on written records and recollections by the executive director of The Costume Bank. No other volunteers, customers, or employees were interviewed.

Teaching plan

Teaching plan topic: Entrepreneurial Process and Spirit
60-minute teaching plan

Preassignment: Read the case before class (20 minutes).

	Timing	Activity	Organization	Student Outcomes
I	0–5 minutes (5)	Read case again. Instructor informs the class of a ground rule for class discussion: Assume that Karen Simon's resignation has *not* yet been accepted by the board and that one more	Individually Instructor informs class.	To become familiar with the case facts. To learn boundary of the class discussion on this day.

	Timing	Activity	Organization	Student Outcomes
		round of discussion between Karen and the board is plausible.		
II	5–10 minutes (5)	Role-play organization, In preparation for answering Question 7 about the message Karen might deliver to the board, after the case has "ended."	Select three different Karen Simon characters, from volunteers or by lottery. Privately (e.g., in sealed envelope), give each a different set of directions about what to say. One Karen could be bitter. Another could be exhausted. A third could be apologetic and seeking assistance. While the three Karens prepare, have the rest of the class (the board) wait without any word about what is going to happen.	The five minutes that the board waits simulates the cost of poor communications. The board blindsided Karen with their takeover. Now, she is returning "the favor." This waiting period also helps students see that positions of power do not always enable those in power to get their way. This pair of lessons about gamesmanship can be discussed by the instructor in the final 5 minutes. See below.
III	10–30 minutes (20)	Role-plays. One at a time, the three Karens send their message to the board, however they choose (e.g., a prepared statement delivered in person, a television interview). After each Karen has spoken, the board may ask questions, but the board may not make any statements about what they might do next.	Individual role players; class members ask questions of Karens.	Students hear an entrepreneur pour out her heart about how important The Costume Bank is to her. Students (as board members) experience challenges to their established authority.
IV	30–45 minutes (15)	Instructor asks Question 8 about what the board should offer to each Karen, in the way of revised job duties and compensation. The board is not permitted to walk away from Karen Simon.	Individuals, including the three Karen Simon role players, participate in class discussion. Students' oral contributions are listed on the board or sketch pad, by the instructor, who tries to separate the job descriptions into distinctively different scenarios.	Students wrestle with the limited resources at the disposal of the board and with the importance of keeping their "star player" around. Students also learn about how job design and compensation can be made contingent on the talents and needs of specific employees. In entrepreneurship situations, management and governing boards cannot afford to take the impersonal stance that jobs and compensation must not be tailored to specific individual circumstances. An impersonal

	Timing	Activity	Organization	Student Outcomes
				approach to Karen has taken the board, and the very organization, to the threshold of crisis.
V	45–55 minutes (10)	Instructor reads the case epilogue to the class and then asks Question 9.	Individual students participate in discussion with one another and instructor.	Students sharpen their analytical skills about a particular person's talents and drives. This they can use in their own self-assessment processes. Students gain an appreciation of what makes entrepreneurs different and special contributors to the communities in which they work.
VI	55–60 minutes (5)	Instructor calls the class's attention to the five-minute silent period in Step II.	Individual students reflect on what has happened in the role play.	Students are urged to see entrepreneurship as a fragile thing, easily swamped by the routine exercise of formal power.

25-minute teaching plan on entrepreneurial process and spirit.
Preassignment: Read case before coming to class (20 minutes).
Do activities III—two Karens only (10 minutes), IV (10 minutes), V (5 minutes) in preceding 60-minute plan.
This teaching plan is most effective with at least 45 minutes.

Teaching plan topic: Strategic Planning and Organizational Governance
60-minute teaching plan

Preassignment: Students should read the case before class (20 minutes). They should also think about the meaning of "bank" in nonbusiness terminology.

	Timing	Activity	Organization	Student Outcomes
I	0–5 minutes (5)	Scan case. Instructor informs the class that they should assume that the board has accepted Karen Simon's resignation and that Karen Simon has severed all ties with The Costume Bank.	Individually Instructor informs the class.	To become familiar with the case facts. To learn boundary of the class discussion on this day.
II	5–10 minutes (5)	Instructor opens class discussion by asking Question 1 about whom the board should contact about Karen Simon's departure, and what should be said to these constituents. Discussion should be brisk and wide-ranging, in order	Instructor and entire class	Students grasp the context in which opportunities and challenges await The Costume Bank. Students learn that strategic planning is not done in a vacuum, but rather that strategy is always conditioned by the relationships that are crucial to the conduct of the organization. Students appreciate that strategic

30

	Timing	Activity	Organization	Student Outcomes
		to emphasize to students that the board is in a real mess that must be addressed quickly and comprehensively.		planning is not some leisurely, armchair exercise divorced from the complex circumstances of running a business; the board has a big problem that must be solved right away.
III	10–20 minutes (10)	Instructor asks class to answer Question 2 about what The Costume Bank has done consistently well over its eight-year history.	Instructor and entire class	Students learn that demonstrated organizational capability is one starting point for strategic planning.
IV	20–30 minutes (10)	Instructor poses Question 3 about the meaning of "bank" in The Costume Bank name and Question 4 about the organization's nonprofit status.	Class is divided into small groups to discuss the pair of questions and agree on answers to both questions.	Students stretch themselves to consider possible arrangements by which The Costume Bank can stay in business.
V	30–40 minutes (10)	Instructor elicits responses from each small group, concerning Questions 3 and 4, working to draw distinctions among the different answers.	Instructor and entire class	Students are introduced to a rudimentary process of scenario building, learning to imagine a variety of feasible futures for the organization.
VI	40–50 minutes (10)	Instructor poses Question 5 about a job description for the next executive director, again working to separate students responses into distinctly different ideas about the future shape of the organization.	Instructor and entire class	Students learn to connect strategy formulation with the action plans through which a strategy is implemented. Students also learn to link aspirations for an organization's future with the people who could play a key role in achieving those aspirations.
VII	50–55 minutes (5)	Instructor poses Question 6 and leads a brisk discussion about whether there is reason for The Costume Bank to exist.	Instructor and entire class	Students appreciate that strategic planning is about the organization as a whole and about the organization's place in a larger world.
VIII	55–60 minutes (5)	Instructor reads the case epilogue to the class, and gives a mini-lecture about how each organization has a history, including its eventual demise.	Individual reflection	Students begin to recognize that not all organizations are destined to last indefinitely. Vision is one ingredient in the lasting power of an organization. So, too, is the contribution that the organization makes to a network of other people and organizations. If there is no good reason, at this junction of ambition and demand, for an organization to continue, then it is a legitimate outcome of strategic planning to close the doors and turn out the lights. We could infer, from any number of

	Timing	Activity	Organization	Student Outcomes
				points in the case (such as the difficulty in attracting grant monies), that the theatrical community in Sonoma County and beyond did not really value the special contribution that Karen Simon thought she could make, and that the board simply ratified that indifference.

25-minute plan for strategic planning
Preassignment: Read case before class (20 minutes).
Do activities II, III, and VII of 60-minute plan.

Discussion questions and answers

Question 1

In the wake of Karen's resignation from The Costume Bank, whom should the board contact and what should those people be told?
Analysis skills (breaking a concept into its parts and explaining their interrelationships, distinguishing relevant from extraneous material).

Answer

This is a question that gets students thinking about the place a business occupies in a community and, in particular, about the constituencies (more formally, stakeholders) who are crucial to the continued operation of the business. It is also a question that spurs students to think about the proper role of a board in the governance of an organization.

It appears from the case that Karen Simon alone was the contact between The Costume Bank and the "outside" world. Hence, the board now faces double trouble. Board members are not well-acquainted with key stakeholders in the first place. On top of that, board members now must explain, and be prepared to answer questions about, the impending departure of the one person whom these stakeholders likely consider the personification of The Costume Bank. On the other hand, the board has been handed a golden opportunity to redefine The Costume Bank, now that the founder has indicated her intention of stepping aside.

Question 2

Over the eight-year history of The Costume Bank, what has the organization done well consistently and distinctively in its dealings with other organizations and persons?
Diagnostic question (probes motives or causes).

Answer

This question calls attention to the concept of distinctive competence (and the companion idea of sustainable competitive advantage). In order to answer this question, students must probe for a common denominator in the actions that Karen Simon and her volunteer colleagues have performed. Students should be encouraged to interpret as "high" a common denominator as possible. What they learn is that an organization's mission can be understood as a de facto concept. What they learn, as a corollary, is that while people can fool themselves with the words that go into a mission statement, a pattern of actions tells a revealing story about what is important to the operators of an organization.

This question is one way to get at the strengths of The Costume Bank. In strategic planning frameworks, leveraging on the strengths of an organization is a central theme. Also important in strategic planning is matching the organization's strengths to opportunities in the organization's pattern of relationships. Students should be encouraged, as a test of their interpretive skills and creativity, to express this de facto mission in their own words, instead of repeating what operators of the business are saying. For instance, one interpretation of The Costume Bank's distinctive competence is this: "We commit ourselves to contribute to a flourishing theatrical community in Sonoma County, even if that means never saying 'no' to a request for costumes." Karen Simon and the board have followed this de facto mission to the letter. And, this has left the organization in a state of crisis.

The question reinforces the importance of stakeholders, per the closing clause.

Question 3

What are some key connotations of operating a "bank," and how appropriate is "bank" as a guide for the future of The Costume Bank?

Analysis skills (breaking a concept into its parts and explaining their interrelationships, distinguishing relevant from extraneous material).

Answer

This question prods students to look behind the observable activities of a business and think about the very meaning of a particular business enterprise. This is one of a set of questions with which students can evaluate the match between the capabilities of The Costume Bank and different scenarios in which The Costume Bank can prosper. This question also encourages students to learn more about the diversity of business practices, as a way to ask questions about one kind of business from the perspective of other kinds of businesses.

The Costume Bank is not a bank, of course, in the federally- and state-regulated meaning of the term. But, we can apply a thoughtful interpretation of banking to The Costume Bank, as a way to assess what the organization has, or has not, done well in its eight-year history.

It is customary to think of a bank as a symbol of continuity, stability, conservative use of resources, confidentiality, protection of valuable property, visibility in the local community, and close ties to other organizations in the community. Apparently, The Costume Bank has consistently embodied these virtues.

At the same time, banks are also symbols of profit-making and capital accumulation. Neither accomplishment stands out in the brief history of The Costume Bank. This leads logically to Question 4.

Question 4

In view of what has transpired in the business environment in which The Costume Bank is located, how appropriate is it that The Costume Bank continue to operate under a nonprofit status?

Diagnostic question (probes motives or causes).

Answer

The world in which The Costume Bank has operated for eight years has not always conformed to assumptions under which Karen Simon and her original board were likely operating when they decided on nonprofit status. Nonprofit status has not consistently been a magnet for grant monies. The local and collegiate theatrical community has thrived, judging from the growth in the volume of business that has come to Karen Simon. Thus, it might now be less important than before that The Costume Bank share nonprofit kinship with its clients. Moreover, the demands of custom production, coupled with funding limitations within which the theaters work, make the price-below-cost condition an impediment to growing the business.

This question gets students thinking about the role that personal values of founders and board members can play in the formulation and implementation of a strategy. In the several additions of *The Concept of Corporate Strategy*, Kenneth Andrews stresses how central a role personal values play in the content of strategic decisions. Now that Karen Simon, and her particular kind of commitment to the theater community, has departed The Costume Bank, board members have a rare opportunity to discuss and decide what is *really* fundamental to them about the business they are governing.

Question 5

What should be included in the job description that the board writes for the next executive director of The Costume Bank?

Synthesis skills (putting parts together to form a new whole; solving a problem requiring creativity or originality).

Answer

Karen Simon's resignation provides the board members with an opportunity to reflect on what has worked and what has not worked in the eight-year history of the organization. In effect, this is an opportunity for the board to "re-start" The Costume Bank concept. One practical way for the board to connect this reflection with an action plan for the coming weeks and months is to write a job description for the next "founder" of The Costume Bank.

The executive director job description goes a long way toward setting limits about how large a business The Costume Bank will entail. Karen Simon did everything from fundraising to cash control to personnel management to customer relations to new business development to facilities management to production to warehousing. Responsibility for any three or four of these activities is a great deal to ask of one person in the executive director's position. As students answer this question, they get the idea that the size of a business is, more perhaps than they first believe, a matter of choice.

Question 6

Why should The Costume Bank business continue after Karen Simon's resignation?
(Or, what difference does it make that The Costume Bank continues in business for one more day?)
Analysis skills (breaking a concept into its parts and explaining their interrelationships, distinguishing relevant from extraneous material).

Answer

This question shines the spotlight on the matter of an organization's mission and does so, subtly yet unmistakably, in a way that links a business to its stakeholders. The instructor can pose this question after reading the epilogue to the class. The epilogue is a bucket of cold water thrown on the enthusiastic support that students can find themselves "giving" to a free spirit such as Karen Simon.

This question is adapted from two recent analyses of the importance of organizational mission. One is *Reengineering the Corporation* (by Michael Hammer and James Champy), and the other is *Built to Last* (by Michael Collins and Jerry Porras). These two books are on the cutting edge of strategic management with regard to the practical value of an organization's mission. Although the case does take us "inside" the board's deliberations, we can nonetheless infer from their decision to close The Costume Bank that they (the board) could not find a sufficiently compelling reason for The Costume Bank's continued existence. An organizational mission can serve a useful purpose as an ultimate standard for deciding whether a business is a legitimate way to spend people's time and money.

This question sobers students to the fact that a business is not destined to last forever. Having a mission is one thing. But, it is another matter whether a business serves a continuing useful purpose for stakeholders in a community. There are other ways for theatrical groups to obtain costumes. For instance, they can sew their own costumes in the kind of on-campus classes and workshops that inspired Karen Simon in the first place.

There are also other organizational arrangements by which costumes can be produced and supplied to theater groups. The guild plays an intriguing role in this regard. The guild might just be one of Karen Simon's most lasting contributions to The Costume Bank. The guild is a network of fellow costumers who can do things in Sonoma County that The Costume Bank board and employees are not capable of doing for themselves. Michael Porter (in his 1985 book, *Competitive Advantage*) argues that it can be helpful if certain competitors, whom he calls "good competitors," took a piece of the market that a firm could not reasonably serve, despite the enticement of "being the biggest." Too great a market share can be a bad idea, Porter and others argue. It is something that The Costume Bank board would do well to take into account.

Question 7

What message should Karen Simon communicate to the board, now that Karen and the board have met to discuss the board's decision to take greater control of Costume Bank operations?
Analysis skills (breaking a concept into its parts and explaining their interrelationships, distinguishing relevant from extraneous material).

Answer

This is a good place for students to sense the zeal and energy of an entrepreneur. Given the opportunity to express her feelings at this turn of events, and given that Karen and the board have apparently not communicated frequently before, Karen is in a position to deliver a "state of The Costume Bank" manifesto. As the case reaches this crescendo, students can concentrate on what is really important to an entrepreneur.

A role-play exercise is useful here. Karen Simon can take several different approaches. She can be the bitter heroine who demands respect from an ungrateful board. She can be the beaten heroine, mentally and physically exhausted. She can be the apologetic, overwhelmed employee who seeks advice from those who are not so closely immersed in the situation. Each of these roles can be enacted without much advance preparation. Other "Karens" are plausible as well. This sets up Question 8.

Question 8:

In the wake of Karen's communication (Question 7) to the board, what kind of revised job description and compensation should the board be prepared to offer Karen in order for The Costume Bank to retain her services?

Analysis skills (breaking a concept into its parts and explaining their interrelationships, distinguishing relevant from extraneous material), relational skills (asks for comparisons of themes, ideas, or issues), and action skills (calls for a conclusion or action).

Answer

This question enables students to grasp the contingency of job design and compensation on the circumstances at hand. With this question, the instructor can initiate a critical discussion of the assumption, often associated with bureaucracy, that a job should be designed without consideration of who will perform the job. This assumption is thrown open to critical debate in entrepreneurial situations. In entrepreneurial settings, it is impossible to separate a job from the person who does that job.

This question also enables students to differentiate between actions that entrepreneurs are expected to perform well and actions that managers are expected to perform well. The Costume Bank is no longer a start-up company. It is a going concern that needs daily attention to matters of control and planning, actions that are customarily assigned to managers. The job description is a device with which students can draw a firm line between entrepreneur and manager.

This question also usefully sets up the instructor's reading of the case epilogue to the class. Students might express shock that the board was "unreasonable" and stubborn in its eventual refusal to negotiate with Karen Simon. Therein lies another lesson, dating to Chester Barnard (in *The Functions of the Executive*), that authority is effective if it is negotiated between the parties. In the case of The Costume Bank, the board certainly maintained its position of power, but the result was the dissolution of The Costume Bank.

Finally, this question touches upon a concern that every organization will face conceivably: how do you keep your "star player"? Entrepreneurial organizations and established organizations alike (e.g., universities and symphony orchestras) must be prepared to deal with this matter.

Question 9:

What do you expect will be Karen Simon's "next stop" in her career as an entrepreneur?

Diagnostic question (probes motives or causes). And synthesis skills (putting parts together to form a new whole; solving a problem requiring creativity or originality).

Answer

This question can also be usefully addressed after the class has heard the epilogue. In effect, who is this person, Karen Simon the entrepreneur? The question gives students the opportunity to infer an entrepreneurial spirit and energy from the several stops that Karen Simon has made in her entrepreneurial activities. As students answer the question, they develop their skill at interpreting common threads, or themes, across an unfolding pattern of actions. That will serve them well as they evaluate complex situations in the future. Their study of strategy and business policy is one place where that diagnostic skill will be tested.

The question also enables students to assess their own capacity for innovative thinking and action. Could I live this way, they could ask themselves, after reading a sketch of how one woman has followed her imagination for nearly twenty years.

References

Andrews, Kenneth (1980). *The concept of corporate strategy*, 3rd ed. Homewood, IL: Dow Jones Irwin.

Barnard, C.I. (1968). *The Functions of the executive*, 30th anniversary ed. Harvard University Press.

Collins, J.C. and Porras, (1997). J.I. *Built to last: Successful habits of visionary companies.* HarperBusiness.

Hammer, M. and Champy (1994). *Reengineering the Corporation: A manifesto for business revolution.* HarperBusiness.

Hawken, Paul (1987). *Growing a business.* New York, NY: Simon and Schuster.

Porter, M.E. (1985). *Competitive Advantage: Creating and Sustaining Superior Performance.* Free Press.

Bollier, D. (1996). *Aiming Higher : 25 Stories of How Companies Prosper by Combining Sound Management and Social Vision.* AMACOM.

Epilogue

When Karen found out what had happened, she tendered her resignation, effective immediately, and removed most of her personal items from The Costume Bank. She consulted an attorney, who told her that the board could do anything it wanted with regard to The Costume Bank and the money. Karen was, technically, an employee of the board, and completely under its jurisdiction. He did comment, privately, that what the board had done was not entirely ethical.

For months, Karen was confused and upset as she began hearing rumors of her mismanagement of The Costume Bank. It was devastating to realize that her life's work, her passion, had gone up in flames because she had chosen the wrong people to support her vision. She had always felt that, no matter what happened, she would be involved with The Costume Bank in some capacity.

The Costume Bank was her life, her baby. She had nurtured it for almost eight years. Her life revolved around making it work and convincing others that it was a viable entity. When she was betrayed, she cried for months. She couldn't understand how this could happen. She blamed herself for her poor choices—in board members, planning, and in simply not being strong enough, physically, to continue to pursue her dream. This was the biggest failure of her life, and she entered a deep depression.

For the next year, as she worked as a travel agent, Karen searched her soul for answers and only succeeded in formulating more questions regarding the demise of her dream.

By January 1998, The Costume Bank had disbanded and sold all costumes, accessories, office and sewing equipment to pay the outstanding debt. Karen was required to settle the debt that was in her name.

Karen quit her job, and went on disability. She and her husband, David, separated for a time while she lived with, and cared for, her elderly mother in a small coastal community in northern California. After six months, Karen and David purchased a small home near Karen's mother. They started a housecleaning business, in which Karen was the office manager. The business was quite successful, and they were happy to be part of a growing community and close to Karen's mother who continued to have health problems.

As of May 1999, Karen needed one more class to complete her M.A. degree, and was investigating taking it through the Internet because she lived in a rural area. She had confidence that she would complete her degree and find work as an executive director of a nonprofit organization.

Karen recently became involved, as a volunteer, with a nonprofit organization on the coast that advocated for victims of domestic violence. She managed the Hot Line, counseled victims, and wrote temporary restraining orders. In the early 1980s, when attending SRJC, she had been an advocate with the YWCA Women's Shelter in Santa Rosa, California. Karen believed this organization needed her particular talents and abilities and hoped to become a paid staff member. She had come full circle.

Teaching Note
DONOR SERVICES DEPARTMENT IN GUATEMALA

Topics (* = Primary topic with Teaching Plan)
*Work design (analyzing work tasks, workspace design, job enrichment)
*Motivation (McClelland's need theory, Vroom's expectancy theory, social reinforcement theory, goal setting theory.)
*Organizational structure (work specialization, chain of command, departmentalization, informal vs. formal organization)
International: Guatemala
National culture
Nonprofit organizations

Case overview
This case illustrates the effect of poor management and inadequate job design on the motivation of a Guatemalan office of translators. A vacuum of leadership and supervision allowed an informal group with poor work norms to take over, creating a climate that resulted in low productivity and morale. The protagonist, a consultant, must determine what recommendations to make about who should run the department and how the work should be structured.

   The details of cases A and B are too complicated to summarize in this overview. Familiarity with the case is essential to do the work design analysis.

Industry
Nonprofit organizations, clerical services, translation services, donor services, multi-national organizations.

Teaching objectives
1.   To determine and evaluate components of good job design in the case (graduates).
2.   To identify components of good job design (undergraduates).
3.   To design a proposal that will improve motivation and job design in the donor services department.
4.   To analyze the situation using a variety of motivation theories (McClelland's need theory, Vroom's expectancy theory, social reinforcement theory, goal setting theory.)

Other related cases in Volume 1
A Team Divided or a Team United? (group dynamics); *Julie's Call: Empowerment at Taco Bell* (job enrichment); *Shaking the Bird Cage* (organizational structure); *Split Operations at Sky and Arrow Airlines* (organizational structure).

Other related cases in Volume 2
Cafe Latte (equity theory); *Computer Services Team at AVIONICS* (group dynamics); *Cost and Schedule Team at AVIONICS* (group dynamics, workspace co-location); *Groupware Fiasco* (group dynamics); *Preferential Treatment* (equity theory); *When Worlds Collide* (organizational structure).

Intended courses and levels
This case is appropriate for undergraduates, graduates, and executives. Although the setting is a nonprofit organization, the same problems can surface in a business context. It is best positioned at the individual level for organizational behavior courses and at the organizing function for management courses.

---

*Source: Adapted from case prepared by Joyce Osland, University of Portland. The case and teaching note were prepared as a basis for class discussion rather than to illustrate either effective or ineffective handling of administrative situations. Suggestions for improvement of this note should be sent to tompkins@uor.edu. Credit will be given in the next revision.

Analysis

Motivation – Many of the difficulties in this case can be traced back to selecting the wrong people for the job and job design errors. For example, José's personality and interests were more clearly suited for creative program work than the detail-oriented work of donor services. Finding those disparate orientations within the same person is usually a challenge.

Elena is a good example of what happens when the most dependable, competent employee is wrongly promoted to a supervisory position. In terms of McClelland's theory of motivation (1985), Elena had a high need for achievement but virtually no need for power. She lacked the drive to learn to supervise, even if her superiors had taken the effort to teach her the necessary skills. Placing a less educated person in charge of the bilingual secretaries was doomed to failure, given Elena's lack of supervision skills and retiring personality.

The bilingual secretaries were too well educated for their original jobs, another example of lack of fit that resulted in decreased motivation and frustration.

The uneven workflow also caused motivation problems. Expectancy theory can be applied to the overloaded translators who had no expectation of effort leading to performance. No matter how hard they worked, they could never clear away the backlog of work on their desks, which is demotivating.

A failure to understand social reinforcement theory explains some of the difficulties with Juana and her clique. Due to Elena's lack of leadership, there were no negative consequences for dysfunctional behaviors. Until Joanna, no one ever clarified for Juana that gossip and failure to act like a team player were not acceptable or explained that negative consequences would result (no chance of promotion, possible chance of termination). Elena did nothing when they wasted time, thereby reinforcing the negative behavior. In contrast, Joanna rewarded desirable behaviors both verbally and by assigning interesting special projects to people who had their work up to date.

The use of the chart showing goals and output is an example of the efficacy of goal setting as a motivational tool.

Job Redesign – The switch to a regional division of work is an excellent example of job redesign (Hackman et al, 1975). Their previous jobs were simple and repetitive. The new, enriched jobs possessed the following characteristics of motivating jobs:

Skill Variety—The new jobs combined several different tasks involving various skills

Task Identity—Translators were solely responsible for all the work processes done in their region, which made their job more meaningful.

Task Significance—Joanna repeatedly explained the importance of donor services in the grand scheme of the organization and emphasized what good customer service meant to both donors and recipients.

Autonomy—The regional translators had more discretion over scheduling their tasks as long as all were done in a reasonable time frame. Given the level of employee education, a procedures manual was necessary to set standards; the employees did, however, have a say (or veto) in developing the procedures.

Feedback—The work station cubbyholes allowed the employees to see at a glance their work progress. Joanna revised their work and gave them feedback on it. The praise or complaints about the work that they did for their region went straight to them.

Customer contact—The regional translators now dealt directly with two sets of customers—the community representatives and the donors who visited the programs—which further enriched their work.

Management Style—The managers and the supervisor in this case performed only some of the responsibilities in their job domain. Sam and José focused primarily on the parts of their jobs that interested them, and Elena mastered the paperwork but not the "people" part of her supervisor role. While this type of behavior is commonplace and understandable, it does not result in an effective workplace.

The superiors' laissez faire attitude and lack of interest in the translators' work and situation resulted in both low productivity and morale. In managerial grid terminology, the managers showed low concern for both the people and the task

In contrast, Joanna's management style indicated a <u>high emphasis on both task and people.</u> She provided structure, clear expectations, and removed obstacles that kept them from doing a good job. At the same time, however, she was concerned about their feelings and needs and tried to create a harmonious, inclusive workplace so that people looked forward to coming to work. Although Joanna was limited somewhat by the cultural context and a hierarchical organizational culture, she tried to empower these employees. There are four aspects of **empowerment**: meaning, competence, self-determination, and impact (Spreitzer, 1992).

<u>Meaning</u> (Employees see their jobs as having meaning when they care about their work and perceive it as important and meaningful): Joanna emphasized the importance of their role in retaining and attracting new donors and advocated for making the department of equal rank with the other departments.

<u>Competence</u> (Employees are capable of performing all the work that must be done): Joanna placed the translators in jobs that suited their skills and worked to improve their English skills. She also set clear standards and procedures so workers knew what was expected of them.

<u>Self-determination</u> (Employees have significant autonomy, considerable freedom and independence, and are able to use personal initiative in carrying out their work): The job redesign allowed the regional translators to choose which of their various tasks they would do each day, taking into consideration the departmental goals and priorities. The charts let them adjust work targets without having to be told by a supervisor (Mary Parker Follett's "the situation is the boss").

<u>Impact</u> (Employees have some control and influence over what happens in their department): Although they seldom took advantage of the opportunity, Joanna asked employees frequently for their suggestions regarding policies and procedures and did not implement any without their approval (rubber stamp-like as it was).

Joanna's faux pas with the workstations is an example of an issue that fell outside the employees' "<u>zone of indifference</u>" (Barnard, 1938). The new procedures and policies were within this zone, which lulled Joanna into making the mistaken assumption that the employees would accept almost anything she and Sam suggested or decided.

Informal Structure vs. Team Approach – The lack of strong leadership created a power vacuum that Juana was quick to fill. She and her cronies created a "we-they" atmosphere with the rest of the department (in-group or out-group, leisure class or overworked class) that was fueled by gossip and pointed jokes. The informal structure was more powerful than a perceived need to work effectively as a department.

The lack of working meetings in the past also impeded teamwork. In the past, there was no <u>superordinate goal</u> (Sherif and Sherif, 1969) to unite the members into a team. Joanna set the superordinate goal of becoming a topnotch donor services department and structured cooperation into the department with the priorities chart, which made helpfulness a norm.

Organizational Culture – Pride in the organization, belief in its mission, and conscientiousness (to a degree) were the key values of the department's organizational culture. The values of the organization's religion were somewhat prevalent but did not always take precedence. Less positive norms were passivity regarding problems, exclusion of certain members, unresolved conflict, and loafing on the job. Joanna tried to inculcate the following <u>norms</u>: efficiency, respectful treatment for all members, clear expectations, pride in achievement, and a focus on developing skills. In the past, no one had consciously managed the organizational culture or the socialization process by which members were brought into the organization.

Research methodology

This case was the result of a consulting contract by the author, who was the consultant in the case.

Teaching plan

Modify the teaching plans below for undergraduates by having them read cases A and B, and then <u>identify</u> work design and motivation theory. You can lead an interesting discussion based on the analysis earlier in this teaching note. You can also use question 1.

Graduates can <u>diagnose and evaluate</u> work design and motivation theory using the teaching plans below.

Teaching plan topic: Organizational Structure and Work Design
60-minute teaching plan

Preassignment: Read case A prior to class (15 minutes).

	Timing	Activity	Organization	Student Outcomes
I	0–10 minutes (10)	Answer discussion question 1.	Full class discussion	Clarify Joanne's diagnosis of the situation.
II	10–25 minutes (15)	Analyze the situation by examining the components of good job design.	Divide the class into five small groups. Each group works on a separate question.	Group 1: Evaluate each job in the office according to its level of skill variety. Group 2: Evaluate each task in the office according to its level of task identity. Group 3: Evaluate each task in the office according to its level of task significance. Group 4: Evaluate each task in the office according to its level of autonomy. Group 5: Evaluate each task in the office according to its level of feedback.
III	25–35 minutes (10)		Small groups report back to the class as a whole.	Verify they have the concepts of job enrichment correct.
IV	35–45 minutes (10)	Answer discussion question 2.	Continue to work in small groups.	Each group works on a proposal that will improve both motivation and job design in the office.
V	45–55 minutes (10)	Wrap-up.	Each group reports its solution.	Students critique each group's proposal.
VI	55–60 minutes (5)	If you do not choose to do the motivation discussion, suggest they read case B. Alternative design. If you are using the motivation discussion, set the stage for the next segment.	Full class discussion	Students learn outcome of case. Alternative design. Students are prepared to analyze the motivation of various characters in the case.

25-minute teaching plan on work design.

Preassignment: Read case A prior to class

Do activities II and III. Instructor links motivation and work design during discussion. Tell students to read case B on their own.

Teaching plan topic: Motivation
60-minute teaching plan

Preassignment: Read case A prior to class (15 minutes).

	Timing	Activity	Organization	Student Outcomes
I	0–5 minutes (5)	Review the analysis on job design from previous session.	Full class discussion	Orientation to the case.
II	5–10 minutes (5)	Discuss connections between motivation and job design.	Full class discussion	Understand how poor motivation and poor job design are connected.
III	10–25 minutes (15)	Analyze the situation using a variety of motivation theories.	Divide the class into four small groups. Each group works on a separate question.	Group 1: Evaluate Elena's behavior using McClelland's need theory (McClelland, 1985). Group 2: Evaluate the work of the translators using Expectancy Theory (Vroom, 1964) Group 3: Evaluate Juana and the clique's behavior using social reinforcement theory (Steers and Porter, 1979). Group 4: Evaluate the work of the group using Goal Setting Theory (Locke and Latham, 1990)
IV	25–35 minutes (10)	Synthesize the analysis.	Small groups report back to the class as a whole.	Students see differences and similarities between various motivation theories.
V	35–50 minutes (15)	Discuss the effects of the work redesign proposals on employee morale.	Full class discussion	Students apply theories of motivation to their previous recommendations.
VI	50–60 minutes (10)	Wrap-up. Read case B.	Full class discussion	Students understand that low motivation may be a symptom and not the cause of the problems in the case.

25-minute teaching plan on motivation.
Preassignment: Read case A prior to class
Do activities III and IV. Tell students to read case B on their own.

Teaching plan topic: Culture
60-minute teaching plan

Preassignment: None.

	Timing	Activity	Organization	Student Outcomes
I	0–15 minutes (15)	Read case A.	Individually	Familiarity with case.
II	15–20 minutes (5)	Review cultural information provided in the case.	Full class discussion	Orientation to the case.
III	20–30 minutes	Answer discussion question 3 (First part)	Full class discussion	Students list characteristics of Guatemalan culture discussed in the

	Timing	Activity	Organization	Student Outcomes
	(10)			case.
IV	30–35 minutes (5)	Answer discussion question 3 (Second part).	Full class discussion	Students understand some of the key differences between U.S. culture and Guatemalan culture given in the case.
V	35–50 minutes (15)	Review text material on managing in a global environment.	Instructor lecture or discussion	Using the text students have for the course, connect material with the case.
VI	50–60 minutes (10)	Wrap up case. Suggest they read case B for follow-up.	Full class discussion	Students learn outcome of the case, reflect on the appropriateness of their recommendations.

25-minute teaching plan on culture.

Preassignment: Read cases A and B prior to class

Discuss question 3 (15 minutes), and then do activity V (10 minutes).

Discussion questions and answers

Question 1

What was Joanna's diagnosis of the situation in the donor services department?

Comprehension skills (understanding the meaning of remembered material, usually demonstrated by restating or citing examples) if cases A and B are read before answering Question 1. If the students read only case A before answering, then they are using analysis skills (breaking a concept into its parts and explaining their interrelationships, distinguishing relevant from extraneous material).

Answer

Joanna identified the following characteristics of the situation in the donor services department:

All employees are committed to the overall goals of the organization and proud to work for the agency.

The employees are conscientious about doing the work assigned to them but focus only on their tasks rather than the work of the department as a whole.

The distribution of work is unequal. The overloaded workers experience frustration and job stress, because it is impossible for them to finish their work while others have time to waste.

Cooperation and team spirit are lacking due to the unequal distribution of work and the presence of an exclusive subgroup. This results in low morale and low productivity.

Productivity problems also stem from overly complicated work processes and a lack of attention paid to turnaround times and production goals.

Few standards or quality controls are in place.

The translators are overqualified for their job assignments, even though their level of English ability is not advanced. A lack of fit exists between the type of employees hired and the current job descriptions, which constitutes a motivation problem.

Adding further insult to injury, the jobs are boring and repetitive. The clerks experience little variety in their work.

The translators feel they cannot improve their English skills given their current tasks and a supervisor who is not bilingual.

José promoted an employee (Elena) who is not suited for a supervisory role and put her in a no-win situation with regard to authority and discipline.

The lack of attention on the part of Sam and José contributes to these problems. Since management has not established positive norms, the negative norms of the clique dominate the department.

Question 2

What should Joanna recommend to Sam? Note: Students should NOT read case B before answering this question as the answer below is a summary of what happened in case B.
Action question (calls for a conclusion or action).

Answer

Separate donor services from community services, making it a department in its own right at the same level on the organizational chart as community services and accounting. Hire a department head who will ensure that donor services receives the attention, supervision, and importance it deserves. Hiring a department head will allow Elena to gracefully move from a supervisory position that does not suit her.

Assign Elena a job that capitalizes upon her strengths—organization and diligence—and avoids her weaknesses—English and lack of supervisory interest or skills. Change her job title to Community Liaison and let her continue to work with the Spanish-speaking community program representatives, which is a prestigious role in the department and suitable to her skills.

If Magdalena, the most qualified internal candidate, will not accept the position, hire from the outside an experienced manager with excellent English and managerial skills.

Reorganize the work on a geographical basis so that the four translators are responsible for the entire gamut of work processes for a particular region. They would do enrollment figures, donor questions, gift registrations and acknowledgements, etc., giving them responsibility for both translations and clerical work. This would solve the problem of uneven work distribution since all four would then have an equal and reasonable amount of work to do. The variety of tasks assigned would eliminate the boredom problem and the concern about not using their English skills. They would also have contact with community representatives from their region—their clients. Visitors who need the services of a translator would utilize those of the appropriate regional translator, a perk formerly enjoyed only by Juana.

The two specialized jobs, which cannot be easily divided by region, should be assigned to the two most likely candidates. Marisol should continue preparing case histories since it requires a customized computer and only one is available. Due to her superior English skills, Magdalena would take the senior translator job, which could include supervising the outsourced translations and answering difficult donor questions (formerly done by the director's secretary).

Simplify the work processes to improve turnaround times and better utilize human resources.

Encourage the department to work as a team by setting and posting departmental goals and output figures that would be updated daily and weekly. These goals would reflect the changing priorities in the department, and the translators would learn to help out other employees based on the needs of the workflow, rather than friendships.

Encourage teamwork by holding bimonthly meetings in which staff are kept informed of new developments and asked to problem-solve ways to streamline work processes and improve quality.

Make the department a more pleasant place to work. Set norms that promote inclusion and mutual respect.

Prepare a manual that will be used in training and as a reference for current employees that explains how and why the work should be done. Its purpose would be to supply clear work criteria and objectives.

Provide equal opportunities for the translators to increase their English skills so their jobs have more meaning to them. A highly skilled bilingual department head should devote some time to coaching employees and upgrading the English work demanded of employees as much as possible.

Redesign the office so that the traffic flow of visitors to Sam, José, and Elena does not disrupt the other workers. Use the file cabinets to form a hallway that leads to the back offices and place Elena in the front of the office rather than the back corner.

Question 3

What are the cultural factors that influence this case? Would you expect any differences if it had taken place in the United States?
Relational question (asks for comparisons of themes, ideas, or issues).

Answer

Generally speaking, Central Americans expect to meet more of their social needs at work than Americans do. Given a choice between locating their desk so it faces a wall or other employees, they will choose the latter so they can see and talk to other employees throughout the day. This may also be due to a polychronic orientation that allows them to focus on more than one activity at a time. Americans often prefer a quiet workstation that allows them to concentrate with fewer distractions on one task at a time, a monochronic orientation.

In this culture, it is expected that people shake hands and inquire after families whenever they spot an acquaintance, regardless of the setting. Observing this etiquette is very important, so it was necessary to "hide" the translators from the foot traffic so they would have more time to focus upon work and fewer disruptions.

The employees in this case were used to having decisions made for them by their superiors. An autocratic leadership style is still commonly found in this region (although recent research indicates a trend toward more participation). Their lack of suggestions about how to make the necessary changes in the office does not indicate a lack of intelligence but a lack of exposure to participative decision making.

In a country characterized by high power distance and machismo, it is not surprising that Elena, rather than José or Sam, is the target of employee resentment. Elena is not an effective supervisor, but neither are her superiors. Since they are men and senior managers, however, the translators are more likely to overlook the flaws in their management style. Furthermore, José fits the Guatemalan image of a boss—articulate and forceful—while Elena does not.

Gossip and pointed jokes are a means of social control in Latin America where there is more emphasis upon external controls (shame) than internal controls (guilt). This may explain why Juana might be slightly more powerful in this setting than in another culture.

Although one finds cliques in many cultures, Latin American organizations tend to be more riddled with in-group or out-group factions.

References

Barnard, C. (1938). *The functions of the executive.* Cambridge, MA: Harvard University Press.

Hackman, J. R., G. Oldham, R. Janson, and K. Purdy (1975). "A new strategy for job enrichment," *California Management Review,* pp. 57–71.

Locke, E.A. and Latham, G.P. (1990) *A theory of goal setting and task performance.* Upper Saddle River, NJ: Prentice Hall

McClelland, D. (1985). *Human motivation.* Glenview, IL: Scott, Foresman.

Sherif, M. and C.W. Sherif. (1969). *Social psychology.* New York: Harper and Row.

Spreitzer, G.S. (1992). *When organizations dare: The dynamics of individual empowerment in the workplace.* Unpublished dissertation, University of Michigan, Ann Arbor.

Steers, R.M. and Porter, L.W. (1979) *Motivation and work behavior.* New York: McGraw Hill.

Vroom, V.H. (1964) *Work and motivation.* New York: John Wiley.

Epilogue

(Use this epilogue if you decide not to use case B.)

This is the report that Joanna sent to headquarters at the end of the four-month implementation period:

"The major problems within this department were lack of supervision, unequal work distribution, narrow scope of work, absence of controls, and lack of cooperation among employees. During the next four months, I broadened the scope of the work by making employees responsible for geographical areas rather than one process. Staff were reassigned to jobs more in keeping with their skills. With the help of the employees, I wrote a procedures manual and designed new forms in order to streamline and control the processes. I revised the work daily and gave the employees immediate feedback, and quality improved noticeably. With the exception of the case histories sent to headquarters, no one had ever looked at their work before. I also redesigned the physical layout of the

44

department to form work stations and eliminate traffic from certain areas. Lots of changes took place in a short period, and many hours were spent discussing them with staff. One employee quit, but the rest appeared to be happier with their jobs and more motivated. Looking back, I'd say it was a successful project, but I'd be less of a bulldozer if I had to do it over again."

Note: Joanna's job is not atypical for the educated spouses of expatriate managers on 2- to 3-year assignments in other countries. Although spouses are usually barred from official full-time work due to host country labor regulations, competent spouses are sometimes offered part-time jobs as a result of their social connections.

FIRED!

Topics (* = Primary topic with Teaching Plan)
*Career fit
*Career development
Motivation and rewards
Termination
Large business context
Sales context

Case overview

Tony Marks, a sales representative for Rykoff-Sexton, Inc., was just given a written warning by his sales manager, Hank Smith, for poor performance on the job. After hearing the bad news, he sat sort of puzzled because he did not know his performance had been substandard. It was the first time in his professional career that he ever received such a warning from an employer. The next month, Tony is terminated for poor performance. What happened, and what should he do now?

The case describes the training, feedback, and reward systems of Rykoff-Sexton. It is a good case for evaluating career fit and can be used as a starting point for students to examine their own career choices.

Industry

Manufacturer and distributor of food, paper products, cleaning supplies, and heavy equipment. This national corporation provides goods and services to restaurants, hotels, schools and other organizations; Employs approximately 25,000.

Teaching objectives
1. To examine career development and career fit.
2. To begin evaluating the student's own career strengths and where they might fit in a career.

Other related cases in Volume 1

A Team Divided or a Team United? (termination); *Heart Attack* (termination); *Problems at Wukmier Home Electronics Warehouse* (termination).

Other related cases in Volume 2

Angry Branch Manager (termination); *Changing quotas* (rewards, sales context); *Unprofessional Conduct* (career fit); *When Worlds Collide* (rewards).

Intended courses and levels

This case is intended for undergraduate and graduate students in organizational behavior, management, and human resources management. The topic is career development. It is best positioned early in the course, or during discussion of career fit and development. The topic of motivation and rewards is discussed in the teaching plans in relation to sales jobs.

---

*Source: Adapted from case prepared by Teri C. Tompkins. University of Redlands, Jonnetta Thomas-Chambers, and Tony Marks. The case and teaching note were prepared as a basis for class discussion rather than to illustrate either effective or ineffective handling of administrative situations. Suggestions for improvement of this note should be sent to tompkins@uor.edu. Credit will be given in the next revision.

Analysis
All related analysis and references are embedded in the answers to the questions.

Research methodology
This case reflects the recollections of Tony Marks. This case is a true incident based on the perspective of the author. The company is not disguised.

Teaching plan
The teaching plan below is excellent as a launching pad for students to discuss the importance of matching their personal assets to their career. The teaching plan has them evaluate the skills needed at Rycoff-Sexton and the skills that Tony brings to the company. While Tony has some of the skills necessary to make a good sales representative, he lacks others. Students then discuss their own assets and think about the kinds of careers that match.

This case has been divided into A and B. You can use it as a decision case by having the students first read part A and then answer the questions, "Should Tony stay in sales? If so, what kind? If not, what type of career might fit his personal characteristics?" Use case B as an epilogue of what he did.

Teaching plan topic: Career Development
60-minute teaching plan

Preassignment: Read cases A and B before class (20 minutes)

	Timing	Activity	Organization	Student Outcomes
I	0–5 minutes (5)	Review cases A and B.	Individually	Familiarity with case facts.
II	5–15 minutes (10)	*Q1: What type of compensation and rewards did Rycoff-Sexton offer its outside sales representatives?*	Full class discussion or small groups	• Salary first year. • Second year commission likely. • Likely incentives or bonuses for making quota. • Likely benefits.
III	15–25 minutes (10)	*Q2: What is the role of quotas and extrinsic rewards for people in sales jobs?*	Full class discussion or small groups	• Role of quotas: To motivate and provide performance evaluation criteria. • Role of extrinsic rewards: To motivate and provide performance feedback.
IV	25–30 minutes (5)	*Q3: Did Tony seem motivated by meeting quotas?*	Full class discussion or small groups. If meeting in small groups, report back to class.	It doesn't appear so. He was surprised when he was fired, yet apparently the quotas and numbers were available for him to look at any time. It is reasonable to assume that he didn't use the numbers as a motivator.
V	30–35 minutes (5)	*Q4: What was Tony's greatest asset for developing his career?*	Full class discussion	Answers will vary, but make the point that he was very good at developing a network of friends, colleagues, sports teammates, and neighbors who helped him find jobs.
VI	35–45 minutes (10)	*Q5: Is the ability to network a useful tool in sales? If yes, why*	Full class discussion	Yes, Tony's ability to network is an important component of being good sales. Rycoff-Sexton's structure of

Fired!

	Timing	Activity	Organization	Student Outcomes
		was Tony not successful at Rycoff-Sexton? How would open territories affect selling and sales representatives? What type of sales job would Tony be better at?		"open territories" gave advantage to sales people who were good at first impressions because they had to land a deal on lots of "drop-ins." It also increased competition among the sales representatives rather than collaboration. Many sales jobs require aggressive competition to be successful. Tony would do better at sales jobs that depend on long-term relationships. His ability to network could be an asset in goods and services that are not commodities (where best price, not best relationships, gets the job), such as financial planning, insurance sales. In these types of jobs, trust and networking are key to success.
VII	45–50 minutes (5)	*Q6: What stage is Tony in his career development? Optional: mini-lecture/reminder of the five stages in career development (exploration, establishment, midcareer, late career, decline).*	Full class discussion	Tony is in the establishment stage, which is characterized by steadily improving job performance, making mistakes, and learning from mistakes.
VIII	50–60 minutes (10)	*What are your greatest career assets? What kind of career do you think matches those assets?*	Student pairs or small groups. Or you could assign a short written paper.	This question helps students generalize the case to their own lives. The short paper, if done early in the course, can help you get to know your students and their writing ability. It gives you an opportunity to give them feedback on their writing, if you choose.

25-minute teaching plan on career development.
Preassignment: Read case before class (15 minutes)
Activities. Do activities III, IV, V, and VI in the 60-minute plan.

Discussion questions and answers

Question 1
What type of compensation and rewards did Rycoff-Sexton offer its outside sales representatives?
Exploratory question (probes facts and basic knowledge).
Answer

- Salary first year
- Second year commission likely

48

- Likely incentives or bonuses for making quota
- Likely benefits.

Based on the evidence from the case, we know that Tony's first year was based on a salary. This is in recognition that it takes a while for a sales representative (in any job) to build a territory, especially one that is not divided geographically. It's not clear from the case about his compensation from the second year. He could be on salary plus commission or strict commission. Apparently the newer sales guys get to split accounts if a sales representative leaves, which was the case when Tony argued that he should be given some of the accounts from a person who was leaving. Many sales jobs include some sort of incentive or bonus if you make quota (see *Changing Quotas* case as an example). Since Tony didn't make quota, we don't know if that were true for Rycoff-Sexton. The company promoted its sales force regularly, as we can see from Tony's managers receiving promotions. We can assume with a company as large as Rycoff-Sexton that the company offered benefits.

Question 2

What is the role of quotas and extrinsic rewards for people in sales jobs?
Relational question (asks for comparisons of themes, ideas, or issues).

Answer

- Role of quotas: To motivate and provide performance evaluation.
- Role of extrinsic rewards: To motivate and provide performance feedback.

Frequently sales people are highly motivated by challenge and extrinsic rewards, such as making quotas, receiving bonuses. For example, in the case *Changing Quotas* (volume 2), the highly successful sales person is extremely motivated by meeting her quota and the financial benefits that come with it.

Quotas give sales people a sense of challenge, risk, and reward. Usually a report is generated at regular intervals telling the salesperson how he or she is doing. Most sales people monitor the report very carefully.

Extrinsic rewards, such as commissions, praise, and special prizes are also used frequently to motivate sales people. For example, real estate professionals like not only the reward of the sales commission, but they also like putting "top 1% in sales" on their business cards.

Question 3

Did Tony seem motivated by meeting quotas?
Application skills (using information in a new context to solve a problem, answer a question, or perform a task).

Answer

It doesn't appear that Tony was motivated by meeting quota. If Tony were motivated by the sales figures, he would refer to them frequently to see how he was doing. He would notice how his sales were compared to the other sales representatives. If we assume that the sales figures were published on a regular basis, then it is also reasonable to assume that the numbers were not a motivator for him.

Question 4

What was Tony's greatest asset for developing his career?
Diagnostic question (probes motives or causes).

Answer

Answers will vary, but make the point that he was very good at developing a network of friends, colleagues, sports teammates, and neighbors who helped him find jobs. For example, Rob Resnick, was on his softball team and helped him get the job at Rykoff. In case B, Tony got a call from a long-time friend and neighbor and got his next job. We can assume that Tony has the ability to network, an important component for career development.

Question 5

Is the ability to network a useful tool in sales? If yes, why was Tony not successful at Rycoff-Sexton? How would open territories affect selling and sales representatives? What type of sales job would Tony be better at?

<u>Challenge question</u> (examines assumptions, conclusions, and interpretations).

Answer

Yes, Tony's ability to network is an important component of being good at sales. One explanation of why Tony was less successful at Rycoff-Sexton was that its structure of "open territories" gave advantage to sales representatives who possessed charisma, had high energy, and moved quickly. To find and sell to new customers required a lot of cold calling and "drop ins," and the advantage was to these type of sales reps. The case facts state that Tony was placed in a group of "heavy hitters" and that he was in the middle of the pack of the trainees. It can be inferred that out of 150, perhaps 25 were trainees. We can imagine that they were toward the bottom of the pack because they had not yet built up their territories. Therefore, Tony was probably in the bottom quartile in sales. It's possible that Tony may have been perceived to have been more successful if he had not begun with the heavy hitters.

Open territories also increased competition among the sales representatives rather than collaboration. Many sales jobs require aggressive competition to be successful. Tony does not appear to be a very aggressive person, more like a nice guy.

Tony would do better at sales jobs that depended on long-term relationships. His ability to network could be an asset in goods and services that are not commodities. In commodities, the best price, and not best relationships, gets the sale. Tony might do better in sales jobs that required relationship building, such as financial planning or insurance sales. In these types of jobs, trust and networking are key to success.

Question 6

What stage is Tony in his career development?

<u>Comprehension skills</u> (understanding the meaning of remembered material, usually demonstrated by restating or citing examples).

Answer

Establishment stage.

There are five stages in career development (Robbins and Coulter, pp. 394–395).

<u>Exploration</u>. Begins early in life as we are influenced by parents and relatives. Ends when we finish school, usually by mid-twenties.

<u>Establishment</u>. begins when we search for work and get first jobs. This stage is characterized by steadily improving job performance, making mistakes, and learning from mistakes. Usually ends around mid-thirties.

<u>Midcareer</u>. Individuals are no longer "learners" because mistakes can become costly. Usually ends around 50 or so.

<u>Late career</u>. Can be marked by pleasant time at company as "elder statesman," or feelings of being locked in until retirement. Ages 50 to 70.

<u>Decline</u>. Retirement.

Based on his age and performance, Tony is in the establishment stage, which is characterized by steadily improving job performance, making mistakes, and learning from mistakes.

References

Robbins, S. P. and Coulter, M. (1996). *Management*, 5th ed., pp. 394–400.

Epilogue

U.S. Foodservice, Inc., later bought out Rykoff-Sexton, Inc. At the time of the buyout, many high level executives and salespeople at Rykoff were let go, enabling U.S. Foodservice to bring in their own personnel to run the La Mirada, California, facility. Rob Resnick remained vice president of sales for the La Mirada facility. Hank Smith continued as regional sales manager for the West Los Angeles territory. Mike Bergen left Rykoff shortly after the buyout and is now working for a competitor in the same capacity.

Tony continues to be employed at Financial Management Advisors, Inc., as a marketing associate. This was the position he took after Rykoff-Sexton, Inc., terminated him in February 1997. He does not miss the sales industry and remains excited about his new career. Tony and Rob lost contact with each other after Tony was fired.

*Teaching Note**
HANDLING DIFFERENCES AT JAPAN AUTO

Topics (* = Primary topic with teaching plan)
*Interpersonal conflict
*Interpersonal communication
*Management of conflict
Management styles
Maslow's hierarchy of needs
Motivation
Teamwork
Large corporation context

Case overview

At a parts distribution center for Japan Auto, a Japanese-owned auto manufacturing company, two female employees ended up in a heated argument. Barbara had been employed at Toyota for over seven years. Her coworkers thought she was uncooperative, and a know-it-all, so they tended to steer clear of her. Although the office was relatively small, they managed to ignore her lack of team spirit and the personal insults sometimes directed at them. Another problem was that Barbara was supposed to take cross-training to meet the team's objective for the fourth quarter. Barbara said she was too busy, but members found out it was because she was working on special presentations unrelated to the team's goals, and done mainly to advance her own career. The team approached Chrys, who had just transferred into the department two months prior to talk to their supervisor on behalf of the team. Chrys felt it would be better to first speak with Barbara, before going to the boss.

Although Chrys was at the same management grade as everyone else, she agreed to speak to Barbara. She called Barbara into a conference room and began sharing the department's sentiment. Barbara responded in an angry tone that she had no right discussing departmental matters with her. Chrys got mad and told Barbara in point-by-point detail exactly how she had offended and hurt each member of the department. Barbara backed down and apologized to Chrys. Chrys said she owed an apology to everyone on the team. To Barbara's credit, she asked all the team members into the conference room the next day and apologized. Each member of the team had the opportunity to tell her exactly how she had offended him or her. Then they decided to let it go and focus on the objectives. Although the team still didn't completely trust Barbara, they acknowledged that she was making a much better effort.

Chrys, however, felt bad about the way she had handled herself. Why did she have to lose her temper? Why did she take it so personally when Barbara fought back? Chrys hoped that in the future she would not lose her temper when talking to a fellow associate.

Industry

Unionized auto parts warehouse that was part of a large Japanese automobile manufacturing company. The administrative office was not in a union.

Teaching objectives

1. To introduce students to the concepts of Maslow's hierarchy of needs, managing conflicts, and group dynamics.
2. To recognize how behavioral symptoms can point to the real problem.
3. To evaluate what Chrys did well and what she didn't do well.
4. To decide what steps would be appropriate if you were the manager.

---

*Source: Adapted from case prepared by Nancy Zufferey and Teri C. Tompkins. University of Redlands. The case and teaching note were prepared as a basis for classroom discussion rather than to illustrate either effective or ineffective handling of an administrative situation. Suggestions for improvement of this note should be sent to tompkins@uor.edu. Credit will be given in the next revision.

Other related cases in Volume 1

Julie's Call: Empowerment at Taco Bell (teamwork); *No, Sir, Sergeant!* (interpersonal conflict); *Problems at Wukmier Home Electronics Warehouse* (interpersonal conflict); *Questions Matter* (interpersonal conflict); *The Day They Announced the Buyout* (Maslow's hierarchy of needs).

Other related cases in Volume 2

A Selfish Request in Japan (Maslow's hierarchy of needs); *Angry Branch Manager* (Maslow's hierarchy of needs, teamwork); *Cafe Latte* (interpersonal conflict); *Cost and Schedule Team at AVIONICS* (teamwork); *Incident on the USS Whitney* (interpersonal conflict); *Preferential Treatment* (interpersonal conflict); *Reputation in Jeopardy* (interpersonal conflict); *The Safety Memo* (interpersonal conflict); *Violence at the United States Postal Service* (interpersonal conflict).

Intended courses and levels

This case is intended for undergraduate students in organizational behavior, and management theory courses. The topics include group dynamics, conflict management, Maslow's theory, and management styles. The case can be positioned any time during the term.

Analysis

Analysis can be found in the discussion questions and answers section.

Research methodology

This case reflects the recollection of Chrys in the case. The case is a true incident; however, the company and the names have been disguised.

Teaching plan

This case can provide an excellent opportunity to discuss interpersonal conflict and communication. What are the ways in which to handle conflict? How would you rate Chrys' communication based on conflict management suggestions in textbooks? Was Chrys effective?

Teaching plan topic: Group Development, Communication, and Interpersonal Conflict
60-minute teaching plan

Preassignment: Read case (20 minutes)

	Timing	Activity	Organization	Student Outcomes
I	0–5 minutes (5)	Summarize the case facts.	Ask for or appoint a "volunteer."	Orientation and refresher on case.
II	5–15 minutes (10)	*What factors contributed to the problems between Barbara Smith and Chrys Haber?*	Full class discussion	● Chrys Haber was new, which changed the group dynamics. ● The manager of the team was ineffective at identifying or dealing with the built-up resentment toward Barbara by the other members of the team. ● Barbara had blind spots about her behavior. ● Chrys' and Barbara's desire for career advancement. ● The company culture valued teams and promoted empowered behavior. The team felt responsible for its objective of cross-training.
III	15–25 minutes	*Describe the "noise" barrier at LAPDC.*	Full class discussion	See answer to Question 3.

	Timing	Activity	Organization	Student Outcomes
	(10)			
IV	25–35 minutes (10)	*Using Tuckman's model of group development, at what stage is the administrative team?*	Full class discussion	The group may be going through the second stage on its way to the third stage of development. This is characterized by intense communication and sometimes conflict. The team may have been in the norming and performing stage, but with Chrys' arrival and the new dynamics that caused, the team is once again in the storming phase.
V	35–45 minutes (10)	*Q4: Evaluate Chrys' communication with Barbara in terms of conflict management.*	Full class discussion	Very good technique, despite Chrys' personal feelings about losing her temper. She went directly to Barbara about the problem. She described how Barbara's behavior affected team members, rather than the outcomes (the team doesn't trust you) or her judgment (you are arrogant). She provided feedback, which Barbara had been lacking. On the negative side, she took Barbara's defensiveness personally and became defensive herself. She could have said and acted the same way while having more control over her emotions, which would have felt better to Chrys. It appears that Barbara came to trust Chrys to be honest and direct with her, one in whom she could confide. In terms of results, Chrys appears to be skillful at interpersonal communications.
VI	45–55 minutes (15)	*What recommendations do you have for Chrys and this team now?*	Full class discussion	Continue to provide feedback to each other regarding how behavior affects team performance. Ask the manager to provide mentoring for career development and advancement. Use principled negotiation to iron out differences.
VII	55–60 minutes (5)	Hand out or read epilogue found in this teaching note. Ask for reactions.	Individual or full class reading, followed by full class discussion	Student reactions will vary. Point out or ask for places where there was agreement and disagreement between student analysis and actual outcome.

25-minute teaching plan on group dynamics.
Preassignment: Read case before class (20 minutes).
Activities. Lecture on group development (10 minutes). Do activities IV and VII in the 60-minute plan.

25-minute teaching plan on communication.
Preassignment: Read case before class (20 minutes).
Activities. Mini-lecture on communication noise barriers and feedback (10 minutes). Do activities III and VII in the 60-minute plan.

25-minute teaching plan on conflict.

Preassignment: Read case before class (20 minutes).

Activities. Mini-lecture on conflict management (10 minutes). Do activities V and VII in the 60-minute plan.

Discussion questions and answers

Question 1

What factors contributed to the problems between Barbara Smith and Chrys Haber?

<u>Cause-and-effect questions</u> (causal relationship between ideas, actions, or events).

Answer

- Chrys Haber was new, which changed the group dynamics.

    Any time a new person is added to a group, the dynamics change. The team had developed a norm of ignoring Barbara's communication style. Chrys' strong personality changed the dynamics of the team and stirred things up a bit.

- The manager of the team was ineffective at identifying or dealing with the built-up resentment toward Barbara by the other members of the team.

    This caused a leadership vacuum, which Chrys filled. Because the team members accepted Chrys' natural leadership abilities, she was able to speak for the team when she confronted Barbara.

- Barbara had significant blind spots about her behavior.

    Barbara was unaware that her habits left such a negative impression on her coworkers and customers. Barbara's lack of awareness as to how her actions negatively affected others and why she was oftentimes ignored were her "blind spots." A blind spot can be defined as something that is known to one individual or group, but not another. According to J. Luft (1970), author of *Dealing with Blind Spots: The Need for Feedback*, the fewer the number of blind spots one has, the greater the understanding of one's impact on others, and the greater the opportunity to choose alternative behaviors. Barbara's unawareness of how her habits affected others left her vulnerable and without insight as to alternative behaviors conducive to teamwork and respect from her coworkers. Unbeknownst to Chrys, Barbara's conduct was the result of motivation to gain acceptance and further her career. She had never been considered popular in the department, and when Chrys came on board, Barbara felt even more threatened because Chrys was fairly popular and advancing in her career at a much faster rate than Barbara was.

- Chrys' and Barbara's desire for career advancement.

    Chrys and Barbara were both competitive and eager for career advancement. With limited opportunities to demonstrate competence and initiative (e.g., work improvement teams or presentations), conflict is more likely.

- The company culture valued teams and promoted empowered behavior. The team felt responsible for its objective of cross-training.

    The direct communication between Chrys and Barbara would not have happened on many teams because the culture would not have allowed team members to feel so empowered to handle the problems. In other cultures, Chrys would have been expected to go to her boss and let the boss deal with the problems. At Japan Auto Sales' Los Angeles Parts Distribution Center (LAPDC), team decisions and participation were expected. Consequently, the team could hold a one-hour meeting where Barbara apologized without including the manager. In addition, the team developed and accepted team objectives, such as cross-training. The superordinate goal helped members to feel more justified in asking Barbara to participate as a team player.

Question 2

Describe the noise barrier at LAPDC.

<u>Comprehension skills</u> (understanding the meaning of remembered material, usually demonstrated by restating or citing examples).

Answer

The noise barrier faced at the LAPDC was interpersonal in nature. Interpersonal barriers can be caused by differing perceptions, the communicator's status, inferior listening habits, incorrect usage of terminology and language, and/or actual differences in language (Mosley, et al., 1996, 344). Barbara and Chrys faced conflicts in the areas of perception, listening habits, and incorrect usage of terminology and inferior language skills. With the exception of Marcia (the manager), the employees encountered what is known as irritating listening habits. When an employee interrupts another who is speaking, or when someone makes a suggestion that is immediately and abruptly tossed aside, irritating listening habits are at play. Other examples of irritating listening habits are when an employee has a good idea and another employee says "I thought of that too," or when an employee is speaking and another attempts to finish the sentence. Another category of interpersonal noise is the imprecise use of language or terminology, which Barbara had a tendency to do. Frequently, Barbara would try to assimilate technical lingo utilized by upper management; however, in doing so, she failed to defend her cause. Instead of impressing the group, she was viewed as an employee who had little to contribute and, therefore, lacked importance and was ignored. In addition, by ordering the dealership employee to do as she said because "these are the policies," Barbara had been, among other things, ineffective as a communicator and had contributed to ineffective listening. Moreover, those who were witness to the conversation had interpreted her vague communication as arrogance.

Question 3
Using Tuckman's model of group development, at what stage is the administrative team?
<u>Application skills</u> (using information in a new context to solve a problem, answer a question, or perform a task).

Answer
Under the group development theory defined by B. W. Tuckman, groups experience four basic stages of development, which are natural and inevitable. Some stages overlap others, and the time span of each stage may vary. However, "the central concept is that a group will usually remain in a stage until key issues are resolved before moving to the next stage" (Mosley, Pietri, Megginson, 1996, p. 459). These four stages include forming, storming, norming, and performing. The first stage—forming—happens when department members first come together. At this stage, employees try to determine their role in the group function and in relation to each other personally. Frequently, members of the group are unsure of what is expected of them and, therefore, they tend to rely on leadership to provide the necessary guidance.

The second stage—storming—is the period of conflict among the group members. In this particular case, a major underlying issue was determining which associate would provide the needed leadership in the group. Another major argument was whether or not Barbara would voluntarily contribute and participate in completing departmental objectives. Moreover, concern regarding each associate's personal and professional goals was an issue. According to *Management: Leadership in Action*, "Relationship behaviors emerge, in that people have strong feelings and express them, sometimes in a hostile manner. It is a mistake to suppress conflict; the key is to manage it" (Mosley, et al., 1996, 459). At first, the associates at the LAPDC's Administrative Office suppressed their discontent. However, tensions escalated, leading to the eventual confrontation between Barbara and Chrys.

The third stage is norming. At this stage, the group members come together. "Members feel good about one another and give each other positive feedback. These desirable characteristics of team development result from establishing agreed-upon goals and finalizing the processes, standards, and roles by which the group will operate" (Mosley, et al., 1996, 459). At the LAPDC, norming occurred after the argument between Barbara and Chrys, when the associates agreed that they must work together in order to reach department and personal objectives.

The fourth and final stage is performing—where the group operates in unity. This stage is when open communication and information is exchanged and leadership is shared by all members (Mosley, et al., 1996, 459). As described in the case epilogue, Barbara accepted her role as a team player by voluntarily learning the claims process, Marcia initiated "a different course of action" for fulfilling department objectives and Chrys, along with the other group members, resolved to show more empathy and understanding toward Barbara.

It is likely that the team had been in the norming and performing stage before Chrys arrived. A new member with a strong personality and on such a small team caused the team to cycle back to the storming stage (see Tompkins 1995; 1997, for an explanation of group development stages and cycling back). Once the team members reestablished their roles, then they were able to move to the norming and performing stages.

Question 4
Evaluate Chrys' communication with Barbara in terms of conflict management.
Evaluation skills (using a set of criteria to arrive at a reasoned judgment of the value of something).

Answer
Chrys did very well communicating with Barbara, despite her feelings about losing her temper. Why?
1. She went directly to Barbara about the problem. Talking to the person directly is a recommendation in interpersonal conflict management.
2. Chrys told Barbara the specific **behaviors** that she did rather than saying such things as "You are arrogant." This helped Barbara recognize how she was affecting people in the office. Talking about specific behaviors is much more effective than speaking about generalities.
3. She provided feedback, which Barbara had been lacking.

On the negative side, she took Barbara's defensiveness personally and became defensive herself. She could have said and acted the same way while having more control over her emotions, which would have felt better to Chrys.

Toward the end of the case and in the epilogue, we can see that Chrys' direct communication style was very well received by her associates, her boss, and even Barbara. It appears that Barbara came to trust Chrys to be honest and direct with her, one in whom she could confide. In terms of results, Chrys appears to be skillful at interpersonal communications.

Question 5
What recommendations do you have for Chrys and this team now?
Synthesis skills (putting parts together to form a new whole; solving a problem requiring creativity or originality).

Answer
- Continue to provide feedback to each other regarding how behavior affects team performance.

Barbara's behavior has improved. It makes sense to continue to provide feedback because she responds well to it.

- Ask the manager to provide mentoring for career development and advancement.

A mentor is normally a more experienced and successful individual who is capable of advising and providing emotional support to a developing employee. This individual also has the capability of opening the doors for an aspiring employee. As well, this mentor has the ability to provide constructive feedback about performance (Mosley, et al., 1996, 568). Both Barbara and Chrys would have benefited by such a mentor. The lack of guidance in the department created much frustration and unnecessary competition between the two women.

- Use the principled negotiation to iron out differences.

Finally, had Chrys realized the theory of principled negotiation to resolve conflicts she would have been better equipped to avoid the unpleasant confrontation. A concept proposed by Roger Fisher and William Ury regarding conflict management and resolution is that "whether negotiation involves a peace settlement among nations or a business contract, people often engage in *positional bargaining.*" (Mosley, et al., 1996, 439). The concept is to propose an idea and then give up certain items, thereby giving up the least important things first. Fisher and Ury (1981) suggest a more successful approach might be *principled negotiation.* The four basic components are:
- Separating the people from the problem.
- Focusing on interests, not positions.
- Generating a variety of possibilities before deciding what to do.

- Insisting that the result be based on some objective standard.

Had Chrys utilized this principle, she might have been able to separate Barbara's positions from the underlying problems. Further she might have been better able to resolve the personal and professional conflicts. In turn, this would have motivated Barbara to behave as a team player and act in accordance with the departmental objectives.

References

Fisher, R. and Ury, W. (1981). *Getting to yes*. Houghton Mifflin.

Luft, J. (1970). *Group processes. Dealing with blind spots: The need for feedback*. Palo Alto, CA: National Press Books.

Mosley, D. C., Pietri, P. H., Megginson, L. C. (1996). *Management: Leadership in action*. New York: HarperCollins College Publishers.

Tompkins, T. C. (1997). "A developmental approach to organizational learning teams: A model and illustrative research." In M. M. Beyerlein, and D. A. Johnson (eds.). *Advances in Interdisciplinary Studies of Work Teams* (Vol. 4, pp. 281–302). Greenwich, CT: JAI Press.

Tompkins, T. C. (1995). "The role of diffusion in collective learning." *International Journal of Organizational Analysis*, 3, 69–84.

Epilogue

In early 2000, Chrys was still a claims specialist at the administrative office, but was hoping for a transfer perhaps to customer service. She had about one year left to complete her bachelor of arts degree. She said that she had one more big conflict with Barbara, which made a difference for the better in Barbara's behavior.

Five months after Chrys' and Barbara's last conflict, Barbara has become very pleasant and is much better at internal and external customer relations. Barbara is still going to school on and off and is pregnant with her third child.

The team has done very well, solidly meeting its goals and objectives.

There has been no change in Marcia's leadership style. She tends to rely on Chrys more to handle certain team problems. Whenever Chrys brings up an idea, she'll say, "Run with it, Chrys."

HEART ATTACK

Topics (* = Primary topic with Teaching Plan)
*Cultural differences
*Hofstede's cultural dimensions (Persian versus American cultures)
*Work ethics
*Termination, legal issues of
Ethnic differences and conflict
Small business context

Case overview
This case is of a young graduate student who was fired from her job of six weeks because she left work to be with her father who was being rushed to surgery after a heart attack. Shauna had been hired for a two-person (husband and wife) property management firm to be the bookkeeper. Shauna LeVeque, emotionally drained from worry, is thunderstruck when her boss fires her. She had never been late for work or missed a day in the six weeks she had worked for Mr. Hamid. She had accomplished the task of transferring his checking account information into a computer program in six weeks when he projected two months and she had done so with much praise from him about her accuracy.

The case opens with her father's heart attack on Sunday evening. The doctors advised the family to go home and wait for word. The next morning Shauna's mother told Shauna to go to work and wait for news. As soon as Shauna arrived at work, her mom paged her and informed her that her dad was going into surgery and to come to the hospital. Shauna rushed in to Mr. Hamid's office and told him quickly what was happening and that she would call him that night. He told her he hoped everything would be okay. That night, she called Mr. Hamid and he told her not to bother to come to work the next day. She was fired because she was undependable and didn't ask permission to leave that morning.

Having never been fired from a job and having always left jobs on good terms, she was shocked that Mr. Hamid would be so heartless as to fire her for telling him, rather than asking his permission to be with her father, brother, and mother at the hospital. The next day, Shauna goes to the office to collect her things and to tell Mr. Hamid off. When she mentioned that he would never do such a thing to his daughters, he became irate and told her that if he left work for every little emergency, he would never have been as successful a business man as he was now. Shauna left relieved to not have to work for him again.

Industry
Small two-person property management firm. Small business context.

Teaching objectives
1. To distinguish cultural differences between Middle Easterners and North Americans
2. To apply the spillover model to Shauna and Mr. Hamid's behavior.
3. To become familiar with employment law for small business.

Other related cases in Volume 1
A New Magazine in Nigeria (small business); *A Team Divided or a Team United?* (termination); *Costume Bank* (small business); *Fired!* (termination); *La Cabaret* (cultural differences); *Problems at Wukmier Home Electronics Warehouse* (cultural differences, termination).

---

*Source: Adapted from case prepared by Shauna Le Veque, James C. Spee, University of Redlands, and Teri C. Tompkins, University of Redlands. The case and teaching note were prepared as a basis for class discussion rather than to illustrate either effective or ineffective handling of administrative situations. Suggestions for improvement of this note should be sent to tompkins@uor.edu. Credit will be given in the next revision.

Other related cases in Volume 2

A Selfish Request in Japan (cultural differences); *Angry Branch Manager* (termination); *Cafe Latte* (small business).

Intended courses and levels

This case can be used for undergraduate, graduate, and executive students in the area of management, organizational behavior, and human resources management. Topics include cultural differences among Iranians and Americans, work ethics, and legal issues of firing.

Analysis

Topic 1: Cultural Differences
(questions 1, 2 3)

Mr. Hamid and Shauna were born and raised from two diverse cultures. Mr. Hamid was born and raised in Iran and, according to that culture, the men were the dominant gender. The role of a woman in Iran is only to support the family and her husband. Shauna, on the other hand, was born and raised in Los Angeles where men and women, in theory, were treated as equals. According to Hofstede (1991), people from Iran tend toward low individualism, large power distance, somewhat in the middle but toward strong uncertainty avoidance, and lean somewhat toward the feminine side. Americans have extremely high individualism, lean somewhat toward small power distance, weak uncertainty avoidance, and lean toward the masculine side. On all dimensions, Persians and Americans are opposite.

Hoecklin (1995, based on Trompenaar, 1993) found that Americans are strongly universalistic in their obligations (rules, legal systems, contracts, higher obligations, objectivity, one right way). They are somewhat affective in their emotional orientation in relationships (physical contact more open and free, expressive, vocal, strong body language). They are very specific in their involvement in relationships (direct, confrontational, open, extrovert, separate work and private life). And they are highly achievement-oriented in the legitimization of power and status (status based on competency and achievements, women and minorities visible in more levels in workplace, newcomers, young people, and outsiders gain respect if they prove themselves).

Topic 2: Work Ethics
(questions 4, 5, 6)

The spillover model from *Psychology Applied to Work* by Paul M. Muchinsky (Zedeck, 1992, pp. 313–314) asserts that the values that the person had growing up would influence his or her work ethics. There is a similarity between how a person deals with his or her family at home and how that person acts in the work environment. It also proposes that a person's work experience can influence what he or she does when he or she is away from work. There are three areas in the spillover model.

The effect of work on family. This area examines what impact that the work has on the family. For instance, if a person has encountered a great deal of stress on the job, that person would be very likely to bring the stress home with him or her. That stress would cause a domino effect to all members of the person's family because the family would then react to that person who was under stress at work. It could also cause the opposite reaction. If the person were relaxed and happy at work, then when that person came home, he or she would be more relaxed and happy around the home.

The effect of family on work. This area focuses on how structural or developmental aspects of the family would impact work behavior. If the person is worried about a certain family issue, then that person would be preoccupied with the situation rather than focusing on the job. But, if the person were relatively stress-free at home, then his or her demeanor at work would represent his or her attitude.

The family/work interaction. This third area looks at work and family as an interaction. There is not a simple or direct link that exists between work and family. When one part of a person's life is not going as well as he or she might have hoped, everything else is affected. It is difficult to tell which is the action and which is the reaction—family or work life.

<u>Topic 3: Legal Issue</u>
(questions 7, 8 9)

In 1993, President William Jefferson Clinton signed into law The Family and Medical Leave Act (FMLA). That act provides employers who have fifty or more employees on the payroll to allow employees up to twelve weeks unpaid leave. The employee could use the act for the purpose of birth of his or her child, adoption or fostering a new child, care for a spouse, parent, or child with serious health or condition, or the employee's own health condition. Employees are eligible if they have worked for a covered employer for at least one year and for 1,250 hours over the previous twelve months.

Unemployment compensation states many details, including the following:

- You must be totally or partially unemployed
- You must establish entitlement to benefits by having sufficient earnings in the base period: annual earnings of at least $2,800 of which $1,200 are in each of two separate calendar quarters (requirement vary by state)
- You must be available for full-time work
- You must be able to perform full-time work
- You must be actively looking for full-time work

Research methodology

This case was written based on the recollection of the casewriter. No other parties were interviewed. The case is a true incident. Some names and the organization are disguised.

Teaching plan

Using the analysis above and the teaching plans below, this case provides a nice variety of topics to address.

Teaching plan topic: Cultural Differences
60-minute teaching plan

Preassignment: Read case (15 minutes)

	Timing	Activity	Organization	Student Outcomes
I	0–5 minutes (5)	Summarize the case facts.	Ask for or appoint a "volunteer."	Orientation and refresher on case.
II	5–20 minutes (15)	Review Hofstede's model: • Individualism • Power Distance • Uncertainty Avoidance • Masculine/Feminine	Mini-lecture	Comprehension of key dimensions of the Hofstede's cultural dimensions.
III	20–30 minutes (10)	*Q1: Using Hofstede's dimensions, how could one understand Mr. Hamid as the boss?*	Group discussion	Understand Mr. Hamid's reaction to Shauna's statement that she was leaving was perceived as lacking respect for him.
IV	30–40 minutes (10)	*Q2: Through the lens of western culture, how would one understand Shauna's reaction to the news of being fired?*	Group discussion	Understand that when Mr. Hamid refused to discuss the decision with her, Shauna felt that her right as a human was taken from her.
V	40–50 minutes (10)	*Q3: Would the outcome for Shauna have been any different if she*	Group discussion	No, probably the outcome would be the same. Shauna's ignorance of Iranian culture made it difficult for her to see

	Timing	Activity	Organization	Student Outcomes
		understood Mr. Hamid's management style?		the meaning behind Mr. Hamid's words.
VI	50–60 minutes (10)	Wrap-up. *Does the comparison model explain differences in your workplace?*	Group discussion	Summarize learning from the case through application to a new situation.

25-minute teaching plan on cultural differences.

Preassignment: Read case before class (15 minutes)

Activities. Skip Activity II in the 60-minute plan. Spend 5 minutes on each of the remaining activities.

Teaching plan topic: Work Ethics
60-minute teaching plan

Preassignment: Read case (15 minutes)

	Timing	Activity	Organization	Student Outcomes
I	0–5 minutes (5)	Summarize the case facts.	Ask for or appoint a "volunteer."	Orientation and refresher on case.
II	5–20 minutes (15)	Review the spillover model (Muchinsky, 1992): The effect of work on family. The effect of family on work. The family/work interaction.	Mini-lecture	Comprehension of key dimensions of the spillover model.
III	20–30 minutes (10)	*Q4: How does the spillover model illustrate Mr. Hamid's behavior?*	Group discussion	Mr. Hamid treated Shauna the way women are treated in his home culture.
IV	30–40 minutes (10)	*Q5: How does the spillover model illustrate Shauna's behavior?*	Group discussion	Shauna was brought up to believe that all people are equal, and that each person should be treated with respect, despite his or her gender, age, race or religion.
V	40–50 minutes (10)	*Q6: Would the next employer's background be a major influence when Shauna applied for a job?*	Group discussion	Shauna should ask more questions regarding what will be expected of her and how long the company plans to keep her. She should read up on the culture of the people she will be working for.
VI	50–60 minutes (10)	Wrap-up. Has spillover occurred in your workplace?	Group discussion	Summarize learning from the case through application to a new situation.

25-minute teaching plan work ethics.

Preassignment: Read case before class (15 minutes)

Activities. Skip Activity II in the 60-minute plan. Spend 5 minutes on each of the remaining activities.

Teaching plan topic: Legal Issues
60-minute teaching plan

Preassignment: Read case (15 minutes)

	Timing	Activity	Organization	Student Outcomes
I	0–5 minutes (5)	Summarize the case facts.	Ask for or appoint a "volunteer."	Orientation and refresher on case.
II	5–20 minutes (10)	Review the Family and Medical Leave Act (FMLA). Review unemployment law.	Mini-lecture	Comprehension of key legal issues.
III	20–30 minutes (10)	*Q7: Was firing Shauna legal?*	Group discussion	Shauna was employed less than six weeks, so she could be terminated without cause.
IV	30–40 minutes (10)	*Q8: Could Shauna be eligible for any type of unemployment benefit?*	Group discussion	Shauna was not employed long enough to be eligible for unemployment.
V	40–50 minutes (10)	Q9: *Did Mr. Hamid misrepresent the truth about the job?*	Group discussion	Although Mr. Hamid did not misrepresent the position, what he failed to mention was that there would not be any additional work for her after she finished all the data entries.
VI	50–60 minutes (10)	Wrap-up. *Is employment law important?*	Group discussion	Summarize learning from the case through application to a new situation.

25-minute teaching plan employment law and legal issues.
Preassignment: Read case before class (15 minutes)
Activities. Skip Activity II in the 60-minute plan. Spend 5 minutes on each of the remaining activities.

Discussion questions and answers

Question 1

Using the Hofstede's cultural dimensions, how could one understand Mr. Hamid as the boss?
Application skills (using information in a new context to solve a problem, answer a question, or perform a task).

Answer

It is important to remember that Hofstede's cultural dimensions are based on a generalization. Variations will occur according to subcultures, regions, and individuals (Deresky, 1997, p. 77). Assuming the stereotype, Mr. Hamid is comfortable and supports an unequal distribution of power in the workplace. Shauna, however, would be uncomfortable with differences in power. Thus, Shauna failed to acknowledge Mr. Hamid's authority and formal position by barging into his office and "telling," rather than asking for permission to go be with her dad in the hospital. For Mr. Hamid, this was an insult. For Shauna, it was appropriate. In addition, Mr. Hamid demonstrated his belief in his authority by the way he gave directions and orders to Shauna.

Americans are highly individualist, which refers to the tendency of people to look after themselves and their immediate family only and neglect the needs of society. Shauna felt that it was more important to be with her father rather than tend to her hours at work. Mr. Hamid would not respect this position, believing that by taking care of work, he contributes more to society and his group.

In terms of masculinity, Mr. Hamid's culture leans toward the feminine, which does not value conflict. Americans lend toward masculine, which means that Shauna is likely to be more assertive than

Mr. Hamid would have liked. Uncertainty avoidance is the last dimension, and it appears to have played less of a role in this case.

Question 2

Through the lens of western culture, how would one understand Shauna's reaction to the news of being fired?

Application skills (using information in a new context to solve a problem, answer a question, or perform a task) and relational question (asks for comparisons of themes, ideas, or issues).

Answer

The cultural style that Shauna was brought up in was more egalitarian. She believed that each person should treat others with the same respect that they would like. When Mr. Hamid refused to discuss the decision with her, Shauna felt that her right as a human was taken from her. She understood the United States version of discussion, and when Mr. Hamid didn't engage in the two-way conversation, she didn't know how to respond except to argue. When she started arguing, he felt he had to defend his position and yell.

Question 3

Would the outcome for Shauna have been any different if she understood Mr. Hamid's management style?

Action question (calls for a conclusion or action) and cause-and-effect question (asks for causal relationship between ideas, actions, or events).

Answer

Even if Shauna understood the cultural difference, the outcome would have been the same. Since she didn't have any experience dealing with the Middle Eastern culture, she could not have known to look for any underlying meaning in the job position. Even though during the job interview Mr. Hamid stressed that he wanted the books to be updated and didn't go into too many details on other assignments, Shauna had no way of knowing that it was only a temporary position. She also wasn't accustomed to questioning people's words. Since Mr. Hamid continued the dialog of long-term employment, Shauna believed him. If he didn't mention it, that might have given her a clue that the job was only for the project.

Question 4

How does the spillover model illustrate Mr. Hamid's behavior?

Application skills (using information in a new context to solve a problem, answer a question, or perform a task) and comprehension skills (understanding the meaning of remembered material, usually demonstrated by restating or citing examples).

Answer

Mr. Hamid was Iranian and, according to his culture's religion and traditions, women were to take care of the home and their children. Men had the final word on every issue, including the raising of the children. If a woman spoke out of turn or contradicted a man, her husband or other males in the family could reprimand or even beat her. Mr. Hamid brought that philosophy into his workplace. Since Shauna was a female, Mr. Hamid treated her as he would any other female outside the home. He expected her to be submissive to him.

Question 5

How does the spillover model illustrate Shauna's behavior?

Application skills (using information in a new context to solve a problem, answer a question, or perform a task) and comprehension skills (understanding the meaning of remembered material, usually demonstrated by restating or citing examples).

Answer

Shauna was brought up in southern California where the rich diversity of ethnic cultures meant she was probably taught to accept differences in people. She had her own apartment and was self-sufficient when she applied for the bookkeeping position at ESD demonstrating that she believed that women could live away from home before marrying. It is probable that she believed that people are equal, and that each person should be treated with respect, despite their age, race or religion.

One of the problems that Mr. Hamid and Shauna faced was that they each took their "spillover" into the workplace. Mr. Hamid viewed Shauna as just a woman working for him. He believed that he did not have to treat her with respect, and he didn't believe that he owed her any explanation when he let her go. If he wanted to let her go, he believed that that was his prerogative. Shauna was accustomed to American candor. If she had a problem with someone, she would feel free to discuss the issue with the person she was having the problem with. And, when she confronted Mr. Hamid about being fired, she might have been shocked or surprised that he was so angry when she wanted to discuss it. Mr. Hamid felt that his decision was final; it was not up for debate.

Question 6

Would the next employer's background be a major influence when Shauna applied for a job?
Summary question (elicits syntheses).

Answer

Shauna probably learned a very valuable lesson from this incident. Though she grew up in a culture that respects the cultural background of others, she was quite naïve to overlook that the person's heritage could play a major role regarding business. When she interviews for her next job position, she might want to be sure to not only ask more questions regarding what would be expected of her, and how long the company would plan to keep her, but she might also read about the culture of the people she would be working for.

Question 7

Was firing Shauna legal?
Action question (calls for a conclusion or action) and application skills(using information in a new context to solve a problem, answer a question, or perform a task).

Answer

In short, yes. Because Shauna was employed at ESD for less than six weeks, either party could terminate the commitment. The probationary period for the employer or the employee is three months. If the employer decides after that probationary period that he or she didn't need the employee, he or she must either have sufficient cause to let the employee go, or he or she must compensate the employee financially by paying for unemployment insurance or severance pay. If the company fired the employee without sufficient cause, the employee could sue for wrongful termination. Shauna had the same right to quit the position within the first three months, without giving Mr. Hamid adequate time to find a replacement as the company had in terminating her.

Question 8

Could Shauna be eligible for any type of unemployment benefit?
Evaluation skills (using a set of criteria to arrive at a reasoned judgment of the value of something).

Answer

No. Because she was employed there for only less than six weeks, and there were less than fifty employees on Mr. Hamid's payroll, she was not entitled to any type of unemployment benefit. The law in California is very specific as to who is eligible for unemployment compensation. Even if she worked at ESD for longer than the required three months, she would have a hard time collecting unemployment benefits because she was a full-time student. And, she could not request severance pay because of the same reasons that she wasn't eligible for unemployment benefits. Firing Shauna was completely legal, though she regarded it as unethical.

Question 9

Did Mr. Hamid misrepresent the truth about the job?
Evaluation skills (using a set of criteria to arrive at a reasoned judgment of the value of something).

Answer

In Shauna's eyes, he did. When Shauna applied for the job, she understood it to be a part-time bookkeeping position. During the initial job interview, Mr. Hamid and Shauna discussed what he expected from her. She understood that her main job was to enter the data from the checkbook into the computer program. He mentioned that after that project was completed, he would have other assignments for her but he didn't tell her what those assignments were and she did not ask. It was only after the fact that Shauna realized that though Mr. Hamid did not misrepresent the position, what he failed to mention was that there would not be any additional work for her after she finished all the data entries. In Mr. Hamid's eyes, he likely saw this as a business decision that was entirely ethical.

References:

Badawy, M.K. (1980). Style of mideastern managers. *California Management Review* 22 (3).

Deresky, H. (1997). *International Management: Managing Across Borders and Cultures*, 2nd ed. Reading, MA: Addison-Wesley.

Hoecklin, L. (1995). *Managing Cultural Differences*. Wokingham, England: Addison-Wesley.

Hofstede, G. (1991). *Cultures and Organizations: Software of the Mind*. London: McGraw-Hill U.K. Ltd.

Muchinsky, Paul M. (1992). *Psychology applied to work*. (Zedeck, pp. 313–314).

Epilogue

Hindsight is 20/20. Shauna had no way of knowing that she was hired only to enter data when she accepted the position at ESD and that anything Mr. Hamid said to her was a lie or spoken only under false pretenses. If Shauna had known that the position was only temporary, she probably wouldn't have accepted the position.

Shauna is now a graduate student at Claremont Graduate University, studying Human Resources. She accepted a job as personnel director at a management consulting firm a week after she was fired from ESD. That job allowed her to work around her school schedule, and she enjoyed her coworkers, boss, and her position. Her father survived the heart attack, changed his eating habits, and exercises religiously. He even talked Shauna into quitting smoking because there was now a known heart disease risk in the family.

Shauna hasn't seen or spoken with Mr. Hamid since she walked out of the office. Once in a while, she will pass by one of his properties and reflect back on those six weeks that she worked for him. She assumes that he is doing well. She harbors no ill will.

Teaching Note[*]
JENNA'S KITCHENS, INC.

Topics (* = Primary topic with teaching plan)
*Status
*Constrained decision making
Medium-sized business context

Case overview
Judi Singleton, a regional manager of a chain of franchised family-style restaurants, was faced with declining morale among the regional office employees. Recently, these office employees had been moved from a downtown location to the regional warehouse in the industrial section of the city. Office morale had plummeted. In response, Judi had increased office and warehouse wages, but office morale has continued to decline—leading to another decision-action opportunity.

Industry
Fast-food restaurant chain. Medium-sized company. Regional market.

Teaching objectives
1. To provide students with an opportunity to apply an appropriate conceptual framework to a modest set of data and begin to appreciate the discovery power of related ideas.
There are two secondary teaching objectives also:
2. To show and therefore appreciate constrained decision-action (i.e., prior managerial action severely reduces the action that can now be taken), and,
3. To highlight ideas (status, status incongruity) that are under-represented and under-appreciated in contemporary management/OB texts.

Other related cases in Volume 1
Temporary Employees: Car Show Turned Ugly (constrained decision making).

Intended courses and levels
Undergraduate students in management and organizational behavior courses with modest exposure to the case method will find this case interesting and useful. It is a relatively short case about a little known type of business that has a clear and important need for action at the end. That the case is about a female manager in a woman-run business also attracts interest. This case was written for an undergraduate course that utilized case discussions approximately a third of the class time. It was intended to be used fairly early in the course.

Analysis
Case analysis is provided in the answers to the discussion questions.

Research methods
The case information was gathered in field work during the summer of 1994. The contact and access was initiated by the case writer who, as a restaurant customer, overheard a conversation between a restaurant manager and a regional office representative. After identifying himself and expressing an interest in the company, he was introduced to Judi Singleton, subsequently interviewing her and several other regional employees on two occasions.

---

*Source: Adapted from case prepared by Craig C. Lundberg, Cornell University, James C. Spee, University of Redlands, and Teri C. Tompkins, University of Redlands. The case and teaching note were prepared as a basis for class discussion rather than to illustrate either effective or ineffective handling of administrative situations. Suggestions for improvement of this note should be sent to tompkins@uor.edu. Credit will be given in the next revision.

Teaching Plan
Teaching plan topic: Status Incongruence and Distinguishing Types of Objectives
60-minute teaching plan

Preassignment: None

	Timing	Activity	Organization	Student Outcomes
I	0–10 minutes (10)	Read the case.	Full group discussion	Better comprehension of the situation.
II	10–20 minutes (10)	Q1: What are the symptoms in the case that indicate that something isn't working the way it should or indicate that some managerial action is needed?	Full group discussion	Clarify symptoms and objectives.
III	20–30 minutes (10)	Q2: What are Judi Singleton's probable objectives as regional manager for her region and for herself?	Full group discussion	Distinguish between organizational and personal objectives.
IV	30–40 minutes (10)	Q3: What ideas, models or theories seem most useful for understanding the situation Judi Singleton faces?	Full group discussion	Apply group dynamics model to the situation.
V	40–45 minutes (5)	Q4: As of the end of the case, what appear to be the factors that constrain what Judi Singleton might do?	Full group discussion	Identify constraints to action.
VI	45–55 minutes (10)	Q5: As of the end of the case, what specific action or series of actions do you recommend to Judi Singleton?	Full group discussion	Make recommendations.
VII	55–60 minutes (5)	Wrap up discussion.	Full group discussion	Reflect on key learning points.

25-minute teaching plan on status incongruence.
Preassignment: Read case before class (10 minutes).
Follow segments II, IV, and V above.

Discussion questions and answers
Question 1
What are the symptoms in the case that indicate that something isn't working the way it should or indicate that some managerial action is needed?
<u>Diagnostic question</u> (probes motives or causes).

68

Answer

Understanding the continuing decline in morale among the regional office employees of Jenna's Kitchens turns on seeing and appreciating two sets of case information. First, while the company as a whole and the region are successful (e.g., sales and profits are high, the chain continues to expand), top management is pushing hard to reduce costs (e.g., moving the regional office out of high priced office space downtown to the warehouse) which is easily perceived by employees as inconsistent and symbolically open to misunderstanding. Second, the status differential between office and warehouse personnel was initially considerable (e.g., high priced, downtown facilities, parking garages needed, downtown shopping close by, etc. versus a warehouse in an industrial area with poorer, immediate parking, restaurants, etc.). After the move, this differential was substantially reduced and even symbolically reversed (e.g., office employees begin work before warehouse employees, work simplification). The office women may have especially felt the warehouse area undesirable after the center-city offices. The manager's response to the predictable griping and complaining (i.e., raising wages) was a response to the symptoms of reduced status and did nothing to restore status differentials (warehouse employees also received increases).

Question 2

What are Judi Singleton's probable objectives as regional manager for her region and for herself? Analysis skills (breaking a concept into its parts and explaining their interrelationships; distinguishing relevant from extraneous material).

Answer

The problems that Judi is facing suggest that she is not achieving her objectives; hence, listing organizational and personal objectives will help to focus action on this problem. Students learn to differentiate between personal and organizational goals, which is a fundamental managerial ability.

Some potential answers include:

Organizational
- ROI; profits
- Increased sales, reduced expenses
- Survive through recessions
- Ability to grow the business
- Productive workforce

Personal goals
- To meet organizational needs
- To receive financial rewards for meeting goals
- To have a motivated workforce
- To have opportunity for promotion and advancement
- To work for a successful company
- To have the flexibility to make decisions

Question 3

What ideas, models, or theories seem most useful for understanding the situation Judi Singleton faces? Application skills (using information in a new context to solve a problem, answer a question, or perform a task.).

Answer

The symptoms identified in the case point to low performance and morale of the whole group, not just a single individual. This suggests that the root causes could be found in group dynamics rather than individual dynamics. Whatever is occurring seems to be happening to the entire work group. Work groups have several structural properties, including group structure, work group norms, role relationships, group cohesiveness, and status relationships (Steers, 1984, p. 225). After moving to the new location, the group did not change in size. Work group norms did not change substantially within the group after the move. Roles within the group did not change either. No one was promoted or demoted as a result of the move.

This leaves the issue of status relationships. Status differentiates people and groups from each other. Sources of status include birth, personal characteristics, achievement, possessions, and formal authority. In this case, the office staff felt that higher status was ascribed to them when their office was in downtown Spokane. They came to believe that they deserved to have an office in a prime location because of their importance to the company.

Status incongruence occurs when a person feels that he or she deserves a higher status than he or she receives within the organization. One example is someone who is promoted on a fast track ahead of "old-timers" who feel that they should have been promoted first. In the case, we don't see one individual experiencing status incongruence; we see an entire group. Status differentiation between the office staff and the warehouse staff served the following purposes, which were not clear until the office staff moved to the warehouse location (Steers, 1984, p. 233):

<u>Motivation</u>. After the move, motivation was much lower throughout the group. Higher status was linked with higher achievement. Status incongruence reduced their desire to achieve.

<u>Identification</u>. The downtown office was a status symbol that helped the group identify itself as important. It was a symbol of their value to the company. When they were moved to the warehouse location, they felt that they could no longer be differentiated from the warehouse workers, who held lower status in their eyes.

<u>Dignification</u>. As downtown office workers, the staff felt they deserved a higher level of respect. They may have believed that they should have been consulted before the move was made. Their loss of dignity from moving to the warehouse contributed to the low morale in the group.

<u>Stabilization</u>. The downtown location was a source of stability for the group. It clarified their relationship with others in the company and may have been seen as a source of authority. Without it, they had less leverage to influence the warehouse and other departments to do what they needed to have done.

Question 4

As of the end of the case, what appear to be the factors that constrain what Judi Singleton might do?
<u>Relational question</u> (asks for comparisons of themes, ideas, or issues.)

Answer

Judi is already constrained by her choice of location. It will be too expensive for her to relocate again. She may be risk-averse at this point anyway. If her staff didn't like this move, they might hate another location even more. With her managers focusing on cost cutting, finding another location is out of the question. She is further constrained by the labor cost increases she incurred by trying to buy her way out of the problem with increased wages.

Status tends to be perceived as a zero-sum resource, if someone gains it, someone else must lose it. Judi needs a solution that will reduce the status incongruence felt by her staff.

Question 5

As of the end of the case, what specific action or series of actions do you recommend to Judi Singleton?
Action question (calls for a conclusion or action.)

Answer

At the end of the case, appropriate action would quickly re-establish the office-warehouse employee status differentials—now hard to do and justify, given the constraints of location, labor cost increases, etc. Several short-run, inexpensive actions appear to be feasible, e.g., separate, even named parking spaces; warehouse employee hours earlier than those of office employees; an information system that requires office employees to initiate communication with warehouse employees; an office employee "special" lounge; periodic lunches "downtown" for office employees only; a separate, fancy office entrance, some office jobs enlarged; and so forth. Longer-run action possibilities can only be speculated upon but these should all contribute to reestablishing the status differentials between the office and the warehouse.

References

Steers, R.M. (1984). *Introduction to organizational behavior*, 2nd ed. Glenview, IL: Scott Foresman Co.

Epilogue

None.

JULIE'S CALL: EMPOWERMENT AT TACO BELL

Topics (* = Primary topic with a teaching plan)
*Contingency approach (Routines of task technology)
*Empowerment
Participative management
Job enrichment
Organizational change
Shared decision making
Total quality management (TQM)
Teamwork
Restructuring
Large corporation context

Case overview

This case focuses on the implementation of the empowerment program at a store of Taco Bell. The fast food outlet store is less than a year old, as is the corporate-wide empowerment program. The case describes a one-day visit to Julie's store (Julie is the store manager) by a hospitality management senior student, Marcie, and includes the field notes (observations and interviews) that Marcie made during her visit. The case shows the usefulness of shared decision making which allows team members at the lowest levels of organizations to make decisions. This increases their own work satisfaction and morale, which in turn improves the efficacy and efficiency of their outputs, thereby increasing quality and decreasing the costs.

The case is given focus by requiring students to take Marcie's role. First, they are to think through the situation, consider the employees' and the manager's standpoints and the evidence provided about how the corporate empowerment program has been implemented in Julie's store. Second, they are to outline what they (the students) might or should say to Julie, who is calling Marcie to get her thoughts about "training and empowerment."

The fast food outlet's members are all male, mostly in high school, and have varying degrees of food service experience. The case appendix (i.e., Marcie's field notes) indicates the company's purpose, Julie's and four student employees' conception of empowerment, and describes some of Julie's and the four student employees' behaviors at work as well as several of Marcie's observations about this work setting. With a modicum of comparative analysis, the reader can easily note different motivations and views about empowerment, the work itself, and both the formal as well as informal relationship among the employees and their managers.

Industry

Fast food industry. Large corporation.

Teaching objectives

1. To provide students with an opportunity to think about a popular management practice (empowerment) in context.
2. To provide students with a more proactive role than usual, because the case involves students.
3. To introduce students to the idea of participative management and shared decision making that is taking place in organizations.
4. To increase students' awareness of the importance of teamwork and the required level of communication.

---

*Source: Adapted from case prepared by Craig C. Lundberg (Cornell University), Rasool Azari (University of Redlands), and Teri C. Tompkins. The case and teaching note were prepared as a basis for class discussion rather than to illustrate either effective or ineffective handling of administrative situations. Suggestions for improvement of this note should be sent to tompkins@uor.edu. Credit will be given in the next revision.

Other related cases in Volume 1

A Team Divided or a Team United? (empowerment, participative decision making); *Donor Services Department in Guatemala* (work tasks, job enrichment); *No, Sir, Sergeant!* (empowerment).

Other related cases in Volume 2

Computer Services Team at AVIONICS (participative decision making, TQM); *Cost and Schedule Team at AVIONICS* (empowerment, participative decision making); *Leadership of TQM in Panama* (TQM); *The Safety Memo* (empowerment).

Intended courses and levels

This case is intended for lower division undergraduates. While written for an introductory course in human resources management (where it has been class tested once), it could also be utilized in organizational behavior, management, and service management courses. It should appeal especially to students in hospitality programs.

Analysis

Major points that an analysis should uncover are:
1. Corporate training about empowerment for store managers is general, partial, and imposed.
2. Julie and all other case characters each have a different understanding of what empowerment means.
3. Training is essential to developing empowered employees but corporate formula for store training is unrelated and unrealistic. Little training is being done in Julie's store.
4. Empowerment is probably unrelated to the nature of employees, their needs, and wants.
5. The reward system is also unrelated to the empowerment program and, in fact, does not provide any relevant inducements.
6. Support for Julie's effort to implement empowerment is not forthcoming from her manager.
7. Julie's own needs or wants keep her attention as well as her energy away from the program.
8. Given the high routinization and high control in this type of business and the expected turnover with student employees, empowerment may not be appropriate at all.

Research methodology

An undergraduate student, interested in employment with Taco Bell, visited a store and interviewed the manager and four employees. As the student was leaving, the manager asked the student if she could call and get the students' thoughts on how empowerment was going at her store. Most of the case information is in the form of quotes from the interviews conducted and field notes by the student.

Teaching plan

All relevant contemporary textbooks, whether general management, OB, or HRM, will contain general discussions about empowerment, its purposes, and practices. Most, however, treat it as a stand-alone topic and, therefore, do not emphasize the need for such programs to be congruent with other practices or the firm culture—something instructors should be prepared to add.

Appropriate questions to guide students' preparation will depend somewhat upon the familiarity of the students regarding the topics of empowerment, training, and franchise management. If students are likely to be unfamiliar with these topics, the four questions in the discussion questions and answers section seem appropriate. For students who are somewhat more sophisticated with HRM topics, the following preparation instruction should suffice: Outline, from Marcie's perspective, what you would have her say when Julie calls her.

In class, the discussion can be ordered in two ways—either by first focusing on empowerment (program intentions, how the program is actually being carried out, and how empowerment is perceived by the case characters) and then clarifying relevant situational and contextual factors (the nature of the work, the reward system, formal relationships, managerial style, employee and manager needs and wants, the store manager's relationship to her manager, etc.), or the other way around, i.e., from situation and context to empowerment. A teaching plan is outlined in the table below.

The above presumes that the class discussion revolves around the specifics of the case. In addition or alternatively, the discussion could use the case as a jumping-off place to talk more generally about management fads like empowerment (or, MBWA, Q circles, etc.) and why they may or may not work as intended—leading to the appreciation of a program or practice being consistent with the organizational culture, and other organizational systems, i.e., reward system, communication system, control system, job design, HRM systems, etc.

Teaching plan topic: Empowerment
60-minute teaching plan

Preassignment: Read the case before class (20 minutes). Read about empowerment (in the course text and/or course handouts and/or journal literature).

	Timing	Activity	Organization	Student Outcomes
I	0–15 minutes (15)	*Review what you know about your own experience with fast food outlets, i.e., the types of jobs, management style, and policies/rules that seem to prevail.*	Pose questions to students, and compile a comprehensive list of answers and issues from students.	• Know specifics of the case: • Type of business • Type of employees • Working condition Make the students aware of the crucial issues of this type of business (See question 1)
II	15–30 minutes (15)	*What is the purpose of empowerment? Are there any difficulties such practices entail for managers and employees?*	Let students discuss and work through their questions about empowerment in general. Full class discussion. Lead the class in the discussion of difficulties which may arise with this new program	• Understanding the concept and the purpose of empowerment • Understanding the limitation of practicing empowerment • To understand the difficulties from both management's and employees' perspectives. (See question 3)
III	30–45 minutes (15)	Next, turning to the case, *put yourself in Marcie's shoes and prepare yourself to respond to Julie's call. What will you say to Julie (and why)? How will you say it (and why)?*	Divide the class into several groups (each consisting of 2 to 4 members). Let them form a consultation plan for Julie's situation which then will be presented to the class	Students should consider: • Problem of scheduling • Training and education • Resistance to change • Issue of technology • Corporate goals and objectives • Commitment of top management • Employees' behavior patterns
IV	45–60 minutes (15)	Conclusion: *Is this program appropriate and beneficial for Julie's business. Why? Why not?*	Divide the class into two groups. One group works out the pros; the other works out the cons of this program. Let each group present its results. Let the whole class	Answers will vary. See Question 4 for the pros and cons. This activity also helps students: • Practice working in group • Practice critical and analytical thinking • Make decisions based on documentation

	Timing	Activity	Organization	Student Outcomes
			reach a consensus.	

25-minute teaching plan on empowerment.
Preassignment: Read case before coming to class (20 minutes reading time).
Do activities II (15 minutes) and IV (10 minutes) in preceding 60-minute plan.

Discussion questions and answers

Question 1

Review what you know about your own experience with fast food outlets, i.e., the types of jobs, management style, and policies/rules that seem to prevail.
Exploratory question (probes facts and basic knowledge).

Answer

This type of service-oriented business entails constant change of the workforce—young and high school kids. The job is mainly transitory because the workforce, in general, does not depend on it for its livelihood. Therefore, there needs to be constant training. Also flexibility in work scheduling is very important, because of the constant flux in the workforce personal schedule. Work tends to be simple and routine, requiring standard operating procedures, with little discretionary options, in terms of food operations or cleaning. There are few decisions that need to be made, except in the area of scheduling, and even that is fairly simple.

Traditionally, and unfortunately, many managers and supervisors are unwilling or afraid to relinquish any of their authority or power. Some even insist that employees are not ready or capable of accepting empowerment. This is especially true for managers who lack self-confidence and cannot lead or empower others. Empowerment begins at the top. There must be an organizational culture that supports empowerment.

Question 2

Based on your reading in the text, what have you learned about empowerment?
Knowledge skills (remember previously learned material such as definitions, principles, and formulas).

Answer

"Empowerment is a managerial approach in which employees are given substantial authority and say to make decisions on their own" (Robbins and Coulter, 1996, p. 343). Frederick Taylor, under Scientific Management, wanted workers to do what they were told. This worked fine with less educated employees and less complicated jobs, but today's work can be more complex, requiring better trained employees. By redesigning jobs and letting individual workers and teams make job-related decisions, employees become more empowered (pp. 60 and 61).

Question 3

What is the purpose of empowerment supposed to be? Are there any difficulties such practices entail for managers and employees?
Application skills (using information in a new context to solve a problem, answer a question, or perform a task).

Answer

Empowerment or involvement is one of the basic concepts of TQM. Empowerment depends on the shared decision making by giving the authority to employees at all levels in order to improve organizational performance. As it was discussed in question 1, without an organizational culture supporting empowerment, it is impossible to implement it. People seldom take more responsibility than they have to, especially if it involves doing a dirty job. If there is no appropriate reward system evolving at the same time, empowerment cannot take place.

Managers may be reluctant to relinquish power for various reasons. They may not know how to change their managerial style, they may not trust their employees' competence, they may not be willing to give up their position of perceived power, and they may fear becoming obsolete. On the other hand, employees may not be willing to take on added responsibility and resist change if incentives are not provided.

Finally, a very critical problem with empowerment, is that naïve managers believe that empowerment can improve all worker motivation and commitment. But, the nature of the work does not always lend itself to empowerment. If the work requires routine procedures, and does not allow the worker to make decisions (because the nature of the task requires consistent procedures), then employees will have little say-so about their work. Thus, they will have little empowerment, even if both management and the employee desire it. You can have empowerment over the work only where there is discretion.

Question 4

Put yourself in Marcie's shoes, and prepare yourself to respond to Julie's call. What will you say to Julie (and why)? How will you say it (and why)?
Action question (calls for a conclusion or action).

Answer

There will be a wide variation of responses among students. Because of the concept of empowerment can be so contrary to traditional managerial styles, and even though students were introduced to the new concept, they may have difficulties seeing the validity of its implementation and therefore argue against it. On the other hand, students may embrace its novelty and disregard cautionary considerations, such as the general youth of Julie's employees, the high turnover of this workgroup, and the unrealistic time demand for necessary training.

Further possible issues students will have to consider when discussing how Marcie should advise Julie are 1) possible reluctance of dealing with technology (computer, etc.); 2) is there a reward system to create enough incentive for employees to take on added responsibilities; 3) can Julie develop a set of continuous improvement objectives rather than supervising her work crew; 4) does every employee understand the organizational plans, goals, objectives, vision, and mission (this requires communication).

References

Robbins, S.P., and Coulter, M. (1996). *Management*, 5th ed. Upper Saddle River, NJ: Prentice Hall.

Epilogue

This case provided an active and insightful discussion the one time it was used. The class discussion of the major points of analysis was quite rich. Unexpected, however, was the debate engendered about *how* Marcie should share her thoughts with Julie. The range of student judgment was enormous—from very tentative and polite to telling it like it is. Instructors using this case should be prepared for this!

LA CABARET

Topics (* = Primary with teaching plan)
*Conformity
*Racial oppression
Racial diversity
Racial reasoning
Ethics
Interracial differences and conflict
Cultural differences

Case overview

On a Friday evening, in the summer of 1995, two couples went out to celebrate the conclusion of a hard week of work and school. The first couple consisted of Malcolm, a 29-year-old, easygoing, African American medical student, and Malcolm's girlfriend, Shelly Bina, a 22-year-old communications student of Iranian heritage. Bob and Betty, the second couple, were friends of Malcolm's and both of African American descent. Malcolm, Shelly, Bob, and Betty decided to go to La Cabaret, a local restaurant featuring a live comedy show. Most of the people (including the comedians) at La Cabaret were black.

The two couples chose a table in close proximity to the stage to gain a good view of the comedians. After the first few acts and several rounds of drinks, the crowd began to get a little rowdy. The situation became potentially dangerous when one of the comedians, Harry, immediately spotted and focused on the interracial couple. Harry began to make sneering remarks about their obviously different ethnicity—telling Malcolm "You're not black" because he was with a white woman, and equating being Iranian with being Arabic by calling Shelly a "camel jockey." The jokes were racially inciting to the crowd, and they became more involved in the routine and increasingly hostile toward Malcolm and Shelly.

Malcolm and Shelly stayed until the end of the show and bore the brunt of Harry's jokes because they did not want to give the crowd the satisfaction of seeing them leave. Shelly could feel the tension and anger rising in Malcolm. She also felt completely humiliated and extremely conspicuous as one of the only white people in the predominantly black crowd. Bob and Betty sat quietly watching the show and offered no reaction, defense, or support of any kind.

After the show, Malcolm confronted the comedian but was restrained by Bob before any blows could be exchanged. Malcolm and Shelly left the club and, on their way home, Malcolm apologized continuously to Shelly for their horrible experience.

Industry
Entertainment.

Teaching objectives
1. To analyze social conformity—why do bystanders sometimes fail to help people in distress?
2. To encourage students to examine their feelings surrounding racial injustice.
3. To examine the concept of racial reasoning.

Other related cases in Volume 1
A Team Divided or a Team United? (conformity); *Heart Attack* (ethics); *Problems at Wukmier Home Electronics Warehouse* (diversity).

---

*Source: Adapted from case prepared by Teri C. Tompkins, University of Redlands, Rasool Azari (University of Redlands), Don McCormick (University of Redlands), and the person who shared this story. The case and teaching note were prepared as a basis for classroom discussion rather than to illustrate either effective or ineffective handling of an administrative situation. Suggestions for improvement of this note should be sent to tompkins@uor.edu. Credit will be given in the next revision.

Other related cases in Volume 2

A Selfish Request in Japan (ethics); *Angry Branch Manager* (diversity); *The Safety Memo* (ethics); *The Volunteer* (ethics).

Intended course and levels

This case is appropriate for undergraduate, graduate, and executive students. It is best introduced after some level of trust has been established in the classroom. Depending on the racial composition of the classroom, responses to the issues may vary. It is a useful discussion tool for the topics of diversity and/or ethics.

Analysis

Further analysis might suggest that Shelly and Malcolm may be guilty of attribution errors by attributing Harry's behavior to (internal) personality problems or prejudice. However, it may be true that external factors, such as what the audience finds funny, which is essential to his success as a comedian, may play an integral part in determining the subject matter of his routines.

Research methodology

This case reflects the recollection of one of the main characters in the case. The case is a true incident. Names and organizations have been disguised.

Teaching plan

This case can be taught two ways. The first might feel safer to some students and perhaps the instructor in terms of facilitating students' very divergent feelings regarding race. The first teaching plan focuses on the bystanders and issues of conformity. Instructors can use this case when discussing roles and norms in groups (Robbins, 1998, Chapter 7) or when discussing perceptions and attributions (Robbins, 1998, Chapter 3).

The second teaching plan will involve more controversy in the classroom but has the potential of being a significant case for discussing issues of diversity. The instructor must be flexible because the discussions can go many different directions, depending on the composition of the classroom and the students' values. Many, but not all, students will support the goal of reducing racial oppression. The instructor must be prepared to face students' discomfort with the subject matter, which can lead to strong feelings directed at the instructor or other class members.

Teaching plan topic: Conformity
60-minute teaching plan

Preassignment: None

	Timing	Activity	Organization	Student Outcomes
I	0–10 minutes (10)	Students read case in class	Individually	Knowledge of case facts
II	10–15 minutes (5)	Overview by instructor of case facts by asking someone to summarize the situation in the case.	Full class discussion	Verify that everyone understands the "facts" in the case.
III	15–20 minutes (5)	Ask: "Who would like to begin the analysis of this case by identifying one or two issues it raises?"	As students present their views, ask for clarification and reactions from other students. Keep a list on the board of all issues raised by the case for possibly more in-depth discussion.	Serves as a warm-up and allows students to put their issues on the table right away. This activity could be skipped to allow for a very focused discussion on conformity.
IV	20–35	*Q1: Why didn't Betty and*	Full class discussion or	Students find that conformity is a

	Timing	Activity	Organization	Student Outcomes
	minutes (15)	*Bob defend Malcolm and Shelly?*	small groups. As students provide reasons, instructor sorts them on the board according to the five questions discussed by Aronson: (1) situation serious? (2) require my personal intervention? (3) costly to me? (4) benefit the victim? (5) can I exit easily? (6) other reasons.	strong social pressure that can be explained without regard to "weak" or "radical" personalities and values. Students learn the types of situations and cognitions that lead to conformity. Students learn how powerful pressures are to conform and how difficult they are to overcome even for so-called friends.
V	35–45 minutes (10)	*Q2: What would you do if you were at a meeting at work and someone made a racial (or gender-based, or sexual orientation-based) joke that you personally found offensive?*	Full class discussion or small groups	Students begin to develop their own values and, in some cases, action plans for how to deal with prejudice or stereotypes and how they might overcome the pressures to conform to group norms.
VI	45–55 minutes (10)	*Q3: What lessons might Shelly have gained from the situation at the comedy store?*	Full class discussion or small groups. Could hand out copy of "Reflections from Shelly" at end of this teaching note.	Answers may vary from sit in the back at comedy clubs to some of Shelly's insight in "Reflections from Shelly." By hearing the insights of the more empathic and reflective students and of Shelly, other students will be able to see the benefits of greater perspective taking and empathy with people in other ethnic groups (even in situations like this where empathy is not likely to be the immediate response).
VII	55–60 minutes (5)	Mini-lecture to summarize learning.	Full class	Conformity is a normal social phenomenon that is dependent on many factors including identification with the group (some similarities), the presence of experts in the group, and member(s) who are important to the individual.

25-minute teaching plan on conformity.
Preassignment: Read case before class (10 minutes).
Activities. Do activities IV and V or IV and VI in the 60-minute plan.

La Cabaret

Teaching plan topic: Racism and Racial Oppression
60-minute teaching plan

Preassignment: None

	Timing	Activity	Organization	Student Outcomes
I	0–10 minutes (10)	Students read case in class.	Individually	Knowledge of case facts.
II	10–15 minutes (5)	Ask: *What are some examples of stereotypes from the comedy store incident?*	Full class discussion	Students' list should include Arabic culture—"camel jockey," "interracial couples stereotypes," and "being a real African American."
III	15–30 minutes (15)	*Q2: What would you do if you were at a meeting at work and someone made a racial (or gender-based, or sexual orientation-based) joke that you personally found offensive?*	Full class discussion or small groups	Students begin to develop their own values and, in some cases, action plans for how to deal with prejudice or stereotypes. This list may be idealistic, but you may not have time to demonstrate that fully.
IV	30–40 minutes (10)	*Q5: Imagine that you are an African American in the audience. Why might you agree with Harry's judgment of Malcolm and Shelly? Why might you disagree?*	Full class discussion or small groups	Responses may vary, but the point of this question is to lead to the mini-lecture on the fallacy of racial reasoning.
V	40–50 minutes (10)	Mini-lecture on the fallacy of racial reasoning.	Full class	See answer to question 5 for guidance in this lecture.
VI	50–55 minutes (5)	Hand out or read "Reflections from Shelly" found in this teaching note.	Individual or full class	To see the lessons Shelly learned from the experience.
VII	55–60 minutes (5)	Ask: *What are your reactions to this case and Shelly's reflection?*	Full class	Students will likely mention personal discoveries. Some might remain silent.

25-minute teaching plan on racism.
Preassignment: Read case before class (10 minutes).
Activities. Do activities IV and V and VI in the 60-minute plan. Hand out "Reflections from Shelly" to read later, if desired.

Discussion questions and answers

Question 1
Why didn't Betty and Bob defend Malcolm and Shelly?
Diagnostic question (probes motives or causes). Reference: Robbins, 1998, Chapter 7, pp. 257–258.

Answer

Although Betty and Bob were friends with Malcolm and Shelly, neither one of them seemed outwardly bothered by the routine. Neither one apologized or expressed sympathy for Shelly or Malcolm after the incident. Why?

Elliot Aronson (1995) explores the reasons bystanders fail to help a person in need in his discussion of the Kitty Genovese murder. In the 1970s, a woman by the name of Kitty Genovese was stabbed to death in New York at 3 A.M. No less than 38 people stood at their windows and watched for the 30 minutes it took for her attacker to complete his grisly deed. Yet no one called the police or tried to intervene. Aronson argues that there are five questions that people ask themselves before aiding someone else.

1. Is the situation really serious? If bystanders believe the situation is a true emergency, then they are more likely to become involved. The less ambiguous the emergency, the greater the likelihood of helping.

   It is likely that Betty and Bob did not consider the comedian's routine an emergency. Ribbing the audience is a standard part of many comedy acts. But when Malcolm almost came to blows with the comedian, Bob intervened and pulled Malcolm outside.

2. Does it require my personal intervention? Onlookers are more likely to help if they believe that others cannot or will not help.

   There were many people in the restaurant that evening, so there was less likelihood that Bob and Betty would feel personally responsible for telling the comedian to quit.

3. Will helping be difficult or costly for me? Even if the first two prerequisites are met, that is, the situation is an emergency and the onlooker feels no one else is available to help, he or she is less likely to help if the cost of assistance is high. Thus, if a man witnesses an accident on the highway but is late to an appointment, he is less likely to intervene than if he is on a leisurely drive.

   The cost of intervention might have been perceived to be high for Bob and Betty. The comedians were used to dealing with hecklers from the audience and they might have felt that the comedian would razz them as well if they intervened.

4. Will my help benefit the victim? There is a good deal of evidence that bystanders will aid a victim if they believe that the person needs help and they believe they can make a difference. Thus, if someone knows first aid for choking, he or she is more likely to offer assistance than someone who doesn't know how to help a choke victim. The reasons appear to be based on empathy. It is psychologically uncomfortable to watch someone suffer when you don't know how to help.

   Betty and Bob probably assumed that their protests would not make a difference, stop the comedian, or stop the crowd from making fun of Malcolm or Shelly.

5. Can I easily leave? If bystanders feel that they can exit the situation easily (e.g., drive on down the road), then they are less likely to help. On the other hand, if they are asked directly for help or they are trapped in an elevator with the person in need, they are more likely to offer assistance.

   There is mixed evidence here for Betty and Bob. On the one hand, it would be very difficult for them to make their way out of a crowded show floor; on the other hand, they knew that the routine would only last so many minutes and the comedian would provide the exit for them by leaving the stage.

Question 2

What would you do if you were at a meeting at work and someone made a racial (or gender-based, or sexual orientation-based) joke that you personally found offensive?

Hypothetical question (poses a change in the facts or issues). Reference: Robinson, 1998, Chapter 7, pp. 257–258; Cook, Hunsaker, Coffey, 1997, Chapter 10, p. 328.

Answer

Responses to this question will vary. The point is to get the students talking about what actions they consider appropriate or not. After the question has been explored, it might be helpful for the instructor to give a mini-lecture on conformity.

There are several factors that influence people's decision to say something or not.

A feeling of "common fate" or mutuality may be engendered among people sharing the same interests, pleasures, hardships, and environmental conditions. In such circumstances, the bystander is more likely to "stick his neck out" or state her feelings to the group (Aronson, 1995, p. 43).

In this case, the individual's feeling of identification with the "victim" or feelings of disdain for the jokester (along with the five factors Aronson pointed out in the first question) may make her more willing to say something against the joke.

Aronson (1995) indicates that there are three explanations as to when a group is effective at inducing conformity. He states, "1) it (the group) consists of experts, 2) the members (individually or collectively) are important to the individual, and 3) the members (individually or collectively) are comparable to the individual in some way" (p. 25).

The people in the group were comparable to Betty and Bob, because they were predominantly young African Americans who enjoyed comedy. This may have led Bob and Betty to go along (albeit silently) with the crowd's humiliation of Shelly and Malcolm. They may have felt more camaraderie with the black crowd than with Malcolm's white girlfriend.

So, the composition of the group—a homogeneous group, or a group composed mostly of experts (e.g., a student representative on a faculty committee) or composed of people whom the individual values—can cause an individual to conform.

The Asch experiments pointed out how group pressures for conformity can distort an individual member's judgment and attitude. Asch organized groups of seven or eight people, composed of one unsuspecting subject and the rest informed subjects. The groups sat in a classroom and were asked to compare two cards held by the experimenter. One card had one line a certain length, and the other card had three lines of varying lengths, one of which was the same length as the first card. The difference in the line length was quite obvious (and, in separate experiments, 99% of the attempts by an individual resulted in matching the single line length with the correct line on the second card).

The seating for the experiment was prearranged so that the unsuspecting subject was always the last to answer the question "which of the three lines matched the single line?" In the first two rounds, each person in the group answered correctly. On the third round, the first subject gave an obviously wrong answer, for example saying line A. The rest of the subjects gave the same answer—line A. When it came to the unsuspecting subject's turn, in 35% of the cases, the subject conformed to the group's answer.

The question confronting the unsuspecting subject was "do you publicly state that your perception differs from the rest of the group? Or do you give an answer that you strongly feel is incorrect to go along with the rest of the group members?"

This shows how group norms press us toward conformity. People do not want to appear to be different from the group, even when they know objectively that they are right; it is even more difficult to go against group sentiments with "subjective" events such as derogatory jokes. At La Cabaret, conformity exerted considerable pressure against the impulse to confront the jokester.

On the other hand, Asch's experiments demonstrated that if only one other person in the group gives the correct answer, then the unsuspecting subject is far more likely to give the correct answer. The question facing the unsuspecting subject becomes, "can I risk going against apparent group norms, by stating my feelings about the line knowing that there might be others that feel the same way I do?"

Question 3

What are some examples of stereotypes from the comedy store incident?
Comprehension skills (understanding the meaning of remembered material, usually demonstrated by restating or citing examples).

Answer

Stereotypes are generalizations that "assign identical characteristics to any person in a group, regardless of the actual variation among members of that group" (Aronson, 1995, p. 300). In other words, a stereotype occurs "when someone is identified with a group, then oversimplified attributes associated with that group are linked back to the individual" (Schermerhorn, 1999, p. 337).

Harry, the comedian, referred to Shelly as a "camel jockey." This derogatory term is primarily used to describe people of Middle Eastern descent. Harry incorrectly equated being Iranian with being Arabic. Although both countries are located in the Middle East, their cultures are extremely different.

Both countries have their own distinct language, religion, and culture. Thus, Harry used his preconceived framework of Middle Easterners to comment on Shelly's ethnicity. Furthermore, he also insinuated that in order to be a "true" African American, Malcolm's girlfriend should have also been black. Once again, Harry acted on a stereotype that incorrectly coupled personal relationships with ethnic or racial pride.

Question 4

What lessons might Shelly have gained from the situation at the comedy store?
Summary question (elicits syntheses).

Answer

Ruth Frankenberg (1993) points out that "interracial relationships frequently heightened white women's awareness of social racism" (p. 111). Shelly had the opportunity to experience life though Malcolm's eyes, thus getting a sense of what it was like to be an African American in America. Frankenberg (1993) also states that "white women" who are involved in close relationships with "people of color . . . feel an intimate connection to racial oppression" (p. 110). Shelly reflected on the incident in a student paper, writing that despite her public humiliation, she gained insight about how Malcolm and other African Americans are perceived; she was able to "feel" some of the racial humiliation that African Americans are exposed to on a daily basis from whites. She also became aware that she has the option of being considered a member of the majority group, whereas a black person doesn't.

The situation at the comedy store was difficult for Shelly. Not only did she realize how negatively she was being seen, but she also recognized that other African Americans saw Malcolm in a negative light because he was dating a white woman. When Harry focused his comedy routine on her, and the black audience ridiculed her, Shelly felt betrayed. In dating an African American, she identified more closely with blacks and felt somewhat like an insider. The incident served to remind her that, at least in that incident, she was an outsider. She felt that the audience was holding her accountable for the wrongdoing of white people.

Question 5

Imagine that you are an African American in the audience. Why might you agree with Harry's judgment of Malcolm and Shelly? Why might you disagree?
Diagnostic question (probes motives or causes).

Answer

Some students might agree with Harry's hostility toward Malcolm because they may identify with those African American women who see a shortage of single African American men and resent their dating of white women. Black men dating white women not only makes it more difficult for the women to find black partners, it may suggest that the men have accepted white standards of beauty and attractiveness, and rejected black standards.

On the other hand, students might see problems with Harry's declaration to Malcolm "You aren't black." This kind of thinking is called "racial reasoning" by Harvard theologian and philosopher Cornel West. West laments the type of thinking that leads to accusing others of not being "really black" or not being "black enough." West (1994) writes:

> The claims to black authenticity that feed on the closing-ranks mentality of black people are dangerous precisely because this closing of ranks is usually done at the expense of black women. It also tends to ignore the divisions of class and sexual orientation in black America—divisions that require attention if all black interests, individuals and communities are to be taken into consideration (p. 41).

Mary Gentile (1996) summarizes West's view well when she writes:

> As soon as one's sense of security and legitimacy is based upon racial authenticity, numerous reasons for exclusion emerge, and before we know it, black progress or "black social order" seems to rest upon the subordination and control of certain other blacks . . . [West] calls for a corrective to this limiting and separatist form of thinking that attempts to correct one form of oppression while participating in another. His antidote is a new form of reasoning that bases its claims to moral authority not on "black authenticity" but on a "mature black self-love and self-respect . . . [based] on the moral quality of black responses" to the experience of racism. This reasoning would replace exclusivity and closed ranks with a "coalition strategy," welcoming the support of these genuinely committed to combating racism regardless of their color or ethnicity, and it would embrace true democratic ideals rather than justifying the subordination of some blacks in the service of others.

West's model of "racial reasoning" holds lessons for our thinking about other forms of difference as well. It underscores the diversity that exists within identity groups as well as between them. And it illustrates the ubiquity and limitations of dichotomous, us/them patterns of thinking.

From this point of view, Malcolm would still be an African American male in the eyes of the audience and Shelly would be a member of an African American coalition. In an ideal world devoid of racial reasoning, the Middle Eastern cultures would also benefit from building coalitions and the primarily black audience members would be supportive of Shelly and her Iranian culture.

References

Aronson, E. (1995). *The social animal.* New York: W. H. Freeman and Company.

Cook, C. W., Hunsaker, P. L., and Coffey, R. E. (1997). *Management and organizational behavior,* 2nd ed. Boston: Irwin-McGraw-Hill.

Frankenberg, R. (1993). *The social construction of whiteness: White women, race matters.* University of Minnesota Press.

Gentile, M. C. (1996). *Ways of thinking about and across difference.* Note 9: 395–117. Boston: Harvard Business School Case Clearing House.

Robbins, S. (1998). *Organizational behavior: Concepts, controversies, and applications,* 6th ed. Upper Saddle River, NJ: Prentice Hall.

Schermerhorn, J. R., Jr. (1999). *Management,* 6th ed. New York: Wiley.

West, C. (1994). *Race matters.* New York: Vintage Books.

Epilogue

Shelly and Malcolm stayed together for the next three years but eventually parted ways due to circumstances unrelated to the comedy store incident. Malcolm finished his residency and is a physician in a large medical practice. Shelly is pursuing her master's degree and working in publishing. They are still close friends.

Bob and Betty are still married and friends with Malcolm. Shelly has not maintained her friendship with them, and they never discussed that night.

Reflections from Shelly on the Incident in La Cabaret

The most significant point that I have learned from this situation is the importance of society and its perceptions. Considering this was such an emotionally wrenching experience for me, I had difficulties objectively looking at the incident. Sharing the story with Teri Tompkins allowed me the distance I needed to finally "let go" of the pain.

Initially, I thought I was angry with the comedian, but through this process, I realized I was angry with every single member of that audience. Therefore, I cannot say that I would have reacted any differently. When students look at this case, they need to remember that understanding social psychological theories and being able to apply them to this incident does not take away the emotional pain an incident like this causes. It is hard to rationalize issues when you feel directly "attacked." So, I still would have approached the comedian and would have liked to express my feelings without becoming overly emotional.

However, knowing what I know now, I do not think I would have been so hard on my relationship or myself. It took me a long time to go back to another comedy store. And unfortunately, because I did not have closure on this subject, I indirectly held my boyfriend responsible for the incident. Out of all of the people that were there that night, he did not deserve any grief from me. I was so involved with my own feelings that I never considered this incident was a direct attack on my boyfriend's identity. No matter how betrayed I felt, it probably could not measure up to the betrayal he must have felt from his "own people." He was in the presence of other black people who viewed him as a "sell out," which was not a comfortable feeling for him. In retrospect, it is truly amazing at how much responsibility I placed on him for my pain. For that, I think I will always feel guilty . . . nevertheless, this situation served as a great lesson in empathy.

Teaching Note[*]
MOON OVER E.R

Topics (* = Primary topics in teaching plan)
*Workplace violence
*Emotional Intelligence
Managed health care
Human resource management
Health care context

Case overview
Katia Gore, an emergency room nurse, has been physically assaulted while on her shift by an "impatient" patient. The hospital's executive administrator, Hamilton Bronson, and the head nurse of the emergency room, Edith Warner, are meeting to discuss the facts of the incident. Decisions must be made regarding how to preempt—and protect against—violent attacks.

Industry
Large metropolitan hospital. Company is disguised. No union employees.

Teaching objectives
From studying this case, students should learn the following:
1. To appreciate the seriousness of workplace violence.
2. To associate organizational responses with general and competitive environmental forces.
3. To make decisions regarding the safety and protection of employees.

Other related cases in Volume 1
Problems at Wukmier Home Electronics Warehouse (HRM); *Your Uncle Wants You!* (Emotional Intelligence, HRM).

Other related cases in Volume 2
Violence at the United States Postal Service (workplace violence).

Intended courses and levels
This case would be most appropriately used as the basis for discussion or for a written assignment in undergraduate or graduate courses concerned with human resources management issues. Courses could include Human Resource Management, Principles of Management, and Organizational Behavior. The case would be useful in highlighting issues of workplace violence, organizational responses to environmental change, and emotional intelligence.

Analysis
Violence is one of the most troubling issues facing organizations within American society. Statistics indicate that in 1992 over 1000 Americans were murdered on the job. A recent American Management Association survey of 311 organizations found almost 25% indicated that at least one employee had been attacked or killed on the job since 1990 (Rigdon, 1994). Another survey estimated that, during a recent one-year period, more than 2 million employees were physically attacked and more than 6 million received threats of violence (Northwestern National Life Insurance Company Survey as cited in O'Leary-Kelly, Griffin, and Glew, 1996). This level of violence has tremendous costs for both employees and employers to include the direct consequences of injury or death, decreased employee psychological well-being, and increased legal and medical employer expenses.

---

[*]Source: Adapted from case prepared by Steven J. Maranville, University of Houston – Downtown, and J. Andrew Morris. The case and teaching note were prepared as a basis for class discussion rather than to illustrate either effective or ineffective handling of administrative situations. Suggestions for improvement of this note should be sent to tompkins@uor.edu. Credit will be given in the next revision.

This case draws upon a model of organization-motivated aggression to suggest that the violence directed toward Katia Gore was primarily a function of organizational environment characteristics. The model indicates that perceived aversive treatment (such as waiting) acts as a trigger to outsider-initiated organization-motivated aggression and violence. Further, the model suggests that a key way to decrease aggression and violence is through the manipulation of environmental instigators. Thus, preparation question #3 of this teaching note asks the student to identify ways to change the environmental context so that patients in the emergency room would be subject to less aversive treatment. Two ways that the hospital can reduce the potential for violent behavior is through reduction of waiting time by better forecasting of demand for services and by providing a more complete and better explained emergency room procedure protocol.

A second theoretical issue to be explored concerns emotional intelligence (also known as EQ). Emotional intelligence has been defined as the ability to understand and control one's emotions and the emotions of others (Goleman, 1995). Low EQ individuals may be more susceptible to reacting with violence since they are unaware of their own emotional states and, thus, less able to control emotional displays. Further, awareness of other's emotions (empathy) may act as a buffer to aggressive and violent behavior, since it will be more difficult to harm another if one can empathize with the hurt caused (Morris, 1997). In this case, not only did the actions of the patient indicate low EQ, but Nurse Warner's inability to discern the increasingly agitated state of the patient reflects her own low EQ. It is suggested that a greater ability to understand and recognize the patient's emotional distress may have reduced the waiting patient's willingness to engage in violent behavior.

Research methodology:

This case is based on observations and interviews. The case is a true incident. Names and the organization have been disguised.

Teaching plan

The handouts at the end of the teaching note for *Violence at the United States Postal Service*, Volume 2, are also applicable to this case.

Teaching plan topic: Decision-Focused Case on Workplace Violence
60-minute teaching plan

Preassignment: Read case prior to class (10 minutes).

	Timing	Activity	Organization	Student Outcomes
I	0–10 minutes (10)	Review the facts.	Large group discussion	Understand the situation.
II	10–30 minutes (20)	Discuss forces causing the situation.	Large group discussion	Surface the macro and micro forces causing the situation.
III	30–50 minutes (20)	Identify alternatives.	Large group discussion	Generate and examine alternative solutions to the problem.
IV	50–60 minutes (10)	Plan for implementation.	Large group discussion	Discuss how the selected alternative(s) would be implemented.

25-minute teaching plan on workplace violence.

Preassignment: Read case before class (10 minutes).

Divide the class into small groups. Half the groups answer Q1 and half answer Q2 (15 minutes). As a full class discussion, have the groups report their answers. If time, discuss Q1 or point out the answer.

Discussion questions and answers

<u>Question 1</u>

Who is responsible for what happened to Katia Gore?

<u>Exploratory</u> (probes facts and basic knowledge).

<u>Answer</u>

Certainly individuals are responsible for their own behaviors. Therefore, the patient is responsible for committing the act of violence against Katia Gore. Nevertheless, circumstances may foster the unfortunate opportunity for such violent acts. For example, this incident occurs on the second night of a hot, humid three-day weekend—not to mention the presence of a full moon. Furthermore, Metropolitan is a popular urban hospital that is easily accessed by indigent populations. Hence, as Nurse Warner notes, the situation could have been—and was—anticipated.

<u>Question 2</u>

How has the move toward "managed care" impacted hospitals? What other environmental factors may be making work in hospital emergency rooms more demanding?

<u>Diagnostic</u> (probes motives or causes) and <u>cause-and-effect</u> (ask for causal relationship between ideas, actions, or events).

<u>Answer</u>

Within the "managed-care" system, health maintenance organizations (HMOs) enter into contractual agreements with hospitals to provide medical care for the HMO's subscribing members. A hospital is compensated at a specified annual rate for each HMO member receiving care. This practice is in contrast to the previous era of health care delivery in which health care providers were compensated at the going rate for each service performed. Under managed care, hospitals have been compelled to contain costs, because demand for hospital services has been reduced as a result of health care providers attempting to reduce their own expenses. Cost containment has resulted in more focused services and fewer personnel. While resulting in productivity increases, these responses have at times come under sharp criticism for compromising the quality and responsiveness of health care.

With the changing environment of health care, emergency rooms have become a primary source of medical services for some populations. Sizable segments of society are either unable to obtain health benefits because they are unemployed or marginally employed or are refused health benefits because of preexisting medical conditions. Moreover, the staggering cost of single or family health coverage for even the most basic health services has obstructed many who cannot afford health care coverage. Therefore, people without medical insurance or a primary-care physician are heavy users of emergency room facilities.

In addition, the macro-system of managed care restricts the amount of attention that can be provided to patients. Managed care relies on "wellness" and supports wellness programs as a way to decrease "illness." Although access to a managed care practice can vary greatly by city, corporation, or sponsoring agency, managed care—in an environment without access to urgent care centers—has simply forced more of the population to use ERs as the only entrance into a health care system where appointment times are unrealistic for treating "sickness." Consequently, even with health coverage and a primary physician, some grow impatient with the system and seek faster remedies through emergency rooms.

Further, other factors in the larger social environment are affecting the work performed in emergency rooms. Violent crimes, for example, are generally on the increase. As the level of violent crime increases, the usage of emergency rooms also increases.

These industry and macro-environment forces combined with the statistically expected rate of emergency room usage has led to excessively high levels of demand for emergency rooms. Even without these additional pressures, the emergency room of a hospital is a stressful environment requiring instantaneous life and death decisions. In the context of lean staffing brought about through managed care, the work environment becomes all the more stressful.

Question 3
What should Hamilton Bronson do to safeguard the well-being of emergency room personnel? In addition, was there anything that Nurse Warner should or could have done to defuse the situation before it erupted into violence?
Action (calls for a conclusion or action).

Answer
Workplace violence must be addressed at two levels: 1) the organizational system, and 2) individual behavior. As executive administrator, Bronson can institute systems to preempt violent actions and protect personnel. These systems could consist of measures such as the following: installation of security screening devises such as metal detectors and video cameras, assessing patients at check-in for mental or emotional state as well as physical condition, posting of security guards as a passive deterrent and for active enforcement, stationing volunteers who can provide compassionate attention to patients as they wait, providing the services of hospital social workers to patients or family members who are in distress, and organizing emergency response teams of hospital personnel who can converge to subdue dangerous situations.

These measures taken at the systems level of the organization can do much to prevent and protect personnel. Nevertheless, every employee must exercise prudent measures as well. Employees who interact with patients under highly stressful conditions should possess skills enabling them to identify potentially dangerous and violent personalities. In addition, these same employees should possess effective communication skills enabling them to communicate without encouraging offense.

References

Goleman, D. (1995). *Emotional intelligence: Why it can matter more than IQ*. New York: Bantam Books.

Morris, J. A. (1997, October). "Emotions in organizations and the importance of emotional intelligence." Paper presented at the meeting of the Institute of Behavioral and Applied Management Annual Meeting. San Antonio, Texas.

O'Leary-Kelly, A., Griffin, R., and Glew, D. (1996). "Organization-motivated aggression: A research framework." *Academy of Management Review*, 21, 225–253.

Rigdon, J. E. (1994). Companies see more workplace violence. *Wall Street Journal*, April 12: B1.

Epilogue

There is no epilogue for this case.

NO, SIR, SERGEANT!

Topics (* = Primary topic with teaching plan)
*Power, basis of
*Empowerment
*Authority, acceptance of
Stress
Interpersonal conflict
United States military
Government context

Case overview

Newly noncommissioned officer, Sergeant Mitre (E-5 rank), is proud of the work that he and his 12 men have done in a 30-day war exercise in White Sands, New Mexico. Averaging only two to three hours of sleep a day for over 30 days, he and his troops managed to move heavy artillery each night to new launching pads. His team had accomplished every mission without a hitch, and distinguished themselves as the only section in the entire battalion with all 6 of its vehicles having completed the entire 30-day combat simulation without a single malfunction. This was unheard of in military launching rocket systems battalions. The work was strenuous and his men were looking forward to the relative luxury of the "staging" area, where they would spend the remaining three days before going home to see their families.

Sergeant Mitre and his troops washed their trucks and then went to take showers and sleep in a bed for a full eight hours! As Sergeant Mitre was heading for the barracks himself, Sergeant First Class Fenceroy (E-7 rank) approached him and said, "Sergeant Mitre, I just inspected your vehicles, and they need to be re-washed." "Yes, sir," was Sergeant Mitre's immediate reply. Sergeant Mitre rounded up his troops to rewash the vehicles. As he waited for his troops to reassemble, he inspected the vehicles. They were as clean as or cleaner than the other sections' trucks. Sergeant First Class Fenceroy was a rehabilitation transfer who was to take over command, and Sergeant Mitre had never met the man. It was unusual for a senior noncommissioned officer to be a rehab transfer, and he had obviously been in trouble in some capacity. Sergeant Mitre was sad that their first meeting had to be over this. The 100-degree desert heat sapped his men's energy, and he could feel their morale plummeting. The men finished the job, and he told them to literally "disappear."

A short time later, Sergeant First Class Fenceroy stopped Sergeant Mitre again. "Sergeant, I thought I told you and your men to rewash those vehicles!" Sergeant Mitre's eyes narrowed, "We did, Sergeant; I inspected them myself." "I'm the one who does the inspections around here, and I'm telling you to rewash those vehicles." Sergeant Mitre, extremely angry and afraid of what he might say, turned to walk away from Sergeant First Class Fenceroy. "Sergeant, I gave you a direct order." Sergeant Mitre turned deliberately back to face Fenceroy. Case B is a brief description of Sergeant Mitre going to the first sergeant and captain about his frustration with Fenceroy. They seem okay with his disobedience and tell him to go relax and they'll take care of it.

Industry

United States Military—Army artillery battalion.

---

*Source: Adapted from case prepared by Joel Mitre, Amber Borden, James C. Spee, University of Redlands, and Teri C. Tompkins, University of Redlands. The case and teaching note were prepared as a basis for class discussion rather than to illustrate either effective or ineffective handling of administrative situations. Suggestions for improvement of this note should be sent to tompkins@uor.edu. Credit will be given in the next revision.

No, Sir, Sergeant!

Teaching objectives
1. To evaluate how stress affects acceptance of legitimate authority.
2. To explore French and Raven's bases of power theory and to apply it to the case facts.
3. To investigate how empowerment can sometimes contradict legitimate authority.
4. To illustrate the importance of acceptance of authority.
5. To evaluate what might have happened if an alternative course of action had been chosen.

Other related cases in Volume 1
A New Magazine in Nigeria (acceptance of authority, power); *Handling Differences at Japan Auto* (interpersonal conflict); *Problems at Wukmier Home Electronics Warehouse* (interpersonal conflict); *Questions Matter* (interpersonal conflict); *Shaking the Bird Cage* (power); *Split Operations at Sky and Arrow Airlines* (stress); *Temporary Employees: Car Show Turned Ugly* (power); *Your Uncle Wants You!* (U.S. military).

Other related cases in Volume 2
A Selfish Request in Japan (power); *Incident on the USS Whitney* (acceptance of authority, interpersonal conflict, U.S. military); *Insubordination or Unclear Loyalties?* (acceptance of authority); *Preferential Treatment?* (interpersonal conflict, power); *Reputation in Jeopardy* (acceptance of authority, interpersonal conflict); *Saving Private Ryan and Classic Leadership Models* (U.S. military); *The Safety Memo* (interpersonal conflict); *The Volunteer* (acceptance of authority); *Violence at the United States Postal Service* (interpersonal conflict).

Intended courses and levels
This case involves the issue of acceptance of authority when the person receiving the order is under extreme stress and the order is not rational. In this case, there is no doubt about the legitimate power of the person giving the order and, in fact, there would be harsh punishment for not accepting authority. Yet, even in these circumstances, legitimate power is not enough for the authority to be accepted. It is useful in management and organizational behavioral courses for undergraduate, graduate, and executive students.

Analysis
All related analysis and references are embedded in the answers to the questions.

Research methodology
This case was written from the memories of Sergeant Mitre, the author of the case. This incident is true. Only Sergeant First Class Fenceroy's name has been disguised.

Teaching plan
Teaching plan topic: Power, Authority, and Leadership
60-minute teaching plan
Preassignment: Read case A (15 minutes)

	Timing	Activity	Organization	Student Outcomes
I	0–5 minutes (5)	Summarize the case facts	Ask for or appoint a "volunteer"	Orientation and refresher on case
II	5–15 minutes (10)	Review bases of power.	Mini-lecture	Understanding of French and Raven Model. • Reward power • Coercive power • Legitimate power • Control-of-information power • Referential power

	Timing	Activity	Organization	Student Outcomes
				● Expert power
III	15–20 minutes (5)	*Q2: Using French and Raven's bases of power as a frame, describe the types of power evident in this case.*	Group discussion	Understand how all six sources of power affected the outcome.
IV	20–25 minutes (5)	*Q3: Of the six bases of power, which was the most important one to control Sergeant Mitre's actions?*	Group discussion	Analysis should suggest that reward power was the most influential source of power.
V	25–30 minutes (5)	*Q4: How did Sergeant Mitre see empowerment in his role as section chief?*	Group discussion	Empowerment of the noncommissioned officer allows him or her to get around the written law if his or her actions are approved collectively by the chain of command.
VI	30–35 minutes (5)	Review of authority	Mini-lecture	Comprehension of acceptance theory of authority: The theory that subordinates will accept orders only if they understand them and are willing and able to comply with them.
VII	35–40 minutes (5)	*Q5: Why wasn't Sergeant First Class Fenceroy's authority accepted?*	Group discussion	Sergeant Mitre didn't accept Sergeant First Class Fenceroy's authority because he felt that an order had to have some form of rationality to it.
VIII	40–50 minutes (10)	*Q6: If Sergeant Mitre had followed Sergeant First Class Fenceroy's second order, what might have been the consequences?*	Group discussion	• Possibly lowering the expectations of him by his troops ● Lowering the level of respect and confidence in him and his ability to take care of them. ● Being obedient to the rank structure developed in his Army. ● No waves would have been created. ● It would stifle freedom of thought, empowerment to think and make a decision. ● Sergeant Mitre was in charge of his men, but another authority above them directed their ultimate actions, the overall operation. ● Sergeant Mitre could show that he had confidence in Sergeant First Class Fenceroy's position of authority no matter how outrageous his orders may sound. ● Sergeant Mitre expected his troops to respect his authority, but he believed that respect would come only if he earned it by proving his leadership abilities.
IX	50–60 minutes (10)	Read case B. Wrap up	Group discussion	Reflect on appropriateness of power and authority theory to explain events in the case.

25-minute teaching plan on authority.

Preassignment: Read case before class (15 minutes).

Activities. Do activities I, VI, VII, VIII, and IX in the 60-minute plan.

No, Sir, Sergeant!

Discussion questions and answers

Question 1

How was stress a factor in what happened between Sergeant Mitre and Sergeant First Class Fenceroy? Could stress have been managed?
Analysis skills (breaking a concept into its parts and explaining their interrelationships, distinguishing relevant from extraneous material) and hypothetical question (poses a change in the facts or issues).

Answer

The chief factor, which led to the confrontation between Sergeant First Class Fenceroy and Sergeant Mitre, was amount of stress he and his troops had been under. In a training exercise, the US Army went to great lengths to simulate or reproduce a combat environment. There's no mystery of the stress in this type of environment. How the key figures handled the stress made the situation unique. Clearly, job burnout was evident. This type of exercise forced these men to work on a continual basis (24 hours for 30 days), which very likely caused burnout. Without time away from their positions, the stress built itself to a very high level.

In retrospect, the key stressor was invariably the lack of sleep. Unfortunately, none of the troops had any control over how often they were allowed to rest. Sergeant Mitre most likely had to attend briefings and long meetings with his superiors after missions, which would cut deep into his sleep time. This lack of sleep and the job burnout probably exacerbated any conflict between Sergeant Mitre and Sergeant First Class Fenceroy.

The lack of sleep and the stress involved was uncontrollable. Unfortunately, traditional stress reducers like hot tubs, Jacuzzi, sauna, massage, yoga, rest, or a proper diet were not feasible options for Sergeant Mitre. But other strategies could have proven useful in dealing with his stress. For instance, thinking positive, prayer, meditation, deep breathing, and withdrawal were all ways he could have maintained his stress at a manageable level.

Question 2

Using French and Raven's bases of power as a frame, describe the types of power evident in this case.
Application skills (using information in a new context to solve a problem, answer a question, or perform a task).

Answer

All six bases of power were evident in this case:
Reward Power. Sergeant Mitre's knowledge of taking care of his troops, conducting himself as a noncommissioned officer, and performing his duties by the book, gave him the expectation of being rewarded by promotion, or an award. His troops counted on him to present them with a reward for a job well done! It is likely that Sergeant First Class Fenceroy had an expectation of starting all over again to regain the respect he'd lost at his previous unit. He hoped to be rewarded with respect.

Coercive Power. Fear of receiving punishment for disobeying Sergeant First Class Fenceroy's order.

Legitimate Power. The U.S. Army has clear written and unwritten laws of the structure of rank, and power goes to the one with more on his or her shoulder. At the time of the incident, Mitre was an E-5 and Fenceroy, an E-7, which meant that Fenceroy had legitimate power over Mitre.

Control-of-Information Power. The order to rewash the vehicles could have come from above Sergeant First Class Fenceroy. Sergeant Mitre had no way of knowing for certain. In sharp contrast, Sergeant Mitre's soldiers had the same belief as he did in the preceding example, but they knew the order was coming from above.

Referential Power. Confiding in First Sergeant Baker, because of his reputation as one that stands behind his noncommissioned officers to do the right thing, was reinforcement for Sergeant Mitre.

Expert Power. Confiding in First Sergeant Baker because of his many years of experience as a noncommissioned officer.

Question 3

Of the six bases of power, which was the most important one to control Sergeant Mitre's actions?
<u>Analysis skills</u> (breaking a concept into its parts and explaining their interrelationships, distinguishing relevant from extraneous material).

Answer

Reward power was without question the most powerful type of power controlling Sergeant Mitre's actions during this case. His sole focus, upon arriving at the staging camp, was to get his troops their deserved reward for a job well done. Seeing their happiness was his reward and his gratification. Although Fenceroy's coercive power caused Sergeant Mitre to obey his first order, the thought of letting his troops down far outweighed any punishment he might received for disobeying his second order.

Question 4

How did Sergeant Mitre see empowerment in his role as section chief?
<u>Analysis skills</u> (breaking a concept into its parts and explaining their interrelationships, distinguishing relevant from extraneous material).

Answer

As a sergeant in the United States Army, Sergeant Mitre had a duty to his soldiers. The duty was their total care, which included their morale, professional development, job competency, and well-being, just to name a few. And as a noncommissioned officer in the same army, Sergeant Mitre was to see that this duty was accomplished based on the empowerment his superiors granted him. Just as quickly as empowerment is given, it can be taken away. Sometimes in a sergeant's career, a situation arises in which he or she must make a decision that will affect his or her career either negatively or positively. Empowerment—having freedom to make decisions—allows an individual to make a mark. Even though Sergeant Mitre had clear guidelines to follow, Sergeant Mitre was empowered to make a decision that didn't necessarily follow those guidelines. By all rights, Sergeant Mitre should never have questioned his superior's order, as it wasn't dangerous, nor did it jeopardize the health of his troops. In the army, you never disobey an order of a superior unless it is unethical or unsafe; that is what is written in the military laws. However, empowerment of the noncommissioned officers allows them to get around the written law if their actions are approved collectively by their chain of command, whether it is lawful or unlawful. It comes down to one question, "Was it worth sticking your neck on the line?" That is the question that commanders and first sergeants ultimately ask themselves before they consider looking the other way. If the answer is yes, the gamble paid off, and you retain the ability to exercise empowerment. If the answer is no, you will lose empowerment, either by demotion or by being given a nonleadership position.

Question 5

Why wasn't Sergeant First Class Fenceroy's authority accepted?
<u>Analysis skills</u> (breaking a concept into its parts and explaining their interrelationships, distinguishing relevant from extraneous material).

Answer

Acceptance of authority is the theory that subordinates will accept orders only if they understand them and are willing and able to comply with them (Chester Barnard, 1938).

Sergeant Mitre didn't accept Sergeant First Class Fenceroy's authority because he felt that an order had to have some form of rationality to it. Understanding the order was easy, but understanding the rationality behind the order was a bit different. Comprehending a statement spoken in English is either "yes" or "no." But looking deeper into an order, such as re-washing vehicles again and again while the rest of the battalion was relaxing, well, . . . that was not rational. Therefore, Sergeant Mitre had a problem with Sergeant First Class Fenceroy's formal authority in this instance.

Additionally, a leader must be respected by his or her subordinates, and must have credibility with them, in order for the subordinates to accept their authority. In this case, Sergeant First Class Fenceroy's reputation and credibility were tainted because he was a rehab transfer. The outlandish order was understood by Sergeant Mitre, but not accepted.

Question 6

If Sergeant Mitre had followed Sergeant First Class Fenceroy's second order, what message might have Sergeant Mitre sent to the troops and what might have been the reaction of the troops?

Hypothetical question (poses a change in the facts or issues).

Answer

1. Possibly lower the expectations of him by his troops by telling them that some situations are out of his control and that Sergeant Mitre can't always shield them. But, by lowering expectations from his troops, Mitre would be lowering the level of respect and confidence in him and his ability to take care of them. And in a business where you train every day for the possibility of putting your life on the line for your country, there must never be doubt in your leaders and their abilities.

2. Being obedient to the rank structure developed in his army. Never, ever, second guess a superior's directive. To have simply washed the vehicles over and over again until Sergeant First Class Fenceroy was satisfied. No waves would have been created. No one would ever have known there was a problem. It would have been a great teaching aid to his troops that their sergeant respected rank. Sergeant Mitre wouldn't have risked any possible punishment. However, it would stifle empowerment and the freedom to make a decision. Sergeant Mitre might have appeared weak to his troops. In his business, a weak noncommissioned officer is worthless. This can be likened to standing up to the school's bully. With the entire battalion watching, Sergeant Mitre was placed in a position to maintain his reputation.

3. Sergeant Mitre could show that he had confidence in Sergeant First Class Fenceroy's position of authority, and he could remain confident no matter how outrageous the orders may sound, that Fenceroy knows what's best because of his position above Mitre. By his not questioning Fenceroy's directives, Mitre's troops would have accepted Sergeant First Class Fenceroy's authority because Sergeant Mitre was accepting it. Sergeant Mitre knew that even an 18-year old new soldier could see the bigger picture involved in this incident. Sergeant Mitre expected his troops to respect his authority, but Sergeant Mitre believed that respect would come only if he earned it by proving his leadership abilities. Proof came from making sound decisions and being accountable for his word. If Sergeant Mitre had accepted the order based on Sergeant First Class Fenceroy's authority alone, Sergeant Mitre would have let his troops down, because they would understand what the directive meant. It would mean they were being taken advantage of and he had let them down.

References

Barnard, C.I. (1938). *The functions of the executive*. Cambridge, MA: Harvard University Press.

Epilogue

In retrospect, Sergeant Mitre still believed that he acted correctly. However, he came to understand why and how things happened. This was a very important moment in his professional career. There aren't many times in a person's life where he can really see or smell the moment where he can make a mark. This, however, was a moment that was both loud and fragrant.

Sergeant Mitre did understand that he could have consulted peers or the first sergeant prior to making his own decision, and many may argue that that would have been have been the "smart" thing to do. For Sergeant Mitre, "smart" really meant to take the safer option, rather then to act on emotion. The training he had received to lead his men occurred in the classroom and on the battlefield. He valued the hands-on fighting on the front lines far more than the theory. The use of theory did understand why and how things happened, or more accurately put . . . how they fell into place. The risk paid off for him. The U.S. Army was rid of a troublemaker—Sergeant First Class Fenceroy retired shortly after his return to Ft. Sill. And Sergeant Mitre gained the respect of his soldiers and peers, who saw him as a tough noncommissioned officer that would stand up for his troops, which is invaluable in the military.

Sergeant Mitre ended his tour in the military in 1998. He enrolled at the University of Redlands to complete his last two years of his bachelor's degree in management and business. He is employed full-time as a manager of Big Five Sporting Goods store.

Teaching Note©
PEARL JAM'S DISPUTE WITH TICKETMASTER

Topics (* = Primary topic with teaching plan)
*External environment of organizations (especially resource dependence)
*Interorganizational conflict
*Goal setting
*Negotiation and dispute resolution
Positional bargaining
Large corporation context vs. small business context

Case overview
This descriptive case chronicles a dispute that erupted in 1994 between Pearl Jam, arguably the most popular alternative rock band in the United States, and Ticketmaster, the nation's premier ticket distribution company. The dispute was ongoing as of 1996.

For its 1994 summer tour, Pearl Jam decided to try to limit the price of tickets to its concerts to no more than $20, to accommodate the limited resources of its teenaged fans. To this end, the band priced tickets at $18 and proposed to Ticketmaster that service charges be limited to no more than 10 percent of the value of the ticket. Ticketmaster refused, saying it would lose money.

After the first round of negotiations failed, both organizations escalated the conflict. Pearl Jam instructed its attorneys to file a brief with the Justice Department alleging antitrust violations by Ticketmaster, and members of the band testified before a congressional committee in support of these charges. Pearl Jam charged that Ticketmaster held a virtual monopoly of ticket sales, due to its exclusive contracts with most major venue owners, and that the company had used its market power unilaterally to drive up ticket service charges. Ticketmaster, for its part, threatened to sue arena owners and concert promoters if they did business with Pearl Jam and vigorously defended itself against antitrust charges. No major venues with Ticketmaster contracts were willing to book Pearl Jam concerts. Neither side appeared willing to compromise, and attempts at mediation failed.

The dispute, which continued into 1996, harmed both parties. Pearl Jam was unable to proceed with its concert schedule without the cooperation of Ticketmaster and canceled its entire 1994 summer tour. In 1995 and 1996, the band attempted to tour without the company, using small venues and alternative ticketing systems. Both tours were plagued with numerous problems, many related to ticket sales. In 1996, Ticketmaster failed in its bid for the lucrative contract to sell tickets to the Summer Olympic Games, citing distractions caused by its dispute with Pearl Jam.

Industry
Entertainment Industry. The key actors in this dispute (rock hitmakers Pearl Jam and ticket service powerhouse Ticketmaster) are familiar to most college-aged students and add to the classroom appeal of the case.

Teaching objectives
This is a descriptive, not a decision-focused case. The teaching objective is to require students:
1. To analyze the escalation of a business dispute between two organizations.
2. To identify causes of the dispute, reasons for its escalation, and factors inhibiting its successful resolution.
3. To analyze the consequences of an unresolved dispute for both organizations.
4. To speculate about the functions and dysfunctions of conflict.

---

*This case was written by Anne Lawrence, San Jose State University. The case and teaching note were prepared as a basis for class discussion rather than to illustrate either effective or ineffective handling of administrative situations. Suggestions for improvement of this note should be sent to tompkins@uor.edu. Credit will be given in the next revision.

Other related cases in Volume 1

A New Magazine in Nigeria (goal setting); *Temporary Employees: Car Show Turned Ugly* (negotiation, positional bargaining).

Other related cases in Volume 2

A Selfish Request in Japan (negotiation, positional bargaining); *Negotiating Work Hours* (negotiation); *Richard Prichard and the Federal Triad Program* (goal setting); *The Safety Memo* (positional bargaining); *When Worlds Collide* (external environment).

Intended courses and levels

This case is suitable for upper-division undergraduate or graduate level courses in organization theory or organizational behavior. It is especially useful in connection with discussion of theories pertaining to organizational goals, the external environment of organizations (especially resource dependence theory), inter-organizational conflict, and negotiation and dispute resolution. The case works well in connection with discussion of the relevant chapters in organization theory or organizational behavior textbooks (e.g., Richard L. Daft, *Organization Theory and Design*, Chapters 2, 3, and 11; Stephen P. Robbins, *Organizational Behavior*, Chapter 13).

Analysis

Analysis is embedded in the answers to the questions.

Research methodology

This case was written from transcripts of congressional hearings, legal briefs filed by Pearl Jam's attorneys, materials provided to the author by Ticketmaster Inc., material released to the author under a Freedom of Information request to the Department of Justice, and press reports on the dispute in the *Wall Street Journal*, *Business Week*, the *New York Times*, *Billboard*, *Entertainment Weekly*, and other periodicals. A bibliography is provided with the case.

Teaching plan

Teaching plan topic: Conflict Negotiations, Resource Dependency, and Goals
60-minute teaching plan

Preassignment: Read case before class (25 minutes).

	Timing	Activity	Organization	Student Outcomes
I	0–3 minutes (3)	Ask a student to give an overview of the case.	One to several students (or instructor).	Refresh students' memory of the case.
II	3–5 minutes (2)	Organize five groups of students.	Have students count off 1–5, or use existing groups.	To organize five groups of students of similar size.
IIIa	5–25 minutes (20) There are five III rows.	*Q1: On what external resources were Ticketmaster and Pearl Jam dependent? What strategies did each use to reduce its dependence?*	Assign to group 1 (Simultaneous with four other questions. See next four boxes).	Both dependent on resources. Ticketmaster: Dependent on ticket supply, customers, and government regulations. Successful strategy: exclusive contracts of venues, competitive pricing, vigorously defending itself. Pearl Jam: Dependent on access to large entertainment venues; promoters; ad hoc services; record company. Unsuccessful strategy attempted to form alliances with independent ticketing firms; influence government regulatory policy through

	Timing	Activity	Organization	Student Outcomes
				complaint; negotiated a record deal.
III b	5–25 minutes (20) There are five III rows.	*Q2: What were Ticketmaster's and Pearl Jam's goals? Were both organizations' goals internally consistent? How effective were these two organizations in meeting their goals? Were the two organizations' goals compatible with one another's, wholly or in part?*	Assign to group 2.	Ticketmaster's goal: to increase market share of live event ticketing, and to diversify into related services. It is internally consistent. Pearl Jam's goal (mission) was to make great music; and secondarily to promote youth access and political causes; indifferent to business aspects. Ticketmaster's goal of making as much money as possible was in conflict with Pearl Jam's goal of promoting youth access by lowering ticket prices.
IIIc	5–25 minutes (20) There are five III rows.	*Q3: Theorists have examined various sources of horizontal conflict between and among organizations and groups. Drawing on these theories, offer an explanation for why Pearl Jam and Ticketmaster became involved in a dispute.*	Assign to group 3.	Goal incompatibility (as mentioned in Question 2). Cultural differences (venture capitalists vs. counterculture, anticommercial ethos). Personality clash (between Eddie Vedder and Fred Rosen). Mutual interdependence (Pearl Jam needed major venues and to sell tickets, for which Ticketmaster held exclusive rights; Ticketmaster needed tickets to hot shows.) Escalation and polarization (Pearl Jam lost focus on its objective of reduced ticket prices when only 45 cents off). Lack of direct contact (Pearl Jam's members or its manager never spoke to Rosen). Use of threats (Pearl Jam threatened to tour without Ticketmaster; Ticketmaster to sue promoters and venues).
III d	5–25 minutes (20) There are five III rows.	*Q4: In your view, what were this dispute's benefits and costs—if any—for Pearl Jam? With respect to the final outcome, do you think one organization gained more than the other? In general, was this conflict functional or dysfunctional?*	Assign to group 4.	Dysfunctional for both parties, more so for Pearl Jam. Pearl Jam did not lower service charges or increase competition in ticketing industry and lost untold millions in lost revenues due to cancellations. Ticketmaster did not receive revenue from Pearl Jam ticket sales over a three-year period. Its public image was harmed. It was distracted and missed gaining the Summer Olympics contract. On the other hand, it was able to impress on promoters and venue owners its seriousness in enforcing its contracts.
IIIe	5–25 minutes (20)	*Q5: What techniques did these two organizations use to*	Assign to group 5.	Both parties used techniques that had the effect of escalating the conflict and creating a win-lose situation:

	Timing	Activity	Organization	Student Outcomes
	There are five III rows.	*resolve their dispute? Were these techniques effective, in whole or in part? What techniques of conflict resolution do you believe might have worked more effectively?*		Appeal to external authorities Use of threats Appeal to allies Notably, neither side made a serious effort to initiate direct negotiations nor to bring in a third party to mediate the dispute.
IV	25–45 minutes (20)	Students report back their discussion. Instructor adds to students' reports if necessary to accomplish student outcomes.	From their small groups, students face instructor and participate in large group.	See the preceding outcomes above for specific answers to the questions.
V	45–55 minutes (10)	Role-play potential solutions. Alternatively, you can brainstorm ideas for potential solutions.	Ask for student volunteers, or select students based on their comments in class.	Pearl Jam proposed only one solution and forgot to focus on its goal. With only 45 cents difference, there were opportunities to come up with other solutions. Students may have ideas, such as third-party mediator; acknowledgment of the legitimacy of the other's objectives; search for common ground (e.g., their shared interest in increasing the absolute number of ticket sales).
VI	55–60 minutes	Read epilogue. *Reactions?*	Full group	Gives students a chance to have closure to case.

25-minute teaching plan on conflict with resource dependency as important focus.
Preassignment: Read case before class (25 minutes); jot down notes to answer the five questions (50 minutes).
Activities IV (20 minutes) and VI (5 minutes) in preceding 60-minute plan.

Discussion questions and answers

Question 1

Resource dependence theory argues that organizations strive to acquire control over resources in their external environments on which they are dependent for survival. On what external resources was Ticketmaster dependent? What strategies did Ticketmaster use to reduce its dependence? On what external resources was Pearl Jam dependent? What strategies did Pearl Jam use to reduce its dependence?

Application skills (using information in a new context to solve a problem, answer a question, or perform a task) and analysis skills (breaking a concept into its parts and explaining their interrelationships, distinguishing relevant from extraneous material).

Answer

Both Ticketmaster and Pearl Jam were dependent on resources in their external environments for survival, and both attempted to acquire control over these resources.

Ticketmaster's key mission was to sell tickets to live events. Thus, its main requirement was to secure control over the supply of tickets to popular events, especially "one-time" events that did not have regular season ticket holders. To increase its market share of live event tickets, the company under Rosen's leadership embarked on a largely successful strategy of locking up exclusive contracts with owners of the nation's largest entertainment venues and with the promoters of events that used these venues.

Ticketmaster was able to compete successfully for these agreements on the basis of superior technology, lower costs, and its willingness to rebate a portion of its convenience charges to the venue owners and promoters. It worked through <u>trade associations</u> of venue owners and promoters to enforce these contracts.

Ticketmaster was also dependent, of course, on customers (ticket buyers). However, once it had secured exclusive rights to sell tickets to a particular event, customers who wanted to attend that event had no choice but to deal with Ticketmaster. (It should be noted that in most instances customers did have the option of buying directly from the box office.) In order to succeed, Ticketmaster had to offer a competitive price to the venue owner, but not necessarily to the customer.

Ticketmaster also attempted to eliminate competition by <u>acquiring</u> or <u>entering into joint ventures with</u> other ticket service firms.

Government regulation was a source of external uncertainty for the firm. Although the ticketing industry was largely unregulated, Ticketmaster faced antitrust scrutiny twice, first in 1991 when it purchased Ticketron's assets and second in 1994 when it was investigated in connection with Pearl Jam's complaint. It also faced several private antitrust lawsuits. The company's strategy was to defend itself vigorously, through its <u>attorneys and publicists</u>, against charges of antitrust violations. Rosen also provided testimony before a congressional committee.

Finally, Ticketmaster in the mid 1990s sought to <u>change domains</u> by diversifying out of its exclusive reliance on ticket sales (this fact is not discussed in the case, but may be discussed as a hypothetical strategy).

For its part, Pearl Jam was also dependent on external resources. As a highly popular rock band, Pearl Jam found that it was unable to tour without access to large—stadium-sized—entertainment venues. It also required the services of local promoters—event organizers familiar with the local market. For each appearance, the band needed a host of ad hoc services, including security, publicity, and ticketing. To reach its many fans through record sales, it needed a contract with a major record label able to support the distribution, marketing, and sales of the band's CDs, albums, and tapes. To some degree, the band also needed access to media outlets such as radio and television (e.g., MTV and VH1).

Pearl Jam <u>negotiated</u> a record deal with Sony (Epic Records). It attempted to control ticket sales by forming <u>alliances</u> with independent (of Ticketmaster) ticketing firms. It attempted to <u>influence government regulatory policy</u>, through its antitrust complaint filed with the Justice Department. In general, the band was largely unsuccessful in reducing its dependence on external resources.

In terms of resource dependence theory, both organizations were markedly dependent on external parties for resources critical to their survival and commercial success; but Ticketmaster was more adept at controlling environmental uncertainties.

Question 2

An organizational goal has been defined as a desired state of affairs that an organization attempts to realize. What were Ticketmaster's goals? What were Pearl Jam's goals? Were both organizations' goals internally consistent? How effective were these two organizations in meeting their goals? Were the two organizations' goals compatible with one another's, wholly or in part?
<u>Analysis skills</u> (breaking a concept into its parts and explaining their interrelationships, distinguishing relevant from extraneous material), and <u>evaluation skills</u> (using a set of criteria to arrive at a reasoned judgment of the value of something).

Answer

Ticketmaster's primary goal was to increase its market share of the live event ticketing industry and, beyond this, to diversify into other related services. As a profit-driven enterprise, its main goals were to increase its revenues and to decrease its costs. Rosen was a skilled manager who made the owners of Ticketmaster (the Pritzker family and later Paul Allen) as well as himself a lot of money.

Pearl Jam saw its primary mission as cultural. The band defined its goal as "making great music." Secondarily, they wanted to promote youth access to live music, support various political causes (such as abortion rights and voter registration), and support their teenaged fans—with whom they strongly identified. Band members wanted to articulate and promote "alternative," noncommercial values. Although Pearl Jam was highly successful financially, the band seemed almost indifferent to the business aspects of its venture.

Ticketmaster's goal of making as much money as possible off convenience charges was directly in conflict with Pearl Jam's goal of promoting youth access by lowering ticket prices. (Arguably, selling more tickets at a lower price might have netted Ticketmaster more revenue; but as a practical matter, ticket sales for most Pearl Jam concerts were limited not by price but by the size of the venue.)

Question 3
Theorists have examined various sources of horizontal conflict between and among organizations and groups. Drawing on these theories, offer an explanation for why Pearl Jam and Ticketmaster became involved in a dispute.
Synthesis skills (putting parts together to form a new whole; solving a problem requiring creativity or originality).

Answer
Several factors contributed to the intensity of the dispute between Pearl Jam and Ticketmaster. These may be summarized:

Goal incompatibility: As discussed previously (question 2) Pearl Jam and Ticketmaster had very different goals. Although both organizations were commercially successful, Ticketmaster was primarily a commercial organization, while Pearl Jam's primary mission was cultural. Ticketmaster wanted to increase its revenue; Pearl Jam wanted teenagers to be able to afford its concerts. These goals, as discussed in question 2, were basically incompatible.

Cultural differences: The organizations had diametrically opposed cultures. Ticketmaster had been resurrected by venture capitalists, with a strong orientation toward financial return and a tolerance for risk taking. Pearl Jam sprang from the countercultural, anticommercial ethos of the alternative, "grunge" Seattle music underground.

Personality clash: This conflict appears to have been colored by an intense dislike and distrust between Eddie Vedder and Fred Rosen.

Mutual interdependence: Both organizations were dependent on the other to achieve goals. Pearl Jam needed major venues and to sell tickets to these shows; Ticketmaster held exclusive rights to sell tickets at many of these venues. The cancellation of the band's 1994 tour and the difficulties of its 1995 and 1996 tours only underscore this dependence. Pearl Jam also wanted to lower ticket prices and was dependent on Ticketmaster's cooperation to do so in many instances. For its part, Ticketmaster needed tickets to hot shows. Pearl Jam was one of the top rock and roll acts of the mid-1990s. Arguably, however, the band was more dependent on the ticketer than vice versa: There were other hot acts but few other ticketers for major venues.

Escalation and polarization: The 1994 dispute focused initially on the amount of Ticketmaster's convenience fee. The band wanted $1.80; Ticketmaster wanted its standard fee of $3.00 to $4.00. The ticketer later offered to reduce the fee to as low at $2.25. If Pearl Jam had reduced its share of the ticket price by only 45 cents per ticket, it would have achieved its ticket price objective.

Rather than negotiate over this 45 cents, however, both parties escalated their positions. Pearl Jam refused to budge, citing the principle of youth access to culture. Ticketmaster also dug in its heels, citing the principle of the inviolability of its contracts. By framing the dispute as a matter of principle rather than a matter of a few cents, both sides made compromise more difficult.

Lack of direct contact: Because of the particular structure of the music concert industry, the talent rarely has direct contact with the ticketer. Rather, these two organizations do business through a large number of third parties, including the band manager, the promoter, and the venue owner. Incredibly, throughout this entire, costly dispute, Pearl Jam's members or their manager apparently never had any direct discussions with Rosen or his associates. They never had an opportunity to develop the personal rapport or trust that might have made a compromise possible. No institutionalized forums for joint problem solving existed.

Use of threats: The use of threats by both parties helped escalate the conflict. Pearl Jam threatened to tour without Ticketmaster. Ticketmaster threatened to sue promoters and venues that bypassed them in order to accommodate the band. The use of threats caused both parties to become defensive and intransigent.

Question 4

Theorists differ on whether conflict is "good" or "bad" for organizations. In your view, what were this dispute's benefits—if any—for Pearl Jam and Ticketmaster? What were this dispute's costs—if any— to these organizations? With respect to the final outcome, do you think one organization gained more than the other? In general, was this conflict functional or dysfunctional?

Analysis skills (breaking a concept into its parts and explaining their interrelationships, distinguishing relevant from extraneous material) and evaluation skills (using a set of criteria to arrive at a reasoned judgment of the value of something).

Answer

In general, this dispute was dysfunctional for both parties, although it probably hurt Pearl Jam more than Ticketmaster.

Pearl Jam did not meet its central objective of lowering service charges and increasing competition in the ticketing industry. The band also lost untold millions of dollars because of the cancellation of its 1994 tour and the truncation of its 1995 and 1996 tours (and revenue from albums and other products sold as a result of these tours). Arguably, the band developed a reputation as crusaders for youth and consumer rights that may have enhanced its standing among some fans. The publicity generated by the dispute may have generated some record sales.

Ticketmaster also lost. It did not receive revenue on any of the hundreds of thousands of Pearl Jam tickets sold over a three-year period. It was forced to devote considerable managerial attention and a good deal of money on public relations and its legal defense. The company's public image was probably harmed, as Ticketmaster was portrayed as a heartless monopolist in much of the entertainment press. By its own reckoning, the company lost the Summer Olympics contract because of distractions caused by the dispute. Moreover, Pearl Jam's support may have helped several potential rivals (alternative ticketers) to gain experience and name recognition. On the other hand, Ticketmaster probably succeeded in impressing on promoters and venue owners the company's seriousness in enforcing its contracts. It may have deterred other artists from taking the company on. In balance, it appears that Ticketmaster, too, was a loser in this dispute.

The case does not contain enough detail to permit quantification of both parties' losses, but they clearly exceeded the costs to both parties of a compromise.

Question 5

What techniques did these two organizations use to resolve their dispute? Were these techniques effective, in whole or in part? What techniques of conflict resolution do you believe might have worked more effectively?

Analysis skills (breaking a concept into its parts and explaining their interrelationships, distinguishing relevant from extraneous material) and synthesis skills (putting parts together to form a new whole; solving a problem requiring creativity or originality).

Answer

Both parties used techniques that had the effect of escalating the conflict and creating a win-lose situation.

Appeal to external authorities: Pearl Jam appealed to the Justice Department and to Congress to initiate an antitrust investigation of Ticketmaster. This, of course, upped the stakes and angered Ticketmaster executives.

Use of threats: Both parties used threats. For example, Pearl Jam threatened to tour without Ticketmaster. Ticketmaster threatened to sue promoters and venues that bypassed them in order to accommodate the band.

Appeal to allies: Both sides tried to organize their potential allies: Ticketmaster, the venue owners and promoters; Pearl Jam, other politically minded rock groups and their fans.

Notably, neither side made a serious effort to initiate direct negotiations or to bring in a third party to mediate the dispute. Neither side attempted to find common ground in the dispute (for example, their shared interest in increasing the absolute number of ticket sales). Neither side acknowledged the legitimacy of the other's objectives.

Question 6

Was Ticketmaster guilty of antitrust violations?

Evaluation skills (using a set of criteria to arrive at a reasoned judgment of the value of something).

Answer

Pearl Jam's position	Ticketmaster's position
• TM held a monopoly (2/3 of major venues)	• TM controlled ticket sales for only 2% of all live events
• illegal kickbacks used to secure exclusive contracts	• up-front fees not illegal; common in industry; openly disclosed
• used monopoly power to drive up ticket prices; ticket prices exorbitant and not justified	• fee only $3.15 average, 12.5% increased only slightly faster than price of tickets justified by service provided
• organized an illegal group boycott to prevent PJ from mounting an independent tour	• TM took appropriate steps to enforce legal contracts

Students may wish to discuss if Ticketmaster was, in fact, guilty of antitrust violations, as Pearl Jam charged in its complaint. The case is intended to focus on the process, not the substance, of Pearl Jam's dispute with Ticketmaster. Students will not have sufficient information to examine the legal issues surrounding the antitrust charge competently.

However, if the instructor wishes to spend some class time on the substance of the dispute, the essentials can be quickly diagramed on the board as follows:

In summarizing this portion of the discussion, the instructor should point out that the Justice Department announced in July 1995, without comment, that it had not found sufficient evidence to proceed with an antitrust action against Ticketmaster. (The author's freedom of information request to the Justice Department resulted in the release of some correspondence regarding the case, but no information on the basis for the government's decision.) In addition, a federal judge dismissed the consolidated private antitrust suit. The instructor can point out that several legal authorities did not find sufficient basis to proceed with an antitrust case against Ticketmaster.

References

See case endnotes for references in the case.

Daft, R. L. (1997). *Organizational Theory and Design.* Southwestern

Robbins, S.P. (1997). *Organizational Behavior: concepts, controversies, applications.* Upper Saddle River, NJ: Prentice Hall.

Epilogue

There is no epilogue for this case.

*Teaching Note**
PROBLEMS AT WUKMIER HOME ELECTRONICS WAREHOUSE

Topics (* = Primary topic with teaching plan)
*Decision case
*Socialization
*In-group, out-group
*Attribution theory
*Hofstede's cultural dimensions (Mexico compared to United States)
*Investigation and termination HRM procedures
*Drug abuse procedures for HRM
Cultural differences
Mexican American workers
Interracial differences and conflict
Racial diversity
National culture
Organizational culture
Interpersonal conflict
Large corporation context
Labor/management context

Case overview
Christi Titus, human resources manager for Wukmier Home Electronics, must decide what to do about two warehouse employees (Manny *and* Jim) who almost fought in the workplace.

There were nine employees at the warehouse. Eight of them were Mexican or Mexican American and were long-term employees. The one European American (Jim, age 26) joined Wukmier nine months ago when a new position was added. Christi's investigation revealed that Jim did not seem to fit in or appear to try to fit in to the dominant Mexican culture. Jim believed his good productivity should be enough to maintain his job.

The other workers were united in their frustration with Jim. One of the problems was that Jim didn't want to listen exclusively to Spanish music at work. After Jim brought his radio to work and blasted his music to drown out the Spanish music, all workers were told they could no longer listen to any music in the workplace.

Manny had had run-ins with Jim before. The presenting problem was Manny's threat to Jim to "watch his back" after Jim made what appeared to be a benign comment to another worker about some condiments the worker had with his lunch. Students will note that Jim's comment implied that Manny smoked marijuana (Jim was a clean and sober addict). Some students may note that Manny had an anger management problem.

Another issue is that Jose Garcia, the supervisor at the warehouse, had little formal supervisory training, learning his job by starting at the bottom over the last 30 years. Some of the workers believed that Jose was playing favorites with Jim by allowing him to load product his own way and by not insisting that he listen to the same music they had listened to for years.

Industry
Small isolated group at a regional warehouse for a large, unionized manufacturing company; high-end home electronics.

Teaching objectives
1. To introduce students to the concepts of socialization theory, attribution theory, and Hofstede's cultural dimensions.

---

*Source: Adapted from case prepared by Teri C. Tompkins, University of Redlands, and Kathleen Moldenhauer. The case and teaching note were prepared as a basis for class discussion rather than to illustrate either effective or ineffective handling of administrative situations. Suggestions for improvement of this note should be sent to tompkins@uor.edu. Credit will be given in the next revision.

2. To teach students to explain why people behave as they do in the case; that is, to link case facts to course theories.
3. To learn to recognize how behavioral symptoms can point to the real problem.
4. To decide what steps would be appropriate if you were the human resources manager.
5. To learn to recognize appropriate procedures in human resources cases.

Other related cases in Volume 1

A Team Divided or a Team United? (termination); *Donor Services Department in Guatemala* (Latin culture); *Fired!* (termination); *Heart Attack* (interracial differences and conflict, termination); *La Cabaret* (interracial differences and conflict).

Other related cases in Volume 2

A Selfish Request in Japan (Hofstede's cultural dimensions); *Angry Branch Manager* (interracial differences and conflict, termination); *Leadership of TQM in Panama* (Hofstede's cultural dimensions, Latin culture); *Preferential Treatment?* (interracial differences and conflict); *Unprofessional Conduct* (interracial differences and conflict); *Violence at the United States Postal Service* (interracial differences and conflict).

Intended courses and levels

This course is intended for undergraduate (especially questions 1 to 4), graduate, and executive students in human resources management and organizational behavior. Managing a diverse workforce fits well with management courses. The case should be positioned based on the selected topic.

Analysis

All related analysis and references are embedded in the answers to the questions.

Research methodology

This case reflects the recollection of the human resources manager in the case and the written memos resulting from decisions made in the case. The case is a true incident. Names and the organization have been disguised.

Teaching plan

This case can be used as an illustration of socialization, attribution, and diversity issues. For undergraduate students, the questions and answers will serve to guide students to the specific theories related to the case. If used as a decision-focused case, instructors may want students to role-play the parts of Manny, Jim, Christi, and Jose. The discussion section has several useful questions and answers that were not used in the teaching plans but can lead to interesting discussions.

Teaching plan topic: Socialization Theory
60-minute teaching plan

Preassignment: None

	Timing	Activity	Organization	Student Outcomes
I	0–1 minute (1)	1-minute introduction of class activity.	After introduction, form students into small groups of 4 to 5 students.	Prepare students to discuss case.
II	1–15 minutes (14)	Students read case A (B could also be read, but it has little to do with this teaching plan).	Individual	Familiarity with case facts.

	Timing	Activity	Organization	Student Outcomes
III	15–25 minutes (10)	Mini-lecture: Review socialization theory. Alternative 1: Students recall from their chapter reading what socialization theory is.	Mini-lecture while students remain in their groups. Alternative 1: Professor facilitates discussion or students discuss in their groups.	Students become familiar with the three stages of socialization and that socialization must be planned (see answer in socialization question 1).
IV	25–35 minutes (10)	*Give some examples of socialization theory from the case.*	Small group discussion	Students identify that Jim did not recognize or maybe value the group's norms. There was no formal socialization process in place.
V	35–55 minutes (20)	As a group, discuss these questions: *Think of a time when you first entered a new group (new classroom, sports team, new job). How did you feel? What happened over time? What did you learn about entering a new group?*	Small group discussion	Realization that there are common patterns: New entry: awkward, unaware of norms, tentative. At some point, feel comfortable, know what to do, or decide to exit.
VI	55–60 minutes (5)	Summarize and share epilogue.	Students remain seated in small groups.	Socialization is a two-way street requiring both the company and the employee to pay attention to socialization.

25-minute teaching plan on socialization theory.
Preassignment: Students should read the case before coming to class (15 minutes reading time).
Activities I, III, IV, VI in preceding 60-minute plan.

Teaching plan topic: Hofstede's Cultural Dimensions and Attribution Theory
60-minute teaching plan

Preassignment: Students read case A before class (15 minutes). (Case B is not important to this teaching plan.)
Instructor prepares transparency or handout with a table of Hofstede's dimensions, making sure that Mexican and United States characteristics are on the chart. It is more effective if the table displays several countries in addition to Mexico and the United States.

	Timing	Activity	Organization	Student Outcomes
I	0–15 minute (15)	Lecture on Hofstede's four, plus one, dimensions. Define the dimensions, and give examples using the country table to illustrate characteristics. Alternative: Discussion based on students' reading.	Using an overhead transparency, board, PowerPoint, or handout, have students look up on a table several of the countries that are high or low on the dimensions.	Familiarity with the five dimensions.
II	15–35 minutes (20)	*Q4: How do Hofstede's dimensions help explain the warehouse employees' perceptions and attributions*	Form small groups of 4 to 5 students.	Students apply their knowledge to the case facts to explain behavior of the warehouse employees. The power distance dimension explains

	Timing	Activity	Organization	Student Outcomes
		in the case?		the issues the best.
III	35–50 minutes (15)	Debrief students' small group discussion. Share epilogue. Additional mini-lecture, if time: Discuss the ladder of inference (Senge, 1994, p. 243) to show how cultural dimensions affect perception.	Students remain sitting in small groups.	Realization that cultural dimensions affect perceptions and attributions of individuals.
IV	50–60 minutes (10)	Assessment: Students write down the five dimensions on a clean sheet of paper and the definition of each, describing high and low characteristics. Can be done anonymously or with names.	As individuals or in student pairs. Collect papers and check for comprehension. Clarify any misconceptions next class session if needed.	Comprehensive ability to put in their own words the definitions and characteristics of each high and low dimension.

25-minute teaching plan on Hofstede's cultural dimensions.
Preassignment: Students should read the case before coming to class (15 minutes reading time).
Activities II (allow 15 minutes) and III (allow 10 minutes) in preceding 60-minute plan.

Teaching plan topic: Decision-Focused Case on Investigation and Suspension Procedures in HRM
60-minute teaching plan
Preassignment: Students read case A only (15 minutes).

	Timing	Activity	Organization	Student Outcomes
I	0–1 minute (1)	1 minute introduction of class activity.	Case discussion format—full class. Alternative: form students into small groups of 4 to 5 students.	Prepare students to discuss case.
II	1–15 minutes (14)	Answer the question: *What are the problems that Christi needs to solve in this case?*	Full class discussion—case discussion style or small group discussion.	Some possible answers: Short term: 1) To decide on the intervention for Manny. 2) To decide how to ease the tensions at the warehouse. Long term: 1) To decide if it is important to improve the acceptance of diversity at the warehouse. If yes, then how? 2) To improve Jose's leadership skills.
III	15–30 minutes (15)	*Q4: Brainstorm a list of alternatives that Christi could do to solve the short- and long-term problems.*	Full class discussion—case discussion style or small group discussion	*Case B* provides potential short-term alternatives for #1. For graduates, you may want to let them generate the alternatives on their own. Short-term #2: Can't ignore the

	Timing	Activity	Organization	Student Outcomes
				diversity problem, and it's related to Long-term #1. Since there are now two groups at the warehouse, Christi must make the workplace more friendly for both groups such as, diversity training and more meetings to discuss differences. If she ignores the problem, she is by default deciding to go back to a homogeneous all Mexican-culture workforce.
IV	30–45 minutes (15)	*Q8: If you were Christi, what decisions would you make at the end of the case?*	Small group discussion	Realization that the solution for the short-term #1 does not rest just with ignoring or terminating one or both employees. See answer in discussion and answer section.
V	45–60 minutes (15)	Debrief case and share epilogue.	Full class discussion If alternative organization is used, students can remain seated with their small groups.	Intervention on Manny's behalf paid off: he's a less volatile worker, his family benefited, and the other employees saw the company's fair practice and concern. Employees, like Jim, who are very different from dominant culture (e.g., one African American in all European American setting) can find it difficult. Companies and groups and the minority individual must adjust their policies and behaviors to improve socialization; and help long-term workers adjust to an increasingly diverse workforce.

25-minute teaching plan for a decision case.
Preassignment: Read case before coming to class (15 minutes reading time).
Activities III (allow 10 minutes), IV (10 minutes), and V (5 minutes) in preceding 60-minute plan.

Discussion questions and answers

Question 1

What is socialization theory?
Knowledge skills (remember previously learned material such as definitions, principles, and formulas).
Reference: Robbins (1998) Chapter 16, pp. 607–609, Schermerhorn (1999) Chapter 12, pp. 248–249.

Answer

No matter how good a job the organization does in recruiting and selection, new employees are not fully indoctrinated in the organization's culture. Maybe most importantly, because they are unfamiliar with the organization's culture, new employees are potentially likely to disturb the beliefs and customs that are in place. The organization will, therefore, want to help new employees adapt to its culture. This adaptation process is called socialization.

The most critical socialization stage is at the time of entry into the organization. This is when the organization seeks to mold the outsider into an employee "in good standing." Those employees who fail to learn the essential or pivotal role behaviors risk being labeled "nonconformists" or "rebels," which often leads to expulsion.

There are three stages in socialization: (1) prearrival stage, the period of learning that occurs before a new employee joins the organization. (2) encounter stage, the stage in which a new employee sees what the organization is really like and confronts the possibility that expectations and reality may diverge. (3) metamorphosis stage, the stage in which a new employee adjusts to his or her work group's values and norms.

The socialization process is complete when the new member has become comfortable with the organization and his or her job. He or she has internalized the norms of the organization and his or her work group, and understands and accepts these norms. The new member feels accepted by his or her peers as a trusted and valued individual, is self-confident that he or she has the competence to complete the job successfully, and understands the system, not only his or her own tasks, but the rules, procedures, and informally accepted practices as well. Finally, the new employee knows how he or she will be evaluated, that is, what criteria will be used to measure and appraise his or her work.

Question 2

Give some examples of socialization from the case.

Comprehension skills (understanding the meaning of remembered material, usually by restating or citing examples).

Answer

Socialization happened informally through observation and coaching from senior employees. There appeared to be little attention paid to socialization. Before Jim arrived at Wukmier, all the employees were either first- or second-generation Mexican or Mexican American. Their common culture may have made the socialization process easier when they were newcomers, especially if they had little previous warehouse experience.

Jim had been trained at another warehouse for four years, and it was likely that he brought this training with him to his new position at Wukmier. Since training was informal, it is likely that Jim did not acknowledge or value the "coaching" he got from the others. Perhaps if the training had been conducted more formally, Jim might have been more receptive to Wukmier's ways.

It also appears that Jim was more task-oriented than people-oriented. He believed that if he did his job well, then his job security was set. He didn't realize that every newcomer must first become a member in good standing before he can do things his own way. Because Jim did not demonstrate loyalty to the norms of the in-group, he was labeled a nonconformist and became a member of the out-group.

Question 3

Provide some examples as to how Jose and Christi could have helped the newcomer.

Synthesis skills (putting parts together to form a new whole; solving a problem requiring creativity or originality).

Answer

The first problem Jose and Christi faced was one of selection. By choosing a person outside of the cultural norms of the group they needed to provide more training and sensitivity to divergent views. The old-timers at the warehouse did not want to have to change their norms to accommodate a person from outside of their cultural norms. They expected Jim to accept Spanish music and ways of work. This is similar to an all men's group or all white group not wanting to change their ways to accommodate women or another nonwhite person. An interesting dialogue can be exchanged with students as they put themselves first in Jim's shoes and then in an old-timer's shoes.

To avoid the problem, Jose and Christi would have needed to select another Hispanic employee or at least one that had accepted the cultural norms. The question then becomes a dilemma, "Is it ethical to exclude another race or gender because they don't fit in to the dominant cultural norms?"

If Jim was selected, then adequate measures needed to have been taken to help ensure his acceptable entry. Discussions needed to occur with the old employees to help them let go of some of their hard-and-fast beliefs. A single employee of another race or gender cannot stand easily against the onslaught of dissatisfaction aimed at him or her. It is likely that the new employee will either leave or become disruptive.

Steps needed to be taken to accommodate Jim's taste in music as well, perhaps through headphones when it was safe, or rotation in the broadcasting system.

Jim should have received formal training about Wukmier's procedures for loading production. Regardless of what was done, it is likely that a single individual who is different from the majority will not have an easy entry. It will take increasing the number of minorities to make it possible for the group norms to change.

Question 4

How do Hofstede's dimensions help explain the warehouse employees' perceptions and attributions in the case?

Application skills (using information in a new context to solve a problem, answer a question, or perform a task). Reference: Robbins, 1998, Chapter 4, pp. 138 and 140; Schermerhorn, 1999, Chapter 5, pp. 105–106.

Answer

The Hispanic employees of the warehouse shared a common culture. These men were all of Mexican heritage, either first generation or second generation. Jim was of a different culture. As a white male, he was a representative of the "majority" culture in the United States, although in this setting he was the minority. Dutch researcher Geert Hofstede discovered that most differences among national cultures can be described by four dimensions: uncertainty avoidance, masculinity-femininity, individualism-collectivism, and power distance. Hofstede added a fifth dimension, long-term or short-term orientation, uncovered by Canadian researcher Michael Harris Bond. A comparison of cultural characteristics between Mexico and the United States reveals some differences. Mexico is based upon collectivism, where work in the United States is usually designed and assigned to an individual. In Hofstede's study of 53 countries, the United States scored the highest on individualism. In addition, the U.S. national culture favors low power distance, scores masculine but somewhat toward the middle of the scale, and has weak uncertainty avoidance (it is comfortable with uncertainty). In contrast, the Mexican culture is characterized by strong uncertainty avoidance, is high in masculinity, is collectivist, and tolerates a high degree of power distance.

The Mexicans and Mexican Americans at the warehouse expected Jim to work collectively with them (high collectivism). They expected their supervisor, Jose, to be the boss and tell them what to do (high power distance). Jim, on the other hand, believed strongly in individual performance and felt that his abilities should merit respect (high individualism).

The larger group of employees placed greater emphasis on looking after group needs and protecting one another. They may have argued among themselves, but they were united when it came to their feelings about Jim. Jim was more individualistic. He did his work, working quickly to pull his orders. He felt successful in his previous job and expected to be successful in this job. He did not understand the need to "fit in." He did not understand nor was he interested in the cultural differences.

The U.S. culture is weak in uncertainty avoidance (tolerates a lot of uncertainty). Perhaps this contributed to Jim's failure to try to fit in. Weak uncertainty avoidance is expressed in such statements as 1) Deviation from the norm is not threatening, tolerance of differences is essential; 2) conflict and competition can be managed and used constructively; and 3) there should be as few rules as possible.

Question 5

How would you resolve the music issue?

Analysis skills (breaking a concept into its parts and explaining their interrelationships; distinguishing relevant from extraneous material).

Answer

There is no correct answer, but issues to consider include "what gets more value—the collective/group norms or the individual's freedom/rights?" "Tradition or new ways?" "Fitting in or self-expression?"

Help students explore this question by contrasting these assumptions or values.

Question 6

What factors explain the workers' attitudes toward Jim?

Analysis skills (breaking a concept into its parts and explaining their interrelationships; distinguishing relevant from extraneous material).

Answer

Due to the separate location of the warehouse and the long-time working relationships among the employees, it appears a certain ethnocentricity existed. On one hand, the hiring practices seem to favor Hispanics for the job of warehouse employee. Of course, the location of the warehouse in a primarily Hispanic community probably contributed somewhat to the selection. This group of employees had developed a very close relationship, relying on one another to accomplish the day's work and to provide the social aspect of work. They spoke both English and Spanish at work, listened to Spanish music on the radio, and socialized with one another during the work day. This group readily identified with one another. Cox (1993, p. 132) suggests the benefits of working with others who are similar to ourselves include:

- There is a sense that the behavior of others is less uncertain and more predictable.
- One alternative for attributing the causes of actions or reactions from that person is removed.
- There may be some psychic payoff for our need to give back or promote the well-being of the group, to the extent that we are instrumental in providing economic opportunity for others of our group.
- There is another basis on to which to establish a relationship, and this may make it easier to establish rapport.

Attribution theory helps us to understand ethnocentrism (Robbins, 1998, Chapter 3, pp. 94–95). Internal attributions are made for positive outcomes, and external attributions are made for negative outcomes. The opposite is true for out-group members. When conflict occurred within the in-group, they most likely attributed it to outside forces (external attribution) and not personality problems (internal attribution). The opposite appears true for Jim. When he had conflict, other employees appeared to attribute it to his personality or lack of proper respect (internal attribution).

Jim was perceived as an outsider because he had not yet proven himself to the group. Socialization theory tells us that a normal period of initiation for a newcomer to the group should be expected. However, Jim was also perceived as an outsider because he was different from most of the workers (in terms of race and probably his age). Any observable difference increased the lack of trust and made it more difficult for socialization to occur (Robbins, 1998, Chapter 16, pp. 607–609; Schermerhorn, 1999, Chapter 12, pp. 248–249).

Question 7

If you were Jim, what would you do to enter this group effectively?

Action question (calls for a conclusion or action).

Answer

Jim could have done a lot to make his transition easier. He could first have decreased his personal needs and become more accepting of group norms. Establishing himself as one who has accepted the standards of the group will help him gain more credit, which will allow him to deviate from group norms at a later time. He could suggest other ways to load product, and he could request some of his own music out of "fairness" once he is more accepted in the group. A person in the in-group has much more room to bargain than one in the out-group.

Question 8
If you were Christi, what decisions would you make at the end of the case?
<u>Synthesis skills</u> (putting parts together to form a new whole; solving a problem requiring creativity or originality).

Answer
There are many possible answers. Following are a few possible solutions that students might suggest.

1. <u>Place Manny on temporary suspension pending further investigation.</u> A policy of no tolerance of violence is essential. Threatening another employee is considered an act of violence.
2. <u>Determine if Manny has a drug problem.</u> This could be done by referring him to the EAP. He will have to sign a release to make the data available to Christi.
3. <u>No discipline can be given to Jim, because he did not break any rules.</u> However, an immediate formal socialization process should begin, including expectations of group norms.
4. <u>Formal training must be provided to Jose.</u> While he has successfully directed the work of this group of employees for many years, there are some obvious areas for development. Supervisory training will provide improved interpersonal supervisory skills. The supervisor will be expected to learn ways to reduce conflict through communication, negotiation, and respect. If all employees are treated fairly and even-handedly, conflict can be expected to be reduced. The supervisor must have a good understanding of the bargaining agreement and the company rules. The agreed-upon elements of the contract must be followed. Progressive discipline is an important process to correcting any areas of concern. The supervisor needs to delegate work. By increasing the delegation of work, he will be available to provide leadership and manage the group.

References
Cox, T. Jr.. (1993). *Cultural diversity in organizations: Theory, research and practice*. San Francisco: Berrett-Koehler Publishers.

Robbins, S. (1998). *Organizational behavior: Concepts, controversies and applications*, 6th ed. Upper Saddle River, NJ: Prentice Hall:

Schermerhorn, J. R., Jr. (1999). *Management*, 6th ed., New York: Wiley.

Senge, P., C. Roberts, R. B. Ross, B. J. Smith, A. Kleiner (1994). *The fifth discipline handbook: Strategies and tools for building a learning organization*. New York: Doubleday.

Epilogue
Christi wanted to retain Manny as a worker, but she was concerned about his anger and suspected it might be related to drug abuse. She suspended Manny pending an investigation and referred him to the company's employee assistance program (EAP) for professional evaluation. Manny signed a release so the EAP counselor could discuss the case with Christi. He was evaluated on his "fit for duty" status. He was sent for a drug test.

Manny tested positive for marijuana. Manny wanted to retain his job and after some resistance to the requirements, he participated in anger management workshops and regular drug tests made available through his medical provider. He showed consistent improvement. He reported his wife was very grateful to the company for helping him to stop using drugs and for getting control over his anger.

No action was taken against Jim because he did not threaten anyone. Jim continued to have interpersonal problems at work. He developed a poor attitude, began missing work, and was terminated after receiving three warnings.

QUESTIONS MATTER!

Topics (* = Primary topic with teaching plan)
*Control
*Behavioral control
*Motivation (Maslow's hierarchy of needs)
Communication (dysfunctional, barriers to, effective listening)
Leadership (autocratic)
Medium-sized business context

Case overview

Cathy Parker was excited as she made her early morning commute to work to her new job at EBSCO Subscription Services in February, 1998. Her new position, Customer Service Representative, was at the Los Angeles Regional office of EBSCO Subscription Services (ESS). ESS offered libraries and institutions a convenience. They placed their orders through EBSCO, received the invoice, and wrote one check for most of their subscriptions, such as print, CD-ROM, and electronic journals.

The Los Angeles regional office was comprised of approximately 40 employees, including the regional manager. The customer service departments were divided into three areas: Schools and Universities, Corporate Accounts, and Hospitals and Medical Libraries. Cathy began her training in the Schools and Universities Department, under the direct supervision of Julie Trenton, Customer Service Supervisor. Cathy felt comfortable working with Julie, as she found her easygoing. Julie reinforced that she had an open-door policy, should any questions or concerns arise. Although the training, at times, was extremely detail-oriented, Julie felt that Cathy caught on quickly and, after 3 weeks of training, left her to work on her own. Cathy was proud of this accomplishment, for she had always prided herself on working independently with minimum supervision. After working two months in the Schools and Universities Customer Service department, Cathy was promoted to the position of Customer Service Support for the Hospital and Medical Libraries department.

Everything, at that point, had gone well and run smoothly, when suddenly in mid-April an urgent staff meeting was called. It was announced at the meeting that the group's immediate supervisor had accepted a position elsewhere and that Amanda Holt would be the new supervisor.

Amanda had been an accountant with the company for 9 years, but had never managed people. But from discussion amongst employees, Cathy came to the conclusion that she would give Amanda the benefit of the doubt, and that time would prove to be the best indicator of her management skills.

It wasn't long before Cathy realized that Amanda's way of managing employees greatly differed from that of her predecessor. Shortly after Amanda began her new supervisory position, she called Cathy into her office. Effective immediately, Cathy could not ask questions of the coworkers within her department; all questions were to be directed to Amanda. Amanda also instructed Cathy to save all of her daily work. Every afternoon Amanda would go over the work with Cathy, and address any corrections needed. When Cathy explained to Amanda that she was accustomed to working independently, with minimum supervision, Amanda rebutted that she was not "out to get her," and justified her actions as trying to help Cathy understand her job better. However, Cathy believed that Amanda singled her out for some reason, and wondered if this was a "power trip," or if Amanda's intimidating management techniques would continue indefinitely.

As the weeks passed, Cathy's frustration grew even stronger. Cathy began to consider whether or not she should seek employment elsewhere.

---

*Source: Adapted from case prepared by Cathy Paul, Jonnetta Thomas-Chambers and Teri C. Tompkins, University of Redlands. The case and teaching note were prepared as a basis for class discussion rather than to illustrate either effective or ineffective handling of administrative situations. Suggestions for improvement of this note should be sent to tompkins@uor.edu. Credit will be given in the next revision.

Industry

Magazine subscription service offering consolidated program to place subscriptions for schools, universities, hospitals, medical libraries, and corporations. Provide domestic and international customer service. Medium-sized business.

Teaching objectives

1. To analyze the effectiveness of the control systems used by Julie and Amanda.
2. To analyze the communication process and outline methods of improvement.
3. To recognize the importance of positive motivation and the rewards it can provide.

Other related cases in Volume 1

A New Magazine in Nigeria (acceptance of authority, autocratic leadership); *A Team Divided or a Team United?* (autocratic leadership); *Handling Differences at Japan Auto* (Maslow's hierarchy of needs); *The Day They Announced the Buyout* (Maslow's hierarchy of needs).

Other related cases in Volume 2

A Selfish Request in Japan (Maslow's hierarchy of needs); *Angry Branch Manager* (Maslow's hierarchy of needs); *Preferential Treatment?* (interpersonal conflict); *The Safety Memo* (barriers to communication).

Intended courses and levels

This case is well suited for graduate and executive students to analyze the issues of behavioral control, motivation and communication in an organization. Questions 4 and 5 are well suited for lower division undergraduate students. The case fits well in the control function of management. It fits at the interpersonal level for organizational behavior.

Analysis

All related analysis and references are embedded in the answers to the questions.

Research methodology

This case reflects the recollections of Cathy Paul. It is a true incident. The names have been disguised, but the company has not.

Teaching plan

Teaching plan topic: Behavioral Control and Motivation
60-minute teaching plan

Preassignment: None

	Timing	Activity	Organization	Student Outcomes
I	0–10 minutes (10)	Read the case.	Individually	Familiarity with case facts.
II	10–20 minutes (10)	Short lecture on managerial control.	Lecture	Key points: ● One of four functions of management is control. ● Controlling = Monitoring the activities to ensure they are being accomplished as planned and correcting any significant deviations (Robbins, 1998, p. 3).

	Timing	Activity	Organization	Student Outcomes
				The 11 types of behavioral control are listed in the answer to Q1. Three steps to control: measuring, comparing, and correcting.
III	20–25 minutes (5)	Q1: What type of behavioral control(s) did Julie use?	Full class discussion	● Training ● Mentoring by senior employees ● Rewards (promotion)
IV	25–35 minutes (10)	Q2: What type of behavioral control did Amanda use? Why?	Full class discussion	● Direct supervision. ● Why? Amanda's background was in accounting, where strict controls are common.
V	35–40 minutes (5)	Q3: What type of motivation did Cathy prefer?	Full class discussion	● Cathy preferred extrinsic rewards. ● She wanted to be recognized for work well done. ● She responded better to positive reinforcement and poorly to negative reinforcement (which is what Amanda likely used). ● She wanted autonomy.
VI	40–45 minutes (5)	Q4: Use Maslow's hierarchy of needs theory to explain which needs were met under each supervisor.	Full class discussion	Under Julie: Social needs were met, then esteem developed as she mastered job and was promoted. Under Amanda: Not allowed to talk to others, reduced ability to meet social needs. Less autonomy and respect reduced self-esteem.
VII	45–55 minutes (10)	What would you do if you were Cathy? Why? Any downsides to your action?	Full class discussion	Answers will vary.
VIII	55–60 minutes (5)	Want to hear what Cathy decided to do? Read epilogue and ask for comments.	Full class discussion	Cathy's decision to not take it personally appeared to be functional, and resulted in better communication between them and more autonomy for Cathy.

25-minute teaching plan on control.
Preassignment: Read case before coming to class (10 minutes reading time).
Do activities II, III, and IV (5 minutes), and VIII in preceding 60-minute plan.

25-minute teaching plan on motivation.
Preassignment: Read case before coming to class (10 minutes reading time).
Do activities V, VI, VII, and VIII in preceding 60-minute plan.

Discussion questions and answers

What type of behavioral control(s) did Julie use?

Analysis skills (breaking a concept into its parts and explaining their interrelationships, distinguishing relevant from extraneous material).

Answer

- Training
- Mentoring by senior employees
- Rewards (promotion)

Types of behavioral control (Robbins and Coulter, 1996, p. 749).

1. Selection
2. Goals
3. Job design
4. Orientation
5. Direct supervision
6. Training
7. Mentoring
8. Formalization
9. Performance appraisals
10. Organizational rewards
11. Organizational culture

Of the eleven behavioral control techniques listed above, training, mentoring, and rewards appear to be the methods that Julie used to monitor and control Cathy.

Formal training programs teach employees desired work practices, while informal and formal mentoring activities by senior employees convey to junior employees the "ropes to skip and the ropes to know." Rewards act as reinforcers to encourage desired behaviors and to extinguish undesired ones (Robbins and Coulter, 1996, p. 749).

Cathy was trained in the early stages of her tenure at the company. She was also encouraged to talk to senior employees to get her questions answered. Once she mastered the Colleges and University subscriptions, she was promoted to Medical. All of these control methods were acceptable to Cathy.

Question 2

What type of behavioral control did Amanda use? Why?

Analysis skills (breaking a concept into its parts and explaining their interrelationships, distinguishing relevant from extraneous material).

Answer

- Direct supervision.
- Why? Amanda's background was in accounting, where strict controls are common.

Amanda preferred to use direct supervision. We can speculate why. The case mentions that Amanda had never previously supervised people before and was coming from accounting. Some students will be able to imagine what accounting is like. The preferred controls are formalization (strict accounting practices) and direct supervision. Frequent control is common and necessary in accounting because of the need to maintain accurate records and reporting. It is likely that Amanda had been supervised with frequent monitoring of her work. She believed that this was good management practice, and she applied it to her new job as supervisor, unaware of the contingency theory of management that states that management is more effective if the leadership style is appropriately matched to the situation.

Question 3

What type of motivation did Cathy prefer?

Analysis skills (breaking a concept into its parts and explaining their interrelationships, distinguishing relevant from extraneous material).

Answer

- Cathy preferred extrinsic rewards.
- She wanted to be recognized for work well done.
- She responded better to positive reinforcement and poorly to negative reinforcement (which is what Amanda likely used).
- She wanted autonomy.

Cathy was looking for an extrinsic reward from Amanda. "Extrinsic rewards are externally administered. They are valued outcomes given to someone by another person—typically, a supervisor or higher-level manager. Common examples of extrinsic rewards available in the workplace are verbal praise, special assignments, promotion, awards, office fixtures, benefits, incentive pay, time off, and the like (Schermerhorn, 1996, 145)." Cathy wanted Amanda to acknowledge and praise her for the work she perceived she was performing well. In addition, Cathy wanted to be recognized as a competent member of the work team by Amanda. She believed autonomy was an indication that Amanda saw her as competent.

Question 4

Use Maslow's hierarchy of needs theory to explain which needs were met under each supervisor.

Application skills (using information in a new context to solve a problem, answer a question, or perform a task).

Answer

- Under Julie: Social needs were met, then esteem developed as she mastered the job and was promoted.
- Under Amanda: Not allowed to ask questions or discuss business with others, reduced ability to meet social needs. Less autonomy and respect reduced self-esteem.

The five needs within the hierarchy are physiological (hunger, thirst, shelter, sex, and other bodily needs), safety (security and protection from emotional and physical harm), social (affection, belongingness, acceptance, and friendship), esteem (internal—self-respect, autonomy, and achievement, external—status, recognition, and attention) and self-actualization (drive to become what one is capable of becoming; growth, achieving potential, and self-fulfillment). (Robbins, 1998, 169)

When Cathy took the job at ESS, she fit in quickly. She made friends easily, was trusted by coworkers and her immediate supervisor, and felt like she belonged. Therefore, her social needs began to peak. Cathy progressed to the next level, esteem, where she worked autonomously, achieved multiple responsibilities within differing departments, harbored self-respect, and was recognized as a competent performer who needed little supervision.

Then, the environment changed when she received a new supervisor. Immediately, this affected the stability of her social and esteem needs. She felt less accepted, was given less autonomy, and felt lack of recognition and respect. This halted her progression to self-actualization to achieve her potential and become self-fulfilled.

Question 5

Define communication. Describe what was functional and dysfunctional in Cathy and Amanda's communication.

Knowledge skills (remember previously learned material such as definitions, principles, formulas) and comprehension skills (understanding the meaning of remembered material, usually demonstrated by restating or citing examples).

Answer

"Communication can be defined as the process by which information is exchanged and understood by two or more people, usually with the intent to motivate or influence behavior' Communication is not just sending information. This distinction between sharing and proclaiming is crucial for successful management. A manager who does not listen is like a used car salesperson who claims, "I just sold a car—they just did not buy it" (Daft, 1998, p. 481).

"Functional conflict is constructive and helps task performance. Dysfunctional conflict is destructive and hurts task performance" (Schermerhorn, 1999, p. 339).

In Cathy and Amanda's communication process, functional conflict did exist. The fact that Amanda was willing to work with Cathy, and correct her work errors, was functional. However, this is the only component that was functional. Dysfunction conflict prevailed because of Amanda's approach when communicating with Cathy. Specifically, Cathy's overall performance was shadowed with discomfort and frustration. The lack of empowerment that Cathy experienced was damaging to Cathy's motivational needs. Amanda's poor listening skills compounded this process.

Question 6

What could Amanda and Cathy have done to improve the communication process?
Synthesis skills (putting parts together to form a new whole; solving a problem requiring creativity or originality).

Answer

Barriers to effective communication (Daft, 1998, pp. 496–499): The individual barriers harbored by Cathy and Amanda were perceptions and emotions. Cathy and Amanda needed to broaden their perceptions and have understanding for the opposing ones. In addition, Cathy needed to redirect her emotions, this can be attributed to selective listening when emotions are involved. Cathy and Amanda could have omitted these barriers by asking questions to gain understanding of one another. They weren't actively listening to one another.

Negative feedback: Although it may not have been Amanda's intent to communicate negative feedback to Cathy, Cathy perceived her feedback as negative. It's negative because it didn't support Cathy's goals or needs. Amanda, after giving feedback, should have asked Cathy if she was comfortable with her directive and listened to her response.

Effective listening (Robbins, 1998, pp. 323–325): Both Cathy and Amanda could have improved in this area. Amanda, at times, spent too much time talking and not enough time asking questions and actively listening to Cathy. In addition, she would interrupt Cathy when she spoke and disregard what Cathy had to offer. On the other hand, Cathy attached emotions to Amanda's words. Amanda simply said that she wanted to check her work, help her, and ensure she's doing the work correctly. Although Amanda had been doing a good job, it was based upon another supervisor's perception. She could have patiently taken steps to exemplify to her new boss that she was a competent, new employee that fit well into the group.

Role reversal: Both Cathy and Amanda could have looked at the situation from each other's point of view. Amanda may have understood that Cathy needed her support in a different way and just wanted to be validated as a competent employee. Cathy may have understood that Amanda's lack of experience was going to result in some, perhaps unintentional, trial and error. Amanda needed flexibility, honesty, and support from her staff, and vice versa.

Conflicting points of view, resistance, and closed-mindedness: Both Cathy and Amanda seemed to be set in their ways, which countermands communication. Open communication is necessary to be effective for all parties involved. Cathy wanted to work as she had always worked, and Amanda thought she should supervise, most likely, the way she was supervised. They needed to meet each other half way with a willingness to change.

Question 7

How could Amanda have positively motivated Cathy?

<u>Synthesis skills</u> (putting parts together to form a new whole; solving a problem requiring creativity or originality).

Answer

Amanda should have built a relationship with Cathy first. With some rapport, as a foundation, Cathy may have been less resistant to do things Amanda's way. In retrospect, Amanda may have also had more faith that Cathy could do a good job with little supervision.

Amanda could have been more approachable. She should have worked with Cathy as a partner. She could have explained to Cathy that she wanted to work with her with hope of learning something from her and vice versa.

Amanda should have been more open. She could have shared some of her experiences with Cathy to help her understand why she felt she should supervise the way she did. In addition, she should have asked Cathy (and the other employees) how she perceived her working relationship with her thus far and how her managerial approach made her feel.

Amanda needed a creative, candid way to work with Cathy without making her feel apprehensive and frustrated. She may have been more effective if she'd known how to utilize MBO. This approach would have ensured that Amanda was managing to help Cathy reach her personal and professional goals in conjunction with fulfilling the organization's goals.

Question 8

If you were Amanda, what would you have done to transform your leadership style?

<u>Hypothetical skills</u> (poses a change in the facts or issues).

Answer

<u>Seek mentorship from a more experienced supervisor or manager</u>: "A mentor is a senior employee who sponsors or supports a less experienced employee (a protégé). The mentoring role includes coaching, counseling and sponsorship. As a coach, mentors help to develop a protégé's skills. As counselors, mentors provide support and help bolster the protégé's self-confidence. As sponsors, mentors actively intervene on behalf of their proteges, lobby to get them visible assignments, and politick to get them rewards such as promotions and salary increases." Mentoring has proven to be essential to those who have gotten ahead (Robbins, 1998, p. 583).

<u>Attend seminars for new supervisors and managers</u>: Amanda could attend off-the-job training programs (in-house or off-site) to learn new skills while improving current ones. "Off-site programs are typically sponsored by universities, trade or professional associations, and consultants. Management development workshops are special forms of off-the-job training to improve a person's knowledge and skill in the fundamentals of management" (Schermerhorn, 1996, p. 257).

<u>Build relationships with my team</u>: Through informal channels of communication, such as going bowling, playing softball, going to dinner or to the gym together, the team can interact in a more relaxed atmosphere outside of the hierarchical structure within the workplace (Daft, 1998, p. 492). People who play well together have a greater chance of working well together.

<u>Foster a participative team environment</u>: Partnering with team members to get work done and reach organizational goals is an effective approach that builds rapport and team support. "Participative leadership requires involving subordinates in decision making, consulting with subordinates; asking questions from subordinates; using these suggestions when making decisions (This is one of four approaches introduced in Robert House's path-goal theory)" (Schermerhorn, 1996, pp. 105–107).

<u>Become an active listener</u>: There are ten rules for good listening that Cathy could have followed: ". . . stop talking, put the other person at ease, show that you want to listen, remove any potential distractions, empathize with the other person, don't respond too quickly, be patient, don't get mad, hold your temper, go easy on argument and criticism, ask questions, and stop talking . . ." (Schermerhorn, 1996, p. 216)

<u>Maintain an open-door policy</u>: It is important to let subordinates know that a manager cares about their well-being. Having an open-door policy invites employees to approach you with concerns or

suggestions without apprehension. For this to be successful, the manager must be willing to listen with an open-mind and appreciate the effort of the employee for sharing his or her perceptions or concerns. Ultimately, this will strengthen the superior-subordinate relationship as well as the overall team.

References

Daft, R. L.; Marcic, D. (1998). *Understanding management*, 2nd ed. Orlando, FL: Dryden.

Robbins, S. P. (1998). *Organizational Behavior*, 8th ed. Upper Saddle River, NJ: Prentice Hall.

Robbins, S.P. and Coulter, M. (1996). *Management*, 5th ed. Upper Saddle River, NJ: Prentice Hall.

Schermerhorn, Jr., J. R., (1996). *Management and organizational behavior essentials*. New York, NY: John Wiley and Sons,

Schermerhorn, Jr., J. R. (1999). *Management*, 6th ed. New York, NY: John Wiley and Sons.

Epilogue

After weeks of careful thinking, Cathy decided that the best plan of action was to simply try to work together with Amanda. Cathy realized that Amanda, new to the position of supervising employees, possibly knew of no other way of manage. Cathy hoped that, with time, Amanda would initiate a more open approach to manage her staff members. Perhaps, one day, Amanda would realize that employees tend to be happy in their respective jobs and perform these jobs better when they're given the freedom to make decisions on their own, with the assurance that they are trusted and respected by their supervisor.

After approximately two months, Amanda finally realized that Cathy could work independently. Naturally, questions would arise occasionally. Now, both Cathy and Amanda worked together to find the best possible solution for the given situation. Cathy was no longer required to save her work on a daily basis or address her questions only to Amanda.

Unfortunately, the good working relationship that Amanda and Cathy had worked so hard to achieve was short-lived. Amanda left the company and was replaced by Cathy's current manager, Maria. Maria, 42, was a customer service manager that transferred to Los Angeles from ESS's Denver, Colorado office.

Cathy was comfortable working with Maria right from the start because she gave Cathy the freedom to work independently and was willing to listen when given suggestions to improve productivity and service to their customers. Being new to the office, the roles were sometimes reversed. Maria approached Cathy, as well as the coworkers, with questions regarding accounts and customers.

SHAKING THE BIRD CAGE

Topics (* = Primary topic with teaching plan)
*Decision case
*Power
*Decision-making process
*Understanding "interests" of the opposition
*Problem solving
Influence
Status
Resistance to change
Defensive behavior
Organizational change
Organizational structure
Restructuring
Large corporation context

Case overview

The antenna team is a close-knit group of engineers and technicians responsible for developing sensor-seeking devices for the military. Their manager, Dick, is a world-renowned scientist in this area, and their immediate supervisor is Chuck, a project manager but not a scientist. In the past, the team has been successful at developing products that meet or exceed technical expectations, but with reduced military spending, success is less frequent. The case opens with one member's discovery that there are upper management plans to split the team, three members remaining with Dick and the rest to serve under Forrest, known for "micro-managing." The reorganization is like shaking the bird cage; the same birds are still in the cage, but they land on different perches. The rest of the case details the actions the members take to stop the reorganization.

Part B. After brainstorming alternatives, they decide to present their case to upper management about why they should stay together. They also all agree to quit en masse, if their demands are not accepted. Management is surprised at the vehemence the members display, because they thought that the members didn't enjoy working with Dick or Chuck. Forrest believes the members are a bunch of egotists and need to be whipped into shape. The case ends with a stalemate and no reorganization.

Industry

Technical team from a defense industry division of AVIONICS, a large, diverse organization with multiple divisions and products. The subsidiary is responsible for developing electronic sensing devices. The primary output from company is research and development. Little manufacturing occurs at the company.

Teaching objectives
1. To examine the importance of defining the problem first in the decision-making process.
2. To investigate why and how individual and team members contest for power.
3. To recognize the importance of identifying "the opposition's" interests.

Other related cases in Volume 1

A New Magazine in Nigeria (restructuring); *Fired!* (organizational structure); *Jenna's Kitchens, Inc.* (status); *Julie's Call: Empowerment at Taco Bell* (restructuring); *Split Operations at Sky and Arrow Airlines* (organizational change, organizational structure); *The Day They Announced the Buyout* (organizational change, restructuring).

---

*Source: Adapted from case prepared by Teri C. Tompkins, University of Redlands. The case and teaching note were prepared as a basis for classroom discussion rather than to illustrate either effective or ineffective handling of an administrative situation. Suggestions for improvement of this note should be sent to tompkins@uor.edu. Credit will be given in the next revision.

Other related cases in Volume 2

Angry Branch Manager (decision-making process); *Computer Services Team at AVIONICS* (restructuring); *Insubordination or Unclear Loyalties?* (decision-making process); *Leadership of TQM in Panama* (restructuring); *The Safety Memo* (decision-making process); *When Worlds Collide* (organizational structure, restructuring).

Intended courses and levels

This case is appropriate for courses in organizational behavior, power/influence, management, and communications/negotiations. Upper level undergraduate students can use it, but it is especially rich for graduate and executive students. It is best positioned after students have an understanding of motivation, power, and group dynamics.

Analysis

If used to analyze behavior and make decisions:

At a minimum, recognize:

1. fact finding was not used by either the team or upper management
2. solutions were approached before the problem was defined
3. people will resist change, especially if they have no input as to how or what will change
4. if an individual or team is not doing the job, is it because:
   - lack the skills to do it? Then provide the skills
   - lack the willingness to do it? Then examine organizational systems, such as feedback, rewards, supervision, AND worker attitude and motivation.

Advanced concepts:

1. supervision of engineers and scientists requires a balance between freedom to problem solve/create and constraints to control cost and stay on schedule.

If used for a power/influence class:

At a minimum, recognize:

1. any change will cause resistance
2. scarce resources can shift the equilibrium of organizational structures and people
3. people can use power to further their own objectives, which may or may not be in line with the organization's objectives

Advance concepts:

1. Forrest may be making a bid for power because:
   - he has fewer people reporting to him than the rest of the team
   - downsizing could happen due to fewer contracts
   - Forrest may be trying to strengthen his influence within the organization

Research methodology

This case was part of a dissertation study on how collective learning occurs. Data was collected through interviews with the majority of the team members, as well as all layers of management above the team. In addition, observations of team meetings and review of written documents, such as team minutes, were used to support the research. All people and the organization have been disguised.

Teaching plan

This case works well as a decision-focused case, but it can also work as an analysis case. For graduate and executive students, the teaching plan with role-play is fun, but it can also be taught by following a standard decision-focused framework. 1) What are the key issues and stakeholders? 2) What is the primary issue? 3) What are possible alternatives and their consequences? 4) What solution do you recommend?

Undergraduates can also benefit from the role-play, but may feel as if they are learning more by simply answering the questions.

Teaching plan topic: Decision-Making Process, Organizational Structure, and Discovering "Interests"
60-minute teaching plan

Preassignment: None.

	Timing	Activity	Organization	Student Outcomes
I	0–5 minutes (5)	*Read only part A of case.*	Individually	Familiarity with case facts. Students may feel as if they don't have enough information.
II	5–15 minutes (10)	*After reading part A, what should Kathy, Jim and members of the antenna team do?*	Small groups of 4 to 5	Student answers will vary. As you walk around the room, listen for solutions, versus probing into the facts.
III	15–25 minutes (10)	Read part B. *After reading part B, what should members of upper management do?*	Small groups of 4 to 5	Student answers will vary. As you walk around the room, listen for solutions, versus probing into the facts.
IV	25–35 minutes (10)	Role-play round 1: Jim and Kathy (minus other members) meet with upper management (minus Forrest) and try to resolve the issues.	Ask for volunteers to act out their discussion.	The preceding questions ask students to immediately solve the problem, without giving thought to what the real problems might be. The role-play might serve to demonstrate the lack of understanding of the problem
V	35–40 minutes (5)	Review role-play. Ask students: *What went well, and what could improve the situation?*	Full class discussion. Watch the time. Five minutes is usually plenty of time for a role-play, and the shorter time keeps the "audience" from getting bored.	The results of the role-play depend on the skill levels of the students. Some will gloss over problems, and simply agree. Others will get stuck in their positions and get nowhere. There will be some skillful students who may dig deeper and begin to understand the other people's concerns.
VI	40–45 minutes (5)	State: "Let's probe a little deeper into the issues here." Ask students *Q4: How would you characterize this team prior to the reorganization plans?*	Full class discussion	See answers to Q4.
VII	45–50 minutes (5)	*Q5: Why did the antenna team respond the way it did to the proposed reorganization?*	Full class discussion	See answers to Q5.
VIII	50–55 minutes (5)	Role-play round 2. Either with the same players, or new volunteers, role-play based on the added insights from the	You may want to stop the role-play, and coach students to get	Results will vary, depending on student skill level.

	Timing	Activity	Organization	Student Outcomes
		discussion on question 4 and Q5: *Let's try the role-play again, but this time look for ways to meet your interests as we've just discussed.*	them to ask probing questions in which they might learn more about the other parties concerns.	
IX	55–60 minutes (5)	Summarize relationship to chapter. Point out some of your observations (see Analysis for some ideas). Read or hand out epilogue.	Full class discussion	The analysis section contains some ideas.

25-minute teaching plan on decision-making process and discovering interests.
Preassignment: Read case before class (5 minutes). Answer questions 1 and 2.
Activities. Do activities VI (10 minutes), VII (10 minutes), and IX (5 minutes) in the 60-minute plan.

Discussion questions and answers

Question 1

After reading Part A, what should Kathy, Jim and members of the antenna team do?
Action question (calls for a conclusion or action).

Answer

First, they should help the team gather as many facts as they can to determine what upper management concerns are. Second, they should decide, as a team, how they might address these concerns. If upper management is concerned about tight resources and lack of results, then the team needs to make suggestions that address how they might get better results without decreasing cash flow. Thus, if training is something they feel they need, they might show how training costs can be absorbed by greater results due to increased competency. If upper management is concerned about their attitudes, they must decide if their behavior warrants such concern, and, if it does, how they can manage it; if it doesn't, how they can counteract the accusations. Third, the team must evaluate management's reorganization plan; in light of downsizing, it is likely that reorganization will occur sooner or later. Perhaps members of the team can suggest how and when this might occur.

Question 2

After reading Part B, what should members of upper management do?
Action question (calls for a conclusion or action).

Answer

It appears that too few facts were gathered and too few questions asked prior to considering the reorganization plan. Based on the surprise of team members, it also appears that none of them were questioned or consulted about the reorganization. If top management is seriously concerned about the team's performance, target goals need to be specified with team members determining how those goals might be met.

Management must determine if team members aren't meeting expectations due to poor attitudes, lack of worker motivation, or lack of competency or resources. If it is poor attitude or motivation, then interviews with individuals can be done with decisions made about adjusting such things as feedback systems, reward systems, supervision, or other areas that improve worker attitudes or motivation. If it is lack of competency or resources, then management must determine how to increase member's skill and knowledge sets through such activities as external training, learning activities within the group, developing systems to distribute knowledge across groups, transferring in the missing competency.

Finally, upper management must investigate the reasons Forrest made the reorganization plan in the first place. Interviews with him, his former subordinates, peers, and supervisors might yield some answers. He accuses the team of being a bunch of egotists, but it is possible that he is empire building (trying to grab power by positioning important resources or teams under him).

Regardless of whether the antenna team holds a bunch of egotists, the reorganization is unlikely to improve each member's attitude. Engineers and scientists are an interesting bunch of people to supervise; they need emotional/intellectual space to problem-solve, yet they must also be held accountable to cost and budget. Balancing between these two constraints takes a skillful supervisor. Obviously, management tried to insert Chuck's project management skills to support Dick's scientific skills.

During good times, when resources are plenty, there is more freedom to solve problems in creative, less financially constrained ways. But in scarce times, as the company is now facing, serious attention must be paid to staying within budget and delivering on time. Reorganizations can be used to improve work processes, redistribute resources, or disband a group that is disruptive or ineffective, but management needs to be aware of the secondary effects that any reorganization causes (even if only for a short time)—resistance, adjustment in ways of work, confusion, less efficiency, reduced productivity.

Question 3
What are possible ways to end this stalemate?
Action question (calls for a conclusion or action).
Answer
There are many ways to end the stalemate. Certainly, management can decree it, and the team members must either accept the ruling, or quit, as they have threatened to do. They many also look for joint solutions. For example, a task force could be appointed, with representatives from the concerned parties, to investigate the real problems and suggest solutions.

Reorganizing, just for the sake of reorganizing, is like "shaking a bird cage." The frame and the birds are just the same, only they move to different perches. Sometimes executives reorganize just to "do something," or to try to solve personnel problems. Reorganizing can be very effective, when organizing is done to solve important problems (like span of control, fair distribution of work, or to increase motivation). But frequently reorganization is done, ignoring the larger system (birdcage) and thereby making it look as if great things have changed, when the underlying problems still exist. If management and team members can help identify what they really want (their goals), and determine what they can realistically afford to have their limited resources), then it might be possible to come up with creative solutions that will be less resisted by both sides.

Question 4
How would you characterize this team prior to the reorganization plans?
Analysis skills (breaking a concept into its parts and explaining their interrelationships, distinguishing relevant from extraneous material).
Answer
The team itself has felt successful in the past. Success to them may mean good products that meet or exceed customer expectations. They appear to enjoy their work and working together. They seem unaware or unconcerned with upper management's issues. They may be somewhat isolated in their lab, either physically or emotionally.

Question 5
Why did the antenna team respond the way it did to the proposed reorganization?
Analysis skills (breaking a concept into its parts and explaining their interrelationships, distinguishing relevant from extraneous material).

Answer

First, any kind of unexpected news or change will be resisted, even if only temporarily. Change takes adjustment, and the team members haven't had any time to adjust. Their defensive posture is to fight the news; other choices might have been to leave the company (flight), to withdraw and not have the emotional energy to contribute much to the organization, or to be angry and lash out at "enemies." Second, as scientist they are taught to problem-solve. Brainstorming is the first step to problem solving once the problem has been clearly identified. They believe that if management is presented with a rational reason for why they should not be disbanded, then management will make the rational right choice to keep them together. But to problem-solve effectively, they must first understand all the parameters; they must investigate the facts and ask more questions before they can brainstorm solutions. The team members are not acting as good scientists because they fail to first understand the issues. This is likely because they have already determined what the final outcome should be—keeping the team together. Therefore, they focus on reasons the team should stay together, but not on ways to meet the concerns of management.

Question 6

How might power and influence theory explain case facts?
Application skills (using information in a new context to solve a problem, answer a question, or perform a task).

Answer

During times of scarce resources, power issues are more manifest. In this case, the company is facing fewer defense contracts, requiring tighter budgets and more accountability. When people band together, they have greater power than they would individually. In this case, the team has threatened to quit en masse. The question is whether they would follow through with the threat. Management and the team reached a stalemate, resulting in unhappy people on both sides. Personal power can also be an issue. Forrest may have a need for high personal power. The organization chart indicates that Forrest is a peer of Dick's and has few responsibilities under him. It is possible that he is trying to build a stronger base in order to ensure job security or power.

References

Tompkins, T. C. (1997). "A developmental approach to organizational learning teams: A model and illustrative research." In M. M. Beyerlein and D. A. Johnson (eds.). *Advances in interdisciplinary studies of work teams* (Vol. 4, pp. 281–302). Greenwich, CT: JAI Press.

Tompkins, T. C. (1995). "The role of diffusion in collective learning." *International Journal of Organizational Analysis*, 3, 69–84.

Epilogue

After team members threatened to quit as a unit, top management decided to let the team continue to work together. However, no one was very happy with the situation. Members of the team felt that management had sucked out any enthusiasm they had held for work projects. They felt that management saw them as failures and that management did not appreciate their hard work. They wondered when the next attack would occur. On the other hand, management wondered if the team members had the ability to contribute to the bottom line. Management wondered if the team cared about the company or only about protecting their team turf. Both groups adopted a "wait-and-see" attitude.

*Teaching Note**
SPLIT OPERATIONS AT SKY AND ARROW AIRLINES

Topics (*= Primary topics with teaching plan)
    *Organizational culture clashes
    *Inter-group conflict
    *Job stress
    *Organizational structure
    Job satisfaction
    Organizational change
    Large corporation context

Case overview

Jack, an employee of Sky Airlines, experienced a dramatic change in the manner in which he enjoyed his job. The change occurred as a result of a merger between Sky and Arrow airlines. Jack's job at Sky perfectly met his needs as a college student. He could change his schedule to suit his classes, and his outdoor work as a ramper met his needs. He enjoyed the companionship of his fellow rampers and the emphasis on fun and customer service at Sky. He felt that he had many opportunities to make decisions on his own.

All that changed when Arrow management split ground operations at Santa Clara Airport giving Arrow employees responsibility for gate operations, checking in passengers and their luggage, while Sky employees took responsibility for ramp operations, loading and unloading baggage and freight. This change required the employees of Arrow and Sky to work closely with one another and to coordinate their activities with neither group having control over the whole process. The change produced a significant amount of stress for Jack and other employees. Cultural differences existed between the two companies, and they lacked a solid plan on how to make the joint operation work. Arrow Airlines was a much more structured organization than Sky. Jack and his fellow rampers felt that some of the procedures ran contrary to good operations. The result was conflict between the employees of the two companies and failure of the split operations plan. Ultimately, Arrow took over all operations. Jack and many of the other employees lost their jobs.

Industry

Airline Industry. Sky was a small commuter airline operating primarily in the western part of the United States. Employees were nonunion. Arrow was one of the largest airlines in the world.

Teaching objectives:
1. To introduce students to the concepts of inter-group conflict, organizational change, and organizational culture.
2. To teach students to explain "why" and "how" change affects individuals as well as groups in organizations.
3. To illustrate and help students diagnose the components of inter-group conflict caused by a change in organizational structure that intensified the differences between the two companies' cultures.
4. To recognize how job satisfaction is affected when unavoidable changes in the work environment occur.
5. To recognize the dynamics of stress in a changing environment.

---

*Source: Adapted from case prepared by Jeremy Offenstein, Jonnetta Thomas-Chambers, Jim Spee (University of Redlands), and Teri C. Tompkins, University of Redlands. The case and teaching note were prepared as a basis for class discussion rather than to illustrate either effective or ineffective handling of administrative situations. Suggestions for improvement of this note should be sent to tompkins@uor.edu. Credit will be given in the next revision.

Other related cases in Volume 1

A New Magazine in Nigeria (organizational change); *A Team Divided or a Team United?* (job satisfaction); *Donor Services Department in Guatemala* (organizational structures); *No, Sir, Sergeant!* (stress); *Shaking the Bird Cage* (organizational structure); *The Day They Announced the Buyout* (organizational change).

Other related cases in Volume 2

Insubordination or Unclear Loyalties? (organizational structure); *Negotiating Work Hours* (inter-group conflict); *Reputation in Jeopardy* (organizational change); *Saving Private Ryan and Classic Leadership Models* (stress); *Then There Was One* (job satisfaction); *When Worlds Collide* (organizational structure).

Intended courses and levels

This case is best suited for undergraduate students and graduate students for discovering examples from the case that relate to organizational culture and intergroup conflict theory.

Analysis

All related analysis and references are embedded in the answers to the questions.

Research methodology

This case reflects the recollections of one of the participants in the case. It is a true incident. Names and locations have been disguised.

Teaching plan

This case is intended to illustrate theories on the topics indicated. It is not a decision-focused case, although a few questions may be used to focus on a decision. Instructors should encourage students to explore the issues brought up by the case. For undergraduate students, the questions and answers will serve to guide students to the specific theories related to the case.

Teaching plan topic: Intergroup Conflict, Organizational Structure, and Culture
60-minute teaching plan

Preassignment: Read the case before class (15 minutes)

	Timing	Activity	Organization	Student Outcomes
I	0–5 minutes (5)	Review the facts of the case.	Full group discussion	Familiarization with case material.
II	5–20 minutes (15)	*Q1: What situational factors led to conflict between the operations employees of Arrow and Sky?*	Full group	Understand systemic causes of conflict. Understanding the role of organizational structure.
III	20–30 minutes (10)	*Q2: What were the effects of conflict on the Sky and Arrow employees?*	Full group	Students understand negative consequences of unresolved conflict.
IV	30–45 minutes (15)	*Q3: How are organizational cultures characterized and managed? Compare and contrast the cultures of Sky and Arrow.*	Full group	See answer to Q3.
V	45–55 minutes (10)	*Q4: Could cultural issues have caused the failure of the split operations system? Explain.*	Full group	See answer to Q4.

	Timing	Activity	Organization	Student Outcomes
VI	55–60 minutes (5)	Wrap up the discussion	Full group	Reflections on the conflicts in the case.

25-minute teaching plan on intergroup conflict.
Preassignment: Read case before class (15 minutes).
Do Activity II (10 minutes), III (10 minutes), and VI (5 minutes).

25-minute teaching plan on culture.
Preassignment: Read case before class (15 minutes).
Do Activity IV (10 minutes), V (10 minutes), and VI (5 minutes).

Discussion questions and answers

Question 1

What situational factors led to conflict between the operations employees of Arrow and Sky?
Knowledge skills (remember previously learned material such as definitions, principles, formulas) and application skills (using information in a new context to solve a problem, answer a question, or perform a task).

Answer

For conflict to occur between two groups, certain conditions must be present. These conditions are situations or connections that link groups in such a way that they are likely to conflict with each other. Wagner and Hollenbeck have identified nine factors involved in producing conflict (1998, pp. 258–259).

Interdependence: Before two or more groups can conflict in an organizational setting, they must rely on each other to carry out their separate tasks. The Sky rampers and Arrow employees were highly interdependent on each other. Prior to the splitting of ground operations, each company carried out its procedures within each company separately. After the two companies split operations, employees of each company had to work with members of the other company. The Sky employees depended on the Arrow employees to send passengers, bags, and the flight release on time. In turn, Arrow employees depended on Sky employees to deboard the plane, load the bags, and have the flight ready for boarding and departure in a timely manner.

When Arrow managers split the operation, they made an assumption that gate tasks and ramp tasks were not interdependent. They assumed that each group could do its work without relying on the other group. While this may have been true in the long-haul routes Arrow usually served, it was not true in the short-haul environment Jack was used to. In the fast turnaround environment, everyone had to pitch in together to get the planes ready for their next departure. When the whole operation belonged to Sky, this was easy to accomplish because everyone knew one another and was ready to help out. Information flowed informally between the gate and the ramp as people did their jobs. Arrow relied on formal channels that turned out to be nonexistent, so information about late bags and about departure priorities did not move back and forth efficiently. In addition, Arrow employees frequently ignored Sky appeals for help in speeding up departures.

Political indeterminism: Political indeterminism refers to the lack of a clear established pecking order. The people involved are not clear on who is in charge and who has more authority. Prior to the split in operations, each company had an established order. After the split in operations, it wasn't clear who had ultimate authority between and over the operations of the two companies.

Divergent goals: Different groups have separate (different) goals. While both airlines' goals were to "turn the flight," each wanted to turn its own flights first. The Sky crews wanted to get their flights in and out quickly so they could relax during the down time. Arrow crews wanted to appear professional and to follow set procedures and policies.

Time orientations: Groups can have different feelings toward time, some focusing on minutes, others on weeks or years. Sky employees were used to sending out several 30-passenger flights and turning them

128

in a very short time. On the other hand, Arrow employees were used to sending out fewer, larger flights and turning them in a significantly longer time frame.

Resource allocation: Two groups may conflict over how resources are distributed. Resources that groups compete for can include money and supplies. In this case, the two groups were competing for departure slots and people to load and unload planes. Whenever a crunch occurred, Sky would run out of rampers. In the prior structure, other employees would jump in to help. With its more rigid policies, this did not happen with the Arrow employees running the gates.

Rewards and evaluations: Different groups may be evaluated on different criteria. Conflict can occur if one group forces its criteria for evaluation onto another group. Jack and the Sky crew wanted to have fun on the job and work together to solve problems and get passengers on their way. The Arrow crews seemed more interested in following their procedures.

Status discrepancies: Group status within an organization is usually arranged in terms of a hierarchy of authority. However, groups can conflict over which values are considered important in arranging these hierarchies. For example, a group may decide that the knowledge base of its members should give the group a higher status then the seniority of the members of another group. It is possible that Arrow employees felt greater status because their airline was one of the largest in the world, while Sky airlines was an extremely small operation in comparison.

Jurisdictional disputes: Conflict can arise when two groups dispute regarding which of the groups is responsible for something. Disputes surfaced regarding responsibility, such as which airline would ensure that all late-checked bags were on the flight, and which airline would ensure the flight release was sent out to the aircraft.

Values, assumptions, and general perceptions: For example, one group may feel that a process that ensures quality is important, while another group may emphasize the importance of efficiency. Arrow managers did not value teamwork the same way the Sky managers did. They created the perception that the rampers were not doing their jobs, when in fact the rampers felt the same way about the gate staff. No one had ever brought them together to develop jointly agreed-upon procedures.

Question 2
What were the effects of conflict on the Sky and Arrow employees?
Analysis skills (breaking a concept into its parts and explaining their interrelationships, distinguishing relevant from extraneous material).

Answer
When two groups are in a state of conflict, it tends to increase within-group cohesiveness and between-group disputes. Strong polarities of we-they attitudes develop. This leads to a decrease in communication between the groups and a further increase in conflict. Additionally, perceptions of the other group tend to become more distorted and negative. Finally, intra-group conflict can result in heightened surveillance of the other group. (Wagner and Hollenbeck, 1998, p. 260)

In the situation with Sky and Arrow employees, these effects of conflict were present. As time moved on, conflict continued to escalate. Communications between the groups became less productive and more overtly hostile. Negative perceptions were formed of Arrow employees by Sky employees. Sky employees often referred to Arrow workers as "stupid" or "incompetent." Even conditions of increased surveillance of Arrow employees by Sky employees developed. Toward the end of joint operations, Sky employees made daily complaints to their manager regarding Arrow's performance failures.

Question 3
How are organizational cultures characterized and managed? Compare and contrast the cultures of Sky and Arrow.
Knowledge skills (remember previously learned material such as definitions, principles, formulas).
Application skills (using information in a new context to solve a problem, answer a question, or perform a task).

Answer

One way to characterize an organization's culture, is through an ethnographic approach. An organizational culture can be characterized in terms of its values and norms (Wagner and Hollenbeck, 1998, p. 337). The values and norms of an organization are visible and communicated through certain surface elements (Wagner and Hollenbeck, 1998, p. 338). One of these surface elements is ceremony. Ceremonies are important to an organization because they are occasions when the company recognizes its myths, heroes, and the symbols that communicate their culture (Wagner and Hollenbeck, 1998, p. 338). Various rites are often a part of the ceremonies held by organizations. Rites communicate messages and are set up to serve a specific purpose, such as initiating a new employee (Wagner and Hollenbeck, 1998, p. 338). Other surface elements of an organizational culture include the stories and myths that are told within the organization. These stories and myths represent certain ideals and norms of behavior for people within the organization (Wagner and Hollenbeck, 1998, p. 340). The heroes of that organization also represent the values of an organization's culture. The accomplishments of these people represent what is valued in the employees of the organization (Wagner and Hollenbeck, 1998, p. 340). Symbols are also used in an organization to communicate what is of importance in that culture. The location and the size of an executive's office might be a symbol that communicates something about the company, or symbols can take the form of a company logo (Wagner and Hollenbeck, 1998, p. 340). Finally, language can also represent an organization's culture. The use of certain terms for describing procedures and situations can be organization-specific and represent the culture of that organization (Wagner and Hollenbeck, 1998, p. 341).

Organizational culture can also be discerned from understanding the shared mindset of the employees. This shared mindset facilitates certain automatic thoughts that direct the behavior and thoughts of those in the organization (Ulrich, 1997, p. 170). According to Ulrich, automatic thoughts are imbedded in four processes, workflow, communication/information flow, decision making/authority flow, and human resource flow. Workflow processes refer to how work is distributed and performed within the organization. Communication/information refers to how information is shared and created within the organization. Processes that guide how decisions are made and where authority is located within the organization are referred to as decision-making/authority flow processes. Human resource flow encompasses how people are treated within the organization. The shared mindset of these four processes is communicated through information and behavior by both informal and formal structures (Ulrich, 1997, pp. 170–171).

Another way to look at organizational culture is a comparative method. One such way is by looking at the culture with a framework that sees culture as the result of competing values. These values are flexibility and order on one dimension and internal and external on the other dimension. These competing values result in four culture types in paired opposition. On one dimension is a human relations culture (characterized by cohesion, commitment, and participation) as opposed to a rational culture (characterized by productivity, profits, and goal setting). The other dimension opposes an open system culture against a bureaucratic culture (Ulrich, Losey, and Lake, 1997, p. 55). In this model for understanding organizational cultures, the cultures develop favoring one of the opposing values and a merger that brought opposite types together would likely fail.

The two companies, Sky Airlines and Arrow Airlines, differed in their organizational cultures. One way of examining the differences of the two cultures is by examining the different values and norms. Sky placed a high priority on customer service. Customer service was the one thing that Sky could offer its customers that would distinguish it from other airlines. Arrow, too, placed an importance on customer service, since the airline industry is very service-oriented. Efficiency and empowering employees to perform their jobs were also important values at Sky. This contrasts with Arrow, for its culture focuses more emphasis on following procedures. Another difference between the two companies was standards of employee conduct. Sky employees were expected to have fun at work and enjoy their jobs, whereas Arrow employees were expected to behave in a professional manor.

At Sky, values were communicated through different means. Sky's 25th anniversary party, a ceremony, represented some of these values and stories about the company. Also, at Jack's orientation, he

130

was exposed to values such as fun at work and the company's commitment to safety through stories. Both companies shared a language that was fairly consistent across companies and may represent the culture of those who work in the airline industry.

Cooper and Quinn's (1993) framework of competing values is also useful in looking at the cultures of the two companies. Sky's culture seems to have developed around a flexible ethos and resulted in an open-system culture. This is demonstrated by its de-emphasis on the importance of sticking to procedures in support of the value Sky placed on empowering employees. Comparatively, Arrow's culture was a more bureaucratic culture. It adhered to certain procedures, such as the use of belt loaders on every flight.

A final way to view the cultures of the two companies is in terms of how thought processes of an organization guide the thoughts and behaviors of employees. Every organization has standards for how work is assigned, communication of knowledge is shared, decision making is approached, and employees are viewed and treated. Both Arrow and Sky had separate systems for these processes. Flow existed within each company but ceased to exist between the two companies.

Question 4

Could cultural issues have caused the failure of the split operations system? Explain
Application skills (using information in a new context to solve a problem, answer a question, or perform a task).

Answer

Cultural issues between Arrow and Sky contributed significantly to the failure of the split operations plan. For one thing, the companies held different values but were expected to provide a uniform service. The professional conduct of the Arrow employees that a customer encountered at the ticket counter and the gate differed from the more relaxed attitude encountered amongst Sky employees on the ramp. Additionally, the lack of strict adherence to procedures by the Sky employees may have irritated the management at Arrow. These types of conflicting values may have made it difficult for the split operations to succeed.

According to Cooper and Quinn (1993), the culture of an organization can be categorized into competing value systems. A merger between two companies with competing values would likely fail, according to the model. In examining the cultures of the two companies, it is apparent that Arrow's bureaucratic culture opposes the open-system culture of Sky. As predicted by the model, merging these two systems together would, likely, have failed.

Another cultural problem that, perhaps, contributed to the failure of the merger involved the systems of flow, as outlined by (Ulrich 1997, pp. 170–172). Each company had its own processes to determine how work was distributed, decisions were made, communication of knowledge took place, and how employees were viewed and treated. The problem was that there was no shared system between the two companies. This may have produced a large amount of the conflict over jurisdictional issues, communication issues, and decision-making issues. Since no system was established to promote the flow of these processes between the two companies, they eventually failed at sharing a task.

Question 5

What situations cause stress? Are the components of a stressful situation present in Jack's situation?
Knowledge skills (remember previously learned material such as definitions, principles, formulas).
Application skills (using information in a new context to solve a problem, answer a question, or perform a task).

Answer

Certain environmental factors can cause negative stress in an individual (Taylor, Peplau, and Sears, 1997, p. 399). These situations have certain aspects that make them stressful. One such aspect is that an unpleasant or negative event can cause stress. This type of an event includes experiences such as the death of a spouse, the loss of a job, or the changing of schools. Another type of event that causes stress is an event that is perceived as uncontrollable or unpredictable. People experiencing stress attempt to cope with the stressful event. If an event is perceived as being out of an individual's control or unpredictable, the individual cannot adequately plan for that event. Consequently the individual's level of stress increases. Events that are ambiguous, also, contribute to a person's stress. For example, interpersonal interactions are often filled with ambiguous stimuli. If the interaction with an individual is important to someone, then a reaction by the other person that is hard to interpret will be stressful to the perceiver. Finally, an event that cannot be resolved by the person experiencing it will also produce stress.

Unpleasant events cause negative stress in those who experience them. The events of the case constituted an unpleasant event for Jack. He started out in a job that he greatly enjoyed. During the transition, his job contentment decreased. Finally, he lost his job.

Stress is also caused by events that are uncontrollable or unpredictable. Again, these conditions characterized the events that Jack experienced. The decisions made by Arrow and Sky were beyond Jack's control. Furthermore, the events could be characterized as unpredictable. After the split in operations occurred, there was a three-month time lapse, prior to layoff discussions. Even when rumors began to surface, it was difficult to discern how many layoffs would occur and who would be affected. These conditions made the ultimate outcome difficult to predict.

The rumors of layoffs were also a form of ambiguous information, another factor that can cause stress. This ambiguity was present in two forms. One, uncertainty of how many would get laid off. Two, Jack incorrectly assuming that Sky would increase the number of Delta flights to mirror those of previous light levels.

Finally, the transition of the split operations and the layoffs were events that Jack could not control nor resolve; however, he had to live with the effects of these events. Jack's inability to control or resolve these events contributed to the stress he experienced from the overall organizational change and shift in culture.

Question 6

Was Jack's reaction to Andrew at the end of the case a result of stress?
Comprehension skills (understanding the meaning of remembered material, usually demonstrated by restating or citing examples).

Answer

Stress has many negative consequences for an individual. Among these is workplace violence (Wagner and Hollenbeck, 1998, p. 112). Employees under extreme levels of stress have been known to react violently.

When Jack lashed out at Andrew, it was probably due to the stress he was under. The uncertainty of his future represents a situation that is likely to produce stress. Jack was, probably, at the end of his rope after finding out that he would lose his job. As a result, he reacted harshly toward Andrew.

References

Cooper, R. B. and Quinn, R.E. (1993). "Implications of the competing values framework for management information systems." *Human Resource Management*, cited in Ulrich, Losey, and Lake (1997).

Taylor, S. E., Peplau, L. A., Sears, D.O. (1997). *Social psychology*. New Jersey: Prentice Hall.

Ulrich, D. (1997). *Human resource champions: The next agenda for adding value and delivering results*. Boston, MA: Harvard Business School Press.

Ulrich, D., Losey, M.R., Lake, G. (1997). *Tomorrow's HR management*. New York: John Wiley and Sons.

Wagner, J.A. III, Hollenbeck, J.R. (1998). *Organizational behavior: securing competitive advantage*. New Jersey: Prentice Hall.

Epilogue

Jack ultimately lost his job at Sky Airlines. He is now in graduate school in human resources management. Arrow took over full ground operations while Sky employees remained in limited capacities, such as in-flight crew, pilot, co-pilot, and flight attendant. About one-third of Sky employees at the Santa Clara station kept their jobs running Sky flights for Delta Airlines. The remaining employees transferred, took jobs at Arrow, took jobs elsewhere, or were laid off.

Teaching Note[*]
TEMPORARY EMPLOYEES: CAR SHOW TURNED UGLY

Topics (* = Primary topic with teaching plan)
    *Decision case
    *Leadership (informal)
    *Cohesion,
    *Group and intergroup dynamics,
    *Conflict management
    *Training.
    Ethics,
    Power, coalition and basis of
    Constrained decision making
    Positional bargaining
    Negotiation
    Small business context

Case overview

This case is about a temporary employment firm that hired 18 individuals to work at various stations during a car show. The car show was to gather research from specific invitees to determine future sport car design features for a major automobile manufacturer.

The conditions under which the employees were hired became a contested issue between the employees and the temporary employment firm. The research firm sided with the employees. The employees were represented by a very vocal individual that knew many of the individuals employed because they were all members of the same church.

The temporary employment firm finally agreed to the employees' demand for the extra two-day payment. However, after having agreed orally in front of the group of temporary employees, TEA sent a follow-up, legal-sounding letter indicating that the extra two-day payment was a "gift" that they could later attempt to recover by legal means.

There are ethical issues on both sides—whether the firm did misrepresent itself to the employees and then try to hide it or whether the employees were trumping charges and appeared united because of their mutual church membership. There are also a number of behavioral issues that can be discussed embedded within the dynamics of the case: conflict management, cohesion, leadership, and group and inter-group dynamics.

Industry

TEA is a small company (staff of 25) in the temporary manpower employment industry, specializing in high technology manpower. Nonunion.

Teaching objectives
1.   To give the student an opportunity to see and analyze the behavioral forces of leadership, group, and inter-group dynamics that can create an no-win situation between employees and the firm.
2.   To show clearly how principles of organizational behavior can effect very predictable outcomes.
3.   To show how important perception can be in constructing the reality and strength of one's position.
4.   To demonstrate how important training can be in hiring interviews as to how expectations are set and a psychological contract developed between a potential hire and the firm.
5.   To provide an opportunity to discuss the ethics of behavior when there is no agreed-upon reality between accusing parties.

---

[*]Source: Adapted from case prepared by Gary Oddou, Utah State University. The case and teaching note were prepared as a basis for class discussion rather than to illustrate either effective or ineffective handling of administrative situations. Suggestions for improvement of this note should be sent to tompkins@uor.edu. Credit will be given in the next revision

Other related cases in Volume 1

A New Magazine in Nigeria (cohesion, ethics, power of coalitions); *Team Divided or a Team United?* (cohesion, intergroup dynamics); *Jenna's Kitchens, Inc.* (constrained decision making).

Other related cases in Volume 2

A Selfish Request in Japan (ethics, positional bargaining in negotiations, power of coalitions); *Cost and Schedule Team at AVIONICS* (cohesion, informal leadership); *Groupware Fiasco* (intergroup dynamics); *The Safety Memo* (ethics, positional bargaining in negotiations); *The Volunteer* (ethics).

Intended courses and levels

This case could be used in the following upper-division undergraduate and graduate courses: organizational behavior (group and system level), human resources management, management (leading and organizing functions), and ethics courses.

Analysis

The real substance to this case is the analysis of what led to the present situation Anita faces so that students can see management, HR, and OB principles at work. Many of the OB principles related to the case are addressed in the answers to the questions.

Management and HR issues to cover: The following topics can be broached in an HR discussion:

a. possible lack of training of TEA employees such that a mistake was made in presenting the contract information.

b. possible lack of honesty among TEA employees to admit that a mistake was or might have been made.

c. possible lack of communication between TEA management and interviewers with respect to the intent of the contract.

d. what to do when employees present a "union-like" front.

OB issues to cover: It appears as though a serious mistake was made by TEA in either being unaware of the alleged discrepancy in information presented to the interviewees and/or underestimating the power of unity and leadership of the temporary employees. In focusing on the temporary employees' informal power, the following OB topics should be covered in the discussion relative to the group and inter-group dynamics: group, leadership, motivation cohesion (already treated in responding to Question 2) and conflict management.

Conflict management: Given the apparent accusatory-denial approach by both the employees and TEA and the within group cohesiveness as explained above, this set the climate for a win-lose situation. The atmosphere was hostile and not conducive to exploring mutually benefiting solutions to try for a win-win situation if possible.

Each side perceived the other as the enemy rather than the problem as the enemy. This perception helped generate the subsequent correspondence from both sides and the accusations by TEA about the temporary employees' swearing and being uncooperative.

Conflict management styles. In short, the atmosphere for a collaborative or integrative problem solution did not exist because of both groups' "hard line" approach. Nor was a compromise approach likely given the perceptions by both sides. This left either an accommodation, avoidance, or win-lose approach. The problem could not be avoided, so that was not an option. In this situation, the accommodation approach could have surfaced in two ways: 1) either the temporary employees could have decided to accommodate TEA and dropped their demands, or 2) TEA could have accommodated the temporary employees. In either case, the result would have been the same as a win-lose approach, given the strong motivation to win by both sides.

Bringing in the church members' leader was not necessarily a good idea because he was not a neutral party. He obviously had previous experience with the church members and shared all the things that create cohesiveness with these members. If his previous experiences were positive with these members, that combined with the common goals, etc., his perception of the present situation with TEA was likely to be subconsciously biased toward his own "group" if any bias were to take place.

As previously mentioned, the representative from RC was not a neutral party who could serve as arbitrator either. He had interest most of all in seeing the show completed without interruption or other problems. This gave the temporary employees more power than TEA in the negotiations and served to create a clearer "we-they" atmosphere between the temporary employees and TEA.

In short, the role of neutral arbitrating party was nonexistent. Given the cohesiveness of each side, the clear difference in perceptions by both sides, the accusatory atmosphere, and the need to come immediately to a decision created an intense, negative atmosphere where one side (TEA) seemed to have little choice but to grant the temporary employees' wish for pay for the additional two days.

Research methodology

This case was written from interviews held with temporary employees and with TEA management. However, TEA management limited the interview information and did not wish to discuss the case at length. The case is a true incident, but the names and organization have been disguised.

Teaching plan

This case is designed to encourage discussion and analysis of:
1. organizational behavior (informal leadership, group and inter-group dynamics, conflict management, and ethics)
2. human resources management (employee training, particularly as it relates to job hiring and psychological contracts), and
3. ethics.

Two teaching approaches to this case are described below. The first (in part A) asks the students to put themselves in the decision "seat" and to justify the decision, given the behavioral issues in the case. The second requires the students to answer discussion questions that are designed to direct attention to essential issues in the case. The essential issues are presented in three 25-minute teaching plans.

Teaching plan topic: Leadership, Cohesion, Group Dynamics
60-minute teaching plan

Preassignment: Read cases A and B (15 minutes).

	Timing	Activity	Organization	Student Outcomes
I	0–3 minutes (3)	Summarize the case.	A student	To re-familiarize everyone with the case.
II	3–10 minutes (7)	Ask students to describe the problems in the case. (List them on the board.)	Full class	To illustrate the interrelation nature of the problems in the case.
III	10–30 minutes (20)	Divide students into groups of 3 to 4 to do this. Select the most immediate problem of resolving the conflict. Ask students: If they were Anita, what would they do?	Student groups of 3–4	To get them to move from effect to cause to application of OB concepts and theories.
IV	30–35 minutes (5)	List on the board the actions they would take.	Instructor	To make visible the proposed solutions for discussion.

	Timing	Activity	Organization	Student Outcomes
V	35–45 minutes (10)	Analyze the assumptions of each solution and the implications of each.	Full class	To uncover what students think are the root issues that created the problem.
VI	45–60 minutes (15)	*Ask students which solutions should be implemented and why.* Include in the discussion the importance of considering the leadership, motivation, and cohesion of the temporary employees.	Full class	To bring closure to the case and help students to understand that original solutions that involve people must consider individual, group, and inter-group dynamics.

25-minute teaching plan on conflict, cohesion, and leadership.
Pre assignment: Have students read case and analyze it for the following:
1. What problem(s) are presented in the case? (5 minutes)
2. What was the cause? (10 minutes)
3. What would the student do in Anita's place? (10 minutes)

25-minute teaching plan on role of leadership.
Preassignment: Read cases A and B before class (15 minutes).

	Timing	Activity	Organization	Student Outcomes
I	3 minutes	Summarize the case.	A student	Re-familiarize everyone with the case.
II	20 minutes	*Identify the leaders in the case and why they are leaders.*	Students	To get the students to analyze what constitutes leadership in informed contexts especially. At least 3 important leaders: 1) RC employee that sided with the temporaries; 2) president of the women's organization in the church who lent her support to Sue's position; 3) Sue, who became the voice of the group and who followed behind the scenes to organize support when TEA tried to disintegrate support for the temporary employees' position.
III	2 minutes	Conclude the case by summarizing info on leadership that relates to this case.	Instructor	To bring closure to the case and the variable that can create leadership.

25-minute teaching plan on employee training.
Preassignment: Read cases A and B before class (15 minutes).

	Timing	Activity	Organization	Student Outcomes
I	10 minutes	Ask students to relate the problems that developed.	Class as a whole	To prepare to link them to HR issues.
II	10 minutes	Ask students how this conflict might reflect poor employee training.	Class as a whole	To show the important relationship between HR practices and a smooth-

	Timing	Activity	Organization	Student Outcomes
				running organization.
III	5 minutes	Ask students what TEA could do in the future to avoid such problems.	Class as a whole	To conclude the case on a constructive, teaching note.

Discussion questions and answers: Case A

Question 1

What are the basic issues in this case for both sides?
Knowledge skills (remember previously learned material such as definitions, principles, formulas) and analysis skills (breaking a concept into its parts and explaining their interrelationships, distinguishing relevant from extraneous material).

Answer

Some of the basic issues in this case relate to the importance of professional presentation, clear communication between management and one's employees and between interviewers and interviewees, the psychological contract that develops between a firm and even temporary employees via the interviewer, the importance of understanding the sources of group unity, the belief that one's perception is reality, the importance of trust between identifiable groups (i.e., employees and management), the effects that a "hard-line" approach has on the ability to resolve a problem for a win-win outcome, and that "winning" against someone's will has automatic negative consequences as well.

Question 2

What can we learn about the factors that strengthen a group's position or power?
Comprehension skills (understanding the meaning of remembered material, usually demonstrated by restating or citing examples) and analysis skills (breaking a concept into its parts and explaining their interrelationships, distinguishing relevant from extraneous material).

Answer

This question can best be answered by looking at three issues: the cohesion, motivation, and leadership of the temporary employees.

Cohesion. The temporary employees were extremely cohesive. Principles that relate to greater group cohesion include frequency of contact, common goals, perceived similarity among members, having a strong leader and a perceived enemy, etc. Most of these apply to all employees who were protesting TEA's alleged change in policy; however, they especially apply to the temporary employees who were church members. They all took this job to earn some extra spending money—mostly for Christmas (common goal). Those sharing the same religious beliefs also shared a nonmonetary goal, spiritual development and salvation (common super-goal).

Most of the temporary employees knew each other from years of association (frequency of contact) and liked each other (perceived similarity and friendship) as reflected in the fact that they formed the network that was used to interest one another in the job, they had an outspoken leader who was willing to represent their perceived rights and feelings (clear and strong leadership), and certainly they perceived TEA as their enemy.

The temporary employees' position was clearly strengthened by the amount of cohesion they had, the apparent solidarity around perceiving an enemy (TEA and their alleged misrepresentation) and secondarily around the desire to earn money, and the strong informal leadership by Sue.

In addition, there were inter-group dynamics occurring that strengthened each side's position:
1) Competing goals developed. TEA wanted employees to work so the show went smoothly; temporary employees wanted to get paid for the entire time they felt they were forced to commit to;
2) Miscommunication apparently occurred regarding the issue of whether the interviewers committed the recruits to five days and implied or explicitly promised them five days of pay; and

138

3) Perceived value differences and stereotypes (deception vs. honesty—viewed as being infringed on from both sides).

The group's apparent solidarity around perceiving an enemy (TEA and their alleged misrepresentation) and secondary desire to earn money relate to issues of motivation:

Motivation. The primary theory operating here was probably equity theory. Although the initial common interest in taking the position seemed to be the monetary benefit, it appears as though the issue of "justice" became the guiding principle for complaint. "Fairness" has always been a strong motivation for taking a stand and sticking by it. In this case, that was obviously the situation. The temporary employees felt they had a promise and obligation by TEA that TEA was not going to honor. Even worse, they felt that TEA was strategically operating to not honor their obligation as perceived by the temporary help.

Given that the temporary employees were interested in working almost exclusively to earn some extra money, particularly for Christmas, their motivation was high and fairly singular in that regard as well. Losing two days' pay out of five meant losing a significant portion of why they had hired on with TEA.

There was an equity issue relating their time invested to interview, to go down a second day to sign the contract, and then to invest several hours for the orientation relative to the pay expectation. There was also the psychological expectation of counting on a certain amount of money that might have already been spent—actually or in planning. Also, if they felt TEA had required them to be available for the whole time, then an equitable return gesture would be to pay for the entire time.

Finally, some mothers had arranged for day care, and one woman flew from Portland with the expectation that her airfare would be covered by the five-day payment. These commitments, based on an understanding of a five-day payment, would certainly motivate the temporary employees to demand a five-day payment even if they were going to work only two days plus the orientation. The strong leadership the temporary employees experienced also merits analysis:

Leadership. Whether TEA had a clear strategy to discourage the temporary employees from following through with their objective to receive the additional pay is unclear; however, the letter (Appendix F) was interpreted by some of the temporary employees as having the intent to create a division within the temporary employees and the perception as though the cohesion in the general meeting was not reality.

The informal leader, the most vocal member of the temporary employees, saw this as a power play and took it upon herself to counter this perceived strategy (real or not). After the initial correspondence from TEA, stating that the money was a "gift" and could be recoverable by legal means, she contacted all of the employees to reaffirm their conviction and to explain what she felt TEA was trying to do. Her role was absolutely critical in maintaining the conviction among the temporary employees. Were it not for her leadership in the meeting and in this situation, a number of the temporary employees (including those in the same church) said they would probably not have continued their efforts to claim the money.

On the other hand, TEA had no leader with any real power as perceived by the temporary employees. Their perception was that TEA was not well run and somewhat unorganized. The TEA supervisor in the general meeting lost credibility when the RC representative sided with the employees.

Question 3

What would you do if you were Anita?

Synthesis skills (putting parts together to form a new whole; solving a problem requiring creativity or originality).

Answer

This is a question that begets a subjective view. As mentioned later on, TEA could a) give in to the demands, b) refuse to give in, or c) propose a compromise.

1) Agree. Agreeing with the temporary employees' demands would primarily cost money. Secondarily (or primarily, depending on the person), it would cost TEA some pride. Admitting to wrongdoing would require humility; paying the two days while still maintaining innocence would also require some humility in order to ensure the main goal (a good show) is accomplished.

2) <u>Refusal</u>. Disagreeing with the temporary employees' demands would mean a) either the temporary employees would walk, requiring TEA to try to hire and orient new employees in one day, or b) the temporary employees would remain in spite of their "threat" but might perform less well from sensing they were taken advantage of.

3) <u>A compromise decision.</u> A compromise might be to propose paying for one day instead of two. This would still show some good faith yet maintain a certain amount of "air of honor or integrity" in TEA.

If, in my own investigation as a TEA supervisor or manager, I felt that the employees had been misled or that there was sufficient doubt whether the employment interviews had been conducted properly, then I would feel obligated to pay them the entire schedule. In addition, this would help preserve the reputation of the firm to a certain extent.

If, however, I determined that TEA was not at fault, then I would probably assume there was no malicious intent but a misunderstanding and propose a compromise.

Finally, if the temporary employees refused a compromise, then I would go ahead and pay them the full amount but let them know I did not think this was a fair demand. Without saying so, I would never knowingly hire from this particular church group again.

In the final analysis, though, unless a compromise situation is struck, TEA has little choice but to meet the temporary employees' demands. One day is not realistically adequate to find, interview, and orient some 20 new employees.

Depending on which of the above scenarios took place, I might either reprimand some TEA employees for sloppy work (their omission) and/or make sure they were properly trained if that was deemed lacking (TEA's omission).

Discussion questions and answers Case B

Question 1

Who was probably at fault in this case?
<u>Analysis skills</u> (breaking a concept into its parts and explaining their interrelationships, distinguishing relevant from extraneous material).

Answer

It is impossible to know who was at fault. The reader is essentially required to take sides in order to attribute fault. It is unlikely that all of the individuals hired colluded and developed a strategy to get more money from TEA. This is particularly true if the individuals actually were practicing their religion, which presumably incorporates honesty and integrity in its doctrine. Further, more than just the members of the same church challenged TEA's statements.

In addition, if TEA had done the show for the past two years, it should have known exactly what the schedule would be for each employee and should not have needed to hedge itself by committing the employees to the entire show if all the employees were not needed for that time.

There should have been no ambiguity about the temporary employees' schedules.

On the other hand, it is possible that the temporary employees misunderstood the interviewer's statements about the schedule. If so, it is understandable why TEA would stand united and disagree with the extra payment.

Question 2

Do you feel RC's intervention was appropriate? Why or why not?
<u>Evaluation skills</u> (using a set of criteria to arrive at a reasoned judgment of the value of something).

Answer

RC's intervention had or could have had several effects. First, it should have reinforced the employees' position and given them encouragement and more solidarity. Second, it could have created a rift between RC and TEA, which is not very productive if they are to have a continuing relationship. It acts as a divisive effect.

Was it appropriate? Perhaps yes, given the immediate need to see the show go on in order to complete the research. This is a self-interested motive. Again, if the relationship between RC and TEA is critical, then the intervention was probably inappropriate.

Clearly, RC could have discussed its position in private with TEA to allow TEA to strategize and "save face" before the employees. This would have accomplished its goal of having the show continue as expected and given TEA more control in determining, or at least delivering, the expected outcome (i.e., granting the employees their wish) without the protracted "negotiations."

Question 3
What are the contextual factors that contributed to a win-lose result?
<u>Comprehension skills</u> (understanding the meaning of remembered material, usually demonstrated by restating or citing examples) and <u>analysis skills</u> (breaking a concept into its parts and explaining their interrelationships, distinguishing relevant from extraneous material).

Answer
In addition to the points already elaborated in the previous OB theory section, the main discussion points would include these primary contextual factors:
- potential lack of ethical standards within TEA
- potential sloppiness in administering the interviews
- strong cohesion within both groups, but especially within the temporary employees.
- strong leadership within the temporary employees
- clear motivation to restore "fairness" and secondarily earn anticipated income.
- lack of TEA's ability to manage conflict

Epilogue
Clearly, TEA "lost" in some respects. It is doubtful any of these disgruntled temporary employees would ever work for TEA again. TEA also had to pay more money than it had apparently intended. Shelley, the initial TEA contact with the religious organization, suffered a slightly damaged reputation because of the apparent misunderstanding. However, the employees also "lost," particularly those employees who were church members. TEA changed its policy of hiring such that it precluded hiring any "large" numbers of individuals from one source. In addition, the reputation of this church was tarnished by their perceived inappropriate behavior. Finally, the whole incident caused a great deal of stress in Sue McIntyre's life and family. For weeks, she became somewhat depressed (although she was prone to depression anyway), and it began to have a negative effect within her family.

Teaching Note[*]
THE DAY THEY ANNOUNCED THE BUYOUT

Topics (* = Primary topic is teaching plan)
*Communication
*Organizational change
*Perception
Buyouts and mergers
Productivity
Maslow's hierarchy of needs
Restructuring
Banking context

Case overview
This case chronicles the day in the life of a young bank employee who found out at the beginning of her day that her bank may be bought out. It describes in rich detail the emotional impact on Diane Fox and her considerations for her future. Diane Fox began working for Rolling Hills Bank as a temporary worker. Her father, the bank's controller, helped her get the job. Diane worked her way up in the bank and at the time of the case was an administrator in the Human Resources department.

Rolling Hills Bank was a small 15-branch bank primarily owned and controlled by the original board of directors. Board members socialized together and had begun talking among themselves that they would like to sell the bank and have more free time. When Cal State Bank made a generous offer, board members felt it was worth serious consideration. Cal State Bank would keep the branch personnel and service center personnel, but it was likely that administrative personnel would be laid off.

The news of the possible buyout was broken in the morning newspaper. Later that morning, the president met with the employees and apologized that they had to find out about the possible buyout in such an impersonal way. Many of the employees, who always felt they could trust the president, suddenly didn't feel so trusting of him now. Diane felt that the board of director's greed, as well as the president, might cause 60 people to lose their jobs. Diane goes to see her father and finds that he was calm and suggested that she not worry about things, as change was a long way off.

When she returned to her department, her supervisor, the vice president of human resources, called a department meeting. To improve morale they decided to continue to conduct business as usual. They also agreed that, if an employee came to them, they would tell the employee not to worry. Diane agreed to tell employees not to worry, but in her case, she realized that it would be a lie.

Industry
Small regional bank with 250 employees.

Teaching objectives
1. To evaluate the effect of organizational change on employees' productivity, perceptions, and needs during the initial hours of finding out about the change.
2. To diagnose and understand that people's perceptions cause them to react differently to the same news.
3. To evaluate the communications process.
4. To design a communications plan for use after a buyout or merger decision.

---

[*]Source: Adapted from case prepared by Diane Trachsel and Teri C. Tompkins, University of Redlands. The case and teaching note were prepared as a basis for classroom discussion rather than to illustrate either effective or ineffective handling of an administrative situation. Suggestions for improvement of this note should be sent to tompkins@uor.edu. Credit will be given in the next revision.

Other related cases in Volume 1

A New Magazine in Nigeria (communications, restructuring); *A Team Divided or a Team United?* (communications); *Fired!* (communications); *Handling Differences at Japan Auto* (Maslow's hierarchy of needs); *Heart Attack* (communications); *Julie's Call: Empowerment at Taco Bell* (restructuring); *Questions Matter* (Maslow's hierarchy of needs); *Shaking the Bird Cage* (restructuring).

Other related cases in Volume 2

A Selfish Request in Japan (Maslow's hierarchy of needs); *Angry Branch Manager* (Maslow's hierarchy of needs, perception); *Cafe Latte* (perception); *Computer Services Team at AVIONICS* (restructuring); *Leadership of TQM in Panama* (restructuring); *Negotiating Work Hours* (perception); *Reputation in Jeopardy* (buyouts and mergers); *Unprofessional Conduct* (perception); *When Worlds Collide* (restructuring).

Intended courses and levels

The objectives of this case are appropriate for graduate and executive students in organizational behavior and management. Undergraduates will need a little more guidance in the questions, perhaps by specifying the theories that might be used to evaluate the organizational change or providing a framework to design the communication plan.

Analysis

All related analysis and references are embedded in the answers to the questions.

Research methodology

This case is based on the recollections of Diane Fox and an interview with her father. It is a true incident. Rolling Hills Bank and the names of the employees are disguised. Cal State Bank is not disguised.

Teaching plan

Teaching plan topic: Organizational Change, Perception, and Communication
60-minute teaching plan

Preassignment: Read case (15 minutes)

	Timing	Activity	Organization	Student Outcomes
I	0–5 minutes (5)	Summarize the case facts.	Ask for or appoint a "volunteer."	Orientation and refresher on case.
II	5–10 minutes (5)	*What were employees' reactions when they heard about the announcement?*	Full class discussion	Clarify facts from the case. Use the reactions as a basis for discussion for Part III.
III	10–15 minutes (5)	*Why did people react the way they did?*	Full class discussion	Fear of the unknown creates anxiety. Stages of grief (shock). The answer to Q1 can explain some of the reasons.
IV	15–20 minutes (5)	*Q4: Why did some people appear worried, but others, like Diane's dad, appeared calm?*	Full class discussion	See answer to Question 4. We react differently based on our needs, values and beliefs. Our internal perceptions influence us. Some prefer to wait and see; some try to prepare themselves in case the buyout occurred.

	Timing	Activity	Organization	Student Outcomes
V	20–25 minutes (5)	*Q3: Why did some employees stop trusting the president? Use communication theory to analyze this phenomenon.*	Full class discussion	See answer to Question 3. The information, received from another source, was brief. People filled in the blanks. The president was not very believable because his verbal and nonverbal cues did not match.
VI	25–40 minutes (15)	*Q5: Outline how you would improve the communication of the merger announcement. What are the positive and negative aspects of your plan?* *Q6: Design a communication plan that the HR department can use the day the possible buyout decision was announced.*	Divide the class in small groups to speed up discussion and to allow students to get a more hands on feel for the difficulty of the design.	• See answer to Question 5 and 6 • President needs to communicate to large group of people at once to reduce rumor. • Methods to reduce employees' anxiety should be considered. • Basically let them know that you will be communicating any news as soon as it is developed. • Communicate often. • Plans for transitions are critical in times of major change. There is much work to be done in the next few months if this buyout really occurs.
VII	40–50 minutes (10)	Report back on Part VI.	Select a spokesperson to report back to entire class during the last five minutes.	Use the board to write the ideas. If you can, draw connecting lines from the needs of the employees to how it is addressed in the communication plan.
VIII	50–55 minutes (5)	*What have we learned about people's reactions during the early stages of change? What have we learned about communication during these times?*	Full class discussion	Students' answers will vary.
IX	55–60 minutes (5)	Hand out or read the epilogue found in this teaching note. Ask for reactions.	Individual or full class reading, followed by full class discussion.	Student reactions will vary. Point out or ask for places where there was agreement and disagreement between student suggestions and response.

25-minute teaching plan on communication.
Preassignment: Read case before class (15 minutes). Assign questions 1, 3, and 4 as homework before class.
Activities. Do activities VI and VII in the 60-minute plan.

25-minute teaching plan on perception.
Preassignment: Read case before class (15 minutes).
Activities. Do activities I, II, III, IV, and IX in the 60-minute plan.

Discussion questions and answers

Question 1

How does Maslow's hierarchy of needs help explain the drop in productivity on the day of the announcement?

Application skills (using information in a new context to solve a problem, answer a question, or perform a task).

Answer

On the day the impending buyout was announced, employees were very unproductive and scared about the upcoming situation. They were not motivated to work, because their basic needs were now at risk. As Maslow's hierarchy of needs describes, "Individuals are motivated by the urge to fulfill five fundamental needs" (Wagner and Hollenbeck, 1995, p. 173). The first and second fundamental needs are physiological and safety needs. When an individual's future financial security is uncertain because his or her current position is in jeopardy, both physiological and safety needs are threatened. Physiological needs are threatened because, without a job and income, food is usually unattainable. Also, without having a regular financial income, one's shelter is also threatened. Payments for a home or apartment are difficult to make without a job. This basic fear was interrupting the productivity of the employees. It is hard to worry about a project or be friendly to customers when you are unsure of future financial security.

Question 2

Do you agree with Diane Fox that the board of directors and president were greedy? Why would the board and president sell the bank?

Diagnostic question (probes motives or causes).

Answer

Viewed from Diane's perspective, it is easy to see how she might perceive selfish motives by the owners of Rolling Hills Bank. Her perception of the situation was based on "phenomenal absolutism" (Wagner and Hollenbeck, 1995, p. 136), which means, she thought that she knew why this decision was made and she knew she was right. She thought the board of directors and the president decided to sell the bank because they were greedy and they wanted money. They were primary, or majority, stockholders in the company. If Cal State Bank bought out their shares, at the price being discussed, any majority stockholder would make lots of money. In the attention stage (Wagner and Hollenbeck, 1995, p. 141) of perception, "individuals decide what will be processed and what will be ignored." Diane chose to ignore any facts or information that showed her that another reason for selling the bank was possible.

One of an organization's primary functions is to make money for its stockholders. Diane found it shocking and unexpected to be purchased by another bank because she assumed that being purchased was a sign of organizational weakness. But, according to organization development theory, being purchased or sold helps organic organizations to grow and become bigger and stronger (Morgan, 1986, p. 66). To accomplish this, other organizations must not grow or, sometimes, must die out. It is similar to the "survival of the fittest" theory proposed by Darwin, which states that the "fittest" or most successful organism will survive in today's environment. The president and board of directors made the decision to sell their organization because it was a normal process of growth for smaller banks to merge. Business analysts predict that all independent banks will one day be extinct. The president and board of directors did not make the decision to sell because they were selfish and greedy. They made the decision because they realized that any further growth would be a great effort. They were tired of spending all their free time directing the needs of the bank. They hoped that, by selling the bank, they could have more energy to devote to other goals.

Question 3

Why did some employees stop trusting the president? Use communication theory to analyze this phenomenon.

Diagnostic question (probes motives or causes) and application skills (using information in a new context to solve a problem, answer a question, or perform a task).

Answer

Communicating a decision to the individuals that are affected by it is a major responsibility. Communicating effectively and in a timely matter influences the reactions and support you will receive from the recipients. In the Rolling Hills case, the president failed to communicate the decision to consider a purchase offer from another bank. From that point on, his credibility was ruined. The information was still received, but from another source. Because the communication came from the media first, the information was not "decoded" (Wagner and Hollenbeck, 1995. p. 292) and the message was distorted. The distortion was caused by a term known as "noise." When an individual is not communicated to directly, or effectively, they fill in the gaps with their own perceptions.

As discussed earlier, individual perceptions are based on many factors, but in this case they were influenced by fear. Employees' beliefs and values and frame of reference interfered with the message that was communicated. The message was written (in the newspaper), and the information given was brief. This lack of information gave employees' many questions and fears. By the time the president began discussions on the decision, he had some unexpected reactions and ideas about the situation. Most of his time was spent reassuring individuals that this was not supposed to be a secret. He apologized and said he had planned to tell everyone himself. He perceived himself as someone who could alleviate their fears. Unfortunately, he lost credibility by not communicating with his employees openly, as he had done in the past.

The presentation, or nonverbal behavior, exhibited with the president's message was not consistent with the information he was giving. He was trying to be reassuring to the employees but he came across as nervous and uncomfortable. He said nothing was definite, but he also said he couldn't guarantee anyone his or her position in the new organization. He appeared sad, as if the deal was already done. He mentioned that he would not be part of the deal, which meant he would not receive a new position in the new organization. Because his message was full of mixed signals, he did not reassure the staff and the day was full of questions, discussions and unproductive behavior.

Question 4

Why did some people appear worried, but others, like Diane's dad, appeared calm?
Diagnostic question (probes motives or causes).

Answer

Different people react to situations based on their needs, values, and beliefs. Diane felt no sense of control over her financial future and job status. This perception was influenced by other individuals' fears. She had no idea whether she was going to lose her job but other people feared that they would, so she started to worry also. She didn't expect to leave the organization until she was ready to. That decision and control were taken away from her. The feeling of uncertainty affected her motivation and performance as it obviously did others.

But the same behavioral theories that explain why some employees behaved or reacted the way they did do not explain why some did not. These internal factors vary by individual experience and knowledge. For instance, Diane's father's reaction was a nonreaction. When she went to talk to him he was working like he would have on any other day. When she asked him what he thought, and he said it is too soon to worry, it was obvious that he felt differently than she did. But why? The uncertainty that she felt could be attributed to the fact that she had never been through an acquisition or merger before. Also, others could be fearful of losing their jobs because they didn't have enough information or they did not trust the information they were receiving. Diane's dad had been through a few mergers so he realized that it was very early in the process, way too early to start worrying. Another reason he may have been so calm was because he was an executive, so he might have had more information than the line personnel might have. Either way, his individual perceptions of the situation influenced his behavior. But, his perceptions of life and threatening situations were different than some of the other employees and Diane. Predicting how employees will react is difficult for this reason.

Question 5

Outline how you would improve the communication of the merger announcement. What are the positive and negative aspects of your plan?

<u>Analysis skills</u> (breaking a concept into its parts and explaining their interrelationships, distinguishing relevant from extraneous material) and <u>evaluation skills</u> (using a set of criteria to arrive at a reasoned judgment of the value of something).

Answer

With any major change in an organization, communication is one key to success. In this merger situation, it would have helped if the president had communicated the offer and possibilities to the employees before they heard it from someone else. It is very important that he try to communicate the purchase offer to as many people as possible, as quickly as possible. Meeting with a large group of employees is the quickest way to reach them and it offers the employees the opportunity to ask questions immediately. There is little one can do to reduce the shock of a decision like this except to let rumors fly for a year or so that the bank was considering selling. (That can be very impractical).

A positive result of open communication with the president is that employees are less likely to fill the gaps with inaccurate information (as they did with the brief newspaper article). Communication from the president might be received as more factual because it came from the top of the organization. Employees might feel that he cares about them. In addition, they would be able to ask him questions directly rather than communicating through layers of management.

Another way to communicate this type of announcement would be to tell all managers and have them tell their employees. This might allow managers to have a chance to digest the decision before they communicate it to their subordinates. When the subordinates hear the information, the managers may be better able to answer questions due to the smaller group size. A positive consideration for this approach is that employees might feel more comfortable asking questions of their manager than of the president. Most employees feel a hierarchical division between themselves and executives. Asking the president a direct question in front of the whole organization could be stressful. This stress would be avoided.

A con of having the managers tell their employees is some managers will tell their subordinates before others or the information may be distorted. When an announcement of a merger is made, the news will travel fast. Employees from one department might tell employees of another department. This could cause the same reaction that occurred in the actual case. Any kind of announcement of a merger brings risk to the company. Some cons of announcing a merger to employees are that employees might leave the bank as soon as they hear of a pending merger, they might be angry and be unmotivated to work, or they may no longer trust the executives. They may feel that they are no longer working to make the company profitable, but instead, to make the company purchasable.

The president and managers will want to support the company and keep it viable. Many of the employees will continue to work after the merger. Communication should focus on facts. There is not much that one can do to change people's reactions but there are things to help moderate their reactions. First, employees will need solid information to allay their fears and help them know what to expect and how to move forward. People will feel hostile and angry, worried about their jobs, and very likely questioning the buyout itself. We see this reaction with Diane.

It is likely that marketable employees will polish their resumes and may leave as jobs come available. Human Resources and the president must anticipate this and place continual effort to maintain morale.

Question 6

Design a communication plan that the human resources department can use the day the possible buyout decision was announced.

<u>Synthesis skills</u> (putting parts together to form a new whole; solving a problem requiring creativity or originality).

Answer

The human resources department could make themselves available for employees, letting them know that they are free to ask them any questions. This could help them control rumors and calm nerves. Also, human resources, or outside counselors, should be available for one-on-one counseling, or discussions, to alleviate personal fears and problems. Individuals should be allowed to vent as much as necessary. Some individuals need more time than others, depending on their personal situation and coping style.

But human resources can do only so much, and hearing constant fears and complaints could affect the department in a demoralizing way. For instance, human resources personnel might have a problem with their morale because of all the fears and problems they hear from employees. This low morale could also spread if the human resources department was not aware of it. Because of this, the human resources department also needs a source to vent to, whether with a professional counselor or friend.

An action that should be taken to increase motivation might be to continue with work as normal. This would be difficult for a few days after the announcement but a buyout is usually a six-month process. In that six months, the organization could lose a lot of money if motivation decreases. The human resources department can play a major role in the success of this action. One way human resources could increase motivation is to continue with their reward programs. Employees of the month and quarter should continue to be given rewards. Reviews should still be completed. Open positions should still be recruited and filled. This will contribute to the employees' perception that nothing is definite yet.

References

Wagner, J., and Hollenbeck, J. (1995). *Management of organizational behavior*. Upper Saddle River, New Jersey: Prentice Hall.

Morgan, G. (1986). *Images of organizations*. Newbury Park, CA: Sage.

Epilogue

Cal State Bank made the offer to Rolling Hills in June of 1995. Diane started her first real job search in July while she was still working at Rolling Hills Bank. Without too many hassles, her supervisor gave her time off to interview. She found another job, closer to home, with more pay in October of 1995. Rolling Hills Bank officially closed its doors on April 15, 1996. It reopened its doors the following Monday as California State Bank. All of the branch employees were retained. The service center and data processing departments were also retained. Those employees who were not retained received severance packages.

Diane's supervisor, the human resources representative, the lending executives, the financial executives, and the president did not receive positions in the new bank. Diane's father was retained on a temporary basis to help with the conversion of the bank's accounts. He finally left Cal State Bank in August to start a new, regular position with another independent bank. The president of Rolling Hills Bank went to another independent bank.

A year later, the bank which the president had gone to was bought. Cal State Bank was still in existence and growing in 2000. Diane still conducts her banking business there and deals with individuals that she used to work with. Now they are waiting to see who will buy Cal State Bank.

UNMOVABLE TEAM

Topics (* = Primary topics with teaching plan)
*Decision case
*Reward systems
*Resistance to change
*Social system conceptual scheme (adapted from Homans)
*New product development
Innovation
Control, managerial
Organizational structure
Career paths or choice.
Motivation
Group think
Large corporation context

Case overview

This case details the frustration that Paul Riley, manager of the 65-member Analog team, faces as he tries to get members of the management team to see beyond their immediate objective of generating business for the good of their team, to one of helping the entire organization improve profitability. After successfully steering another team into profitable waters, Riley asked for the challenge of working with this team. Members of the Analog management team have worked for AVIONICS for many years and have become very comfortable in their salaries and their positions in the company. Riley has been charged with helping the team take more products to commercial markets, because defense contracts have been drying up. At the end of the case, when he presents a challenge or opportunity to the team, they respond in typical myopic fashion.

Industry

Defense Industry. The team is responsible for developing electronic sensing devices. The primary output from company work is research and development. Little manufacturing occurs at the company.

Teaching objectives
1. To identify the systemic relationships among input factors, such as leadership, rewards, and culture to outcomes factors, such as satisfaction/development/productivity.
2. To devise a plan to overcome resistance and lack of know-how in the group's objective to commercialize some of its defense industry products.
3. To examine the role of rewards in motivation.

Other related cases in Volume 1

A New Magazine in Nigeria (control, restructuring); *A Team Divided or a Team United?* (control); *Costume Bank* (career choice); *Fired!* (rewards); *Julie's Call: Empowerment at Taco Bell* (restructuring); *Questions Matter* (control); *Shaking the Bird Cage* (restructuring); *The Day They Announced the Buyout* (restructuring).

Other related cases in Volume 2

Computer Services Team at AVIONICS (restructuring); *Leadership of TQM in Panama* (innovation, restructuring); *The Volunteer* (career choice); *When Worlds Collide* (rewards, restructuring).

*Source: Adapted from case prepared by Teri C. Tompkins, University of Redlands. The case and teaching note were prepared as a basis for classroom discussion rather than to illustrate either effective or ineffective handling of an administrative situation. Suggestions for improvement of this note should be sent to tompkins@uor.edu. Credit will be given in the next revision.

Intended courses and levels

This case is appropriate for organizational behavior (system level) or management (organizing or controlling function). The case has been classroom tested in a corporation with early to mid-career managers, with good success. It is also useful for undergraduate juniors and seniors or for graduate students.

Analysis

Analysis is imbedded in the discussion questions and answers section.

Research methodology

Data for this case were gathered during a research investigation called "How Collective Learning Occurs." All members were interviewed individually. The team was also interviewed as a group without Dan or John for the purpose of constructing an event history. The company and people are disguised.

Teaching plan

This case provides rich data for examining system-wide issues. It makes a good decision case, and students will enjoy the variety of potential solutions to Riley's dilemmas. To use it as a decision case, the following format is useful (Erskine, Leenders, Mauffette-Leenders, 1998, p. 128). Allow at least 60 minutes.

Preassignment: Read and analyze the case either individually or in groups.

   a) define the issues
   b) analyze the case data with focus on causes and effects as well as constraints and opportunities
   c) generate alternatives
   d) select decision criteria
   e) analyze and evaluate alternatives
   f) select the preferred alternative
   g) develop an action and implementation plan.

The case can also be taught using the social system conceptual scheme (Cohen, Fink, Gadon, and Willets, 1992, adapted from Homans, 1950, 1961). The table following Question 1 and the figure at the end of this teaching note illustrate the social system conceptual scheme. I've found the model useful for analyzing many organizational behavior cases. You may want to teach it as a tool early in your organizational behavior course; then you can use the tool to analyze other OB cases in these volumes. The *Banana Time Case* (Roy, 1997; Cohen, et al., 1995) is a great case for early in the term because it appears so chaotic, but when examined using the social system conceptual scheme, the dynamics of the system become very clear.

Teaching plan topic: Systems Thinking, Group Development, Leadership, and Cohesion.
60-minute teaching plan

Preassignment: Read case (15 minutes). Read about group development.

	Timing	Activity	Organization	Student Outcomes
I	0–5 minutes (5)	Overview of case	Student volunteers	To remind students about the case.
II	5–25 minutes (20)	Explain the Homans' model, then ask: *Q1: Given the case facts, how would you explain the behavior of the Analog management team members using the Homans' social system conceptual scheme*	Mini-lecture followed by discussion in small groups or entire class	See answer to Q1: The system: the general manager's directive caused a shift in Riley's leadership style and a change in the required system (required action: to become market-oriented, rather than product-oriented). The emergent behavior was to look for ways to market internally to other groups and projects. The result is low productivity, low learning, and adequate satisfaction (Sr.

	Timing	Activity	Organization	Student Outcomes
		(Pedagogy in next section)?		Engineers), low satisfaction (Riley).
III	25–35 minutes (10)	*Q2: Analyze the Analog management team members, in light of the theory on reward systems.*	Small groups or entire class discussion	• First, in the past they were rewarded for technological solutions. • Later, rewarded for staying within budget and on time. • Now, they need to be rewarded for bringing in resources.
IV	35–50 minutes (15)	*Q3: What should Paul Riley do to get his Analog management team to meet the challenge of reaching the commercial market?*	Small groups or entire class discussion	• Evaluate whether the Analog Group has the necessary competencies to accomplish the objective. • Provide more guidance and mentoring; perhaps new product development retreat and mentoring of a few junior engineer champions. • Finally, students might question the directive to take products to commercial markets. What is upper management's expectation? What is the feasibility? Where are the resources for training and staffing to help make the venture possible?
V	50–60 minutes (10)	Summarize how related to chapter	Instructor point out key points, or lead class in discussion.	Key points At a minimum, recognize: • the personal systems of long-time employees, comfortable with their salaries, cause the managers of the Analog management team to be complacent. • previously rewarded for technical delivery, now rewarded for financial delivery. • the managers of the Analog management team may lack the knowledge and skills necessary to take their products to commercial markets. Advance concepts: • Paul may need to empower some of the newer engineers on the 65-member team to form new product development groups, and make sure that these teams are supported, perhaps supervising them himself.

25-minute teaching plan on group development.
Preassignment: Read case before class (15 minutes)
Activities. Do activities V and VI in the 60-minute plan.

Discussion questions and answers

Question 1

Given the case facts, how would you explain the behavior of the Analog management team members using the Homans' social system conceptual scheme (Pedagogy in next section)?

Application skills (using information in a new context to solve a problem, answer a question, or perform a task).

Answer

One way to consider organizing student answers to this case is to use the framework from the social system conceptual model. (Homans adapted by Cohen, et al., 1995). The model is especially useful for group and system level analysis.

HOMANS' SOCIAL SYSTEM CONCEPTUAL SCHEME	
The System: Background factors, leadership, and required systems <u>influence</u> *the emergent systems, and emergent systems* <u>influence</u> *consequences. Consequences* <u>feed back</u> *to background factors, leadership, and required systems, which* <u>alters</u> *them. See figure at end of this teaching note.*	
Factors	**Characteristics**
Background Factors (Facts or data that help us understand a person or group)	<ul><li>personal systems (what personality types, what motivations?)</li><li>layout and technology (use of space or technology that influences group)</li><li>external status (status outside of the organization?)</li><li>reward systems</li><li>culture of organization</li></ul>
Leadership (who are the formal and informal leaders, and what are their styles?)	
Required systems (what attitudes, activities, and interactions does the organization require?)	<ul><li>required activities</li><li>required attitudes</li><li>required interactions</li></ul>
Emerging systems (what attitudes and behaviors do we see now?)	<ul><li>activities</li><li>attitudes</li><li>interactions</li></ul>
Consequences or outcomes (what is the current level of productivity, satisfaction, or individual/group development?)	<ul><li>productivity</li><li>satisfaction</li><li>group development</li></ul>

Leadership. Paul Riley was not able to empower his management team and wonders if he must come down hard on them. The directive from above has caused him to modify his normally participative style, to a more directive one.

Background factors. Personal systems: long-time senior engineers who are set in their ways; they enjoy fun and challenging work; they strive for good technological solutions.

Reward systems. Rewarded for technological solutions in the past. Next, they were then rewarded for staying within budget and on time. Now they need to be rewarded for bringing in resources.

Culture. paternalistic, collaborative, friendly, supportive, family-like.

External factors. None noted.

Layout/technology. Focus on engineer solutions that make the customers happy.

Required attitudes. Pay attention to best interest of company;

Required actions. Get business for company; emergent action, get business from within the company.

Required interactions. None noted.

Emergent attitudes, actions, and interactions. Emergent attitude: pay attention to best interest of team.

Consequences. Productivity low, satisfaction adequate, learning low.

The system: the general manager's directive caused a shift in Riley's leadership style and a change in the required system (required action: to become market-oriented, rather than product-oriented). The emergent behavior was to look for ways to market internally to other groups and projects. The result is low productivity, low learning, and adequate satisfaction (senior engineers), low satisfaction (Riley).

Question 2
Analyze the Analog management team members, in light of the theory on reward systems.
Analysis skills (breaking a concept into its parts and explaining their interrelationships, distinguishing relevant from extraneous material).

Answer
People alter their behavior based on what is measured. For example, it appears that on the Analog management team, members used to be measured by how well their product met customer expectations of technical competence. Management team members probably responded by delivering products that met or exceeded customer expectations. During periods of defense cutbacks, greater emphasis was given to delivering a product on time and below cost, even if it meant delivering a product that just barely met customer expectations. It also appears that the company was seeking new ways to leverage their technical competence into the commercial marketplace. Managers on the Analog management team have responded by seeking internal markets as a support staff rather than seeking applications outside the company. Managers on the Analog management team appear to get their personal rewards from affiliating with the other managers. They are satisfied with their salaries and the type of work that they do. Many of them may be close to retirement and are not anxious to create many changes this late in their careers.

Question 3
What should Paul Riley do to get his Analog management team members to meet the challenge of reaching the commercial market?
Synthesis skills (putting parts together to form a new whole; solving a problem requiring creativity or originality).

Answer
First, Paul must evaluate whether or not his current management team members hold the correct competencies to reach commercial markets. If not, he needs to seek ways to build these competencies—training, recruiting an engineer from a targeted commercial industry, seeking these skills from within the organization. Second, Paul must guide his managers into identifying how they can meet the challenge. He might organize a problem-solving retreat, where key project manager and junior engineers from each of his manager's teams brainstorm about applications of their products to commercial products. He could then appoint new product development teams to seek collaborative agreements with large commercial firms in targeted industries. Working closely together, these cross-industry teams may be able to discover new applications for AVIONIC products. Short deadlines and high expectations should be directed toward these product development teams. Paul may even want the product development team managers to report directly to him, to ensure that his management team doesn't prevent (either intentionally or unintentionally) the team from making progress.

References
Cohen, A.R., Fink, S.L., Gadon, H., and Willits, R.D. (1992). *Effective behavior in organizations*, 5th ed. Homewood, IL: Irwin.

Homans, G. C. (1950). *The human group*. NY: Harcourt Brace Jovanovich.

Homans, G. C. (1961). *Social behavior: Its elementary forms*. NY: Harcourt Brace Jovanovich.

Roy, Donald. (1997). "Banana time: Job satisfaction and informal interaction." In J. S. Ott (ed.) *Classic Readings in Organizational Behavior*. NY: Harcourt Brace Jovanovich.

Epilogue
None.

Social System Conceptual Scheme

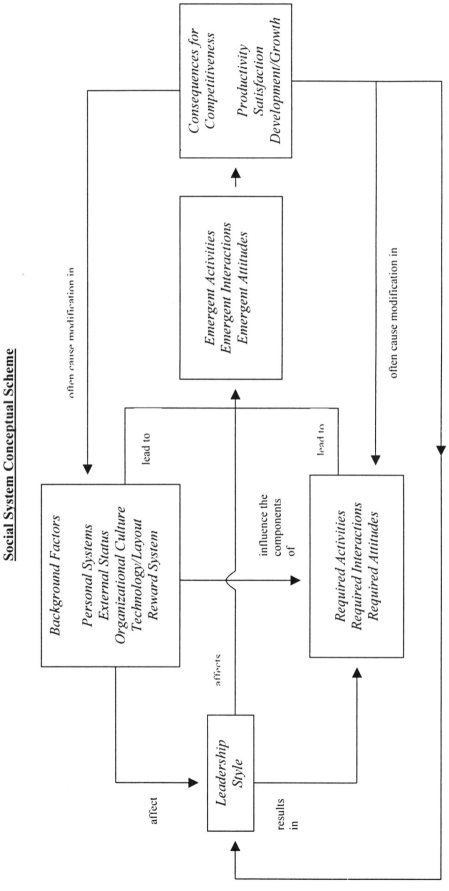

Source: Cohen, A.R., Fink, S.L., Gadon, H., and Willits, R.D. (1992). *Effective Behavior in Organizations*, 5th ed. Homewood, IL.: Irwin, p. 98.

YOUR UNCLE WANTS YOU!

Topics (* = Primary topic with Teaching Plan)
*Job satisfaction
*Recruitment
*Employee selection
*Job fit
Emotional dissonance
Human resource management
United States Military
Government context

Case overview

The E Recruiting Battalion of the U.S. Army has fallen short of its quota of recruits for the past two quarters. The commanding officer of the battalion, Lt. Colonel Tyler Mason, must determine the reasons for this deviation from the quota to ensure the quota is met in future quarters. The case describes the macro-environmental context in which the Army seeks recruits. Further, the case describes the job of the recruiter. To aid his analysis of the situation, Lt. Colonel Mason conducted a job satisfaction survey of the recruiters in his battalion. The case contains quotes from this survey.

Industry

United States Army recruiting battalion.

Teaching objectives
1. To associate macro-environmental factors with job design.
2. To appreciate the usefulness of job satisfaction surveys in analyzing and designing jobs.
3. To make decisions regarding the design of the Army recruiters' job.

Other related cases in Volume 1

Costume Bank (job fit); *Moon over E.R.* (Emotional intelligence, HRM); *No, Sir, Sergeant!* (United States military); *Problems at Wukmier Home Electronics Warehouse* (HRM); *The Unmovable Team* (job fit).

Other related cases in Volume 2

Angry Branch Manager (HRM); *Incident on the USS Whitney* (United States military); *Saving Private Ryan and Classic Leadership Models* (United States military); *The Volunteer* (job fit); *Unprofessional Conduct* (job fit, recruitment).

Intended courses and levels

This case would be most appropriately used as the basis for discussion or for a written assignment in undergraduate or graduate courses concerned with human resources management issues. Courses could include Human Resource Management, Principles of Management, Organizational Behavior, as well as Marketing/Sales Management. The case would be useful in highlighting issues of person-job fit such as job design, selection criteria, and training. Further, the case is one of the first to introduce and apply the concept of emotional labor (the display of organizationally-desired emotion as part of the work role).

Analysis

Person-job fit theory is based on the notion of fit between an individual's personality characteristics and that person's occupational environment (Holland, 1985). Person-job fit suggests that work-related

---
[*]Source: Adapted from case prepared by Steven J. Maranville, University of Houston-Downtown, and Teri C. Tompkins. The case and teaching note were prepared as a basis for class discussion rather than to illustrate either effective or ineffective handling of administrative situations. Suggestions for improvement of this note should be sent to tompkins@uor.edu. Credit will be given in the next revision.

outcomes will be more positive when a high correlation exists between people's personalities and the demands of their jobs. For example, Caldwell and O'Reilly (1990) found that the degree to which people experience person-job fit is positively correlated with the level of performance demonstrated.

This case intimates that one of the factors influencing the comments of the military recruiters was poor person-job fit. Previous research on the emotional labor concept has found that military recruiters report low levels of job satisfaction and high levels of emotional dissonance (conflict between the emotion to be displayed as part of the work role and the emotion actually felt) (Morris, unpublished). Further, the researchers found that emotional dissonance, not emotional labor per se, has a key impact on psychological well-being—such that the greater the emotional dissonance, the lower the job satisfaction and the higher the emotional exhaustion experienced.

These findings suggest that selection, rather than reward systems, may be the most effective way for organizations to manage emotion work (Morris and Feldman, 1996). In other words, instead of forcing employees to comply with display norms that violate felt emotion, organizations should select employees whose expressive styles match emotion display rules (an element of person-job fit). In this case, this means that the Army would be well served by selecting recruiters, not only on their soldiering skills, but on their willingness and ability to appropriately express desired emotion during interactions with potential recruits.

Research methodology

This case is based on observations and interviews. The case is a true incident. Names and the organization have been disguised.

Teaching plan

Teaching plan topic: Recruiting and Person-Job Fit
60-minute teaching plan

Preassignment: None

	Timing	Activity	Organization	Student Outcomes
I	0–10 minutes (10)	Read the case.	Large group discussion	Understand the situation.
II	10–30 minutes (20)	Identify the problem(s).	Large group discussion	Surface the macro and micro forces causing the situation.
III	30–50 minutes (20)	Identify alternatives.	Large group discussion	Generate and examine alternative solutions to the problem.
IV	50–60 minutes (10)	Plan for implementation.	Large group discussion	Discuss how the selected alternative(s) would be implemented.

25-minute teaching plan on recruitment and person-job fit.

Preassignment: Read case before class (10 minutes).

Activities: Divide class into small groups. One-third of the groups do activity II; one third do activity III; one-third do activity IV (10 minutes). Full class discussion and report back (15 minutes).

Discussion questions and answers

Question 1

Describe the factors in the external environment that impact the recruiters' job.

Exploratory (probes facts and basic knowledge).

Answer

The Army's recruitment function has been affected by several changes driven by societal conditions in the past two decades. First, the military has become a totally volunteer force. Second, the Army has changed its strategy of warfare from one of massive deployment of resources to one of flexibility and mobility supported by high technology. Third, the Army has undergone a major downsizing since the end of the Cold War. Fourth, the U.S. workforce has become more diverse; women and ethnic minority groups have found an expanded range of employment opportunities. Fifth, society's values and norms are changing in a way that reflects a diminished level of civic duty, especially among younger Americans who are the Army's target market.

These conditions have had a major influence on the recruiters' job. Although recruitment has always been an important function in the Army, recruitment is now essential, since becoming an all-volunteer force. Rather than performing as "order takers," recruiters must now perform as salespeople—even marketing professionals. The level of selling difficulty has also raised, because the Army has become more selective of its potential recruits, requiring a higher level of education. Moreover, selling the Army to potential recruits has become more difficult, because downsizing has limited the possibilities for promotion and long-term career prospects. These issues of career advancement are of particular concern to women and minority groups that are becoming more difficult to recruit. Overall, the increased difficulty of recruitment is reflected in the way the Army is perceived by its target market. The mission of the Army is a hard sell when the economy is strong and the United States is not faced with an imposing military threat.

Question 2

How might the recruiters' job be changed to make it more satisfying?

Diagnostic question (probes motives or causes) and cause-and-effect question (asks for causal relationship between ideas, actions, or events

Answer

The most fundamental way to improve the satisfaction of recruiters is to have the right people in the position. Every job has its own set of characteristics, and every person is not suited to function effectively in every job. The role of the recruiter is that of a salesperson. Consequently, the theory of person-job fit contends that personnel should be selected for the recruiters' job based on criteria that indicate success in selling. Rather than selecting recruiters on the basis of "soldiering" skills, they should be selected according to criteria such as appearance, friendliness, and interpersonal communication.

Once the right people have been selected, they still need the maintenance and motivating factors that bring continued satisfaction to the job. Maintenance factors would include clearly stated objectives and the proper support for accomplishing those objectives. Motivating factors would include rewards that are clearly linked to successful accomplishment of the objectives and opportunities for professional advancement.

The design of a job, and the extent to which the job design can be changed, depends on the function performed by that job and the organizational culture in which the job performs that function. In the case of Army recruiters, while such factors as person-job fit, more effective communication of expectations, and enhanced rewards seem to be appropriate in terms of making the work more satisfying, the culture of the Army would have a strong influence over the extent to which these factors would be effective, or could even be implemented.

For example, a different set of selection criteria for recruiters may violate deeply held beliefs regarding the central role of the soldier. Recruiters are the Army's front line to the public; consequently, the Army wants personnel in the recruiting position who are the epitome of a soldier. Needless to say, these changes would require system-wide commitment and effort that certainly would require a long-term time frame.

Question: 3

What should Lt. Colonel Mason do now to improve next quarter's recruitment numbers?
Action (calls for a conclusion or action).

Answer

Mason is to be commended for his foresight—even courage—to commission a job satisfaction survey among his battalion's recruiters. Such inquiries into the thoughts and feelings of personnel are not common even in the "new" Army. Although the recruiters' mere responses to this survey are unlikely to change their attitudes as Mason hypothesizes, the survey does provide a vehicle for improved communication. Therefore, Mason should not disregard the findings of the job satisfaction survey. The recruiters' comments represent strong emotions that should be addressed.

Mason should call a meeting with the first sergeants and commanders of the companies within his battalion. In this meeting, Mason should share the results of the survey and initiate a dialogue focused on better understanding the recruiters' concerns. This meeting may lead to another meeting that includes the recruiters at which time collaborative problem solving could be pursued.

These meetings could result in a range of possible solutions. One possible solution could be to enhance the recruiters' training. Currently, the recruiters undertake a structured training program that specifies detailed procedures for conducting their work. This training program might continue to be a useful introduction to the job; but, as recruiters become more familiar with their work, they could benefit from a more problem-centered approach to training that enables them to develop in those areas that are actually troublesome.

This type of training could entail training sessions in which recruiters train other recruiters. The case indicates that, even though the battalion's recruitment quota was not met, some of the recruiting companies within the battalion had met or exceeded their quotas. Obviously, some recruiters have been able to overcome the challenges of selling the Army. These recruiters—if properly motivated and rewarded—could share with other recruiters the lessons they have learned.

Another possible solution could be to allow recruiters to personalize their jobs. The detailed methods and procedures presented in the current training program makes the recruiters' work unnecessarily mechanical. Personalizing the job would not only make the work more satisfying, but would also enhance the recruiters' performance. When trying to make a sale, a mechanical approach is likely to be less effective than a more personal approach.

References

Caldwell, D.F. and O'Reilly, C.A. III. (1990). "Measuring person-job fit with a profile comparison process." *Journal of Applied Psychology*, 75, 648–657.

Holland, J. L. (1985). *Making vocational choices: A theory of vocational personalities and work environments*, 2nd ed. Upper Saddle River, NJ: Prentice Hall.

Morris, J.A. "Predictors and consequences of emotional labor." Unpublished dissertation. University of South Carolina.

Morris, J.A. and Feldman, D.C. (1996). "The dimensions, antecedents, and consequences of emotional labor." *Academy of Management Review*, 21, 986–1010.

Epilogue

None.

Part III

CRITICAL INCIDENT CASE ASSIGNMENT HINTS

If you are like me, you may be concerned about how to help your students think more critically about management theories. You may also be searching for a way to improve students' ability to write, even if you feel that your skills are not that of a professional writer. The critical incident case and analysis will help your students think and write more critically about their own experience. It will also help them learn to apply management concepts to their experience.

According to the North American Case Research Association (NACRA), cases are real-life descriptions of actual organizations. Even so, some students have difficulty believing that a case is real and may discount its value to their learning. A self-written case helps students identify strongly with the facts in the case and increases their understanding of the conceptual material because it directly applies to their own experience. The learning is anchored in an emotional event, so the concepts connected to the analysis of that event are retained over longer periods of time.[1]

The critical incident case also increases students' ability to write and think critically. Professors are being held accountable across every discipline to help improve students' writing skills; yet, designing effective writing assignments that relate strongly to our discipline is not always easy. The critical incident case exercise is divided into distinctive steps, which helps students improve their ability to

- describe vividly, yet objectively
- think critically and conceptually
- explore a topic using different levels and types of questions
- improve clarity and specificity.

The professor doesn't need to be an English teacher to help students improve their writing. Davis (1993, pp. 205–207) writes that the hard work of writing, the use of peer review (where students read and evaluate other student's papers—before the papers are turned into the instructor), and the emphasis on revision helps students improve their writing skills. As management professors, we can concentrate on the theory of the students' case and analysis, while providing students the opportunity to develop their ideas, compose drafts, get feedback from others, revise drafts, edit and present finished work, which supports improving their writing skills.

I have been using some version of student-written cases for seven years. I've also been teaching case method in my Managing Change class about the same length of time. However, it's been only recently that I have taught a case study for a graduate course called Groups and Leaders and assigned the critical incident case as an assignment. I was surprised when I noticed the writing of the critical incident cases improved significantly over previous ones from the same course, and students' analysis of the cases improved after they wrote their own analysis. It appeared to me that there is an interaction effect when students both learn from cases written by others and write their own case and analysis.

There is significant detail in the introduction section of *Cases in Organizational Behavior and Management* to guide you and your students in writing a case and then analyzing it. But I imagine that you would also like some tips in helping students do this assignment. I hope you find the following ideas useful.

Helpful Hints for the Instructor

Class size and planning logistics

What's the ideal class size? Classroom size varies by institution. Here are some suggestions for planning logistics depending on your class size. In half-semester courses, e.g., seven weeks, small classes of 12 students are ideal. This is because turn-around time has to be one week. I've had up to 24, and the one-week turn-around time was challenging.

If you have medium-size classes of around 24, then give yourself two weeks to grade before you promise to turn them back to students. I tell the students on the very first day of class that I will need two weeks to grade each part; otherwise, they wait anxiously for the feedback.

---

[1] Erlbaum. Spear, N.E., & Riccio, D.C. (1994). *Memory: Phenomena and Principles*. Boston, MA: Allyn & Bacon.

Hints for the Critical Incident Case Assignment

If I had large class sizes (I've had 70 students in basic OB courses as an adjunct), I would modify the assignment by having groups of students write and analyze a single case. Groups of 3 to 5 would be ideal. If you use the group writing method, I strongly suggest they do a peer group review to determine how they will distribute their grade. Here's how I explain it to students:

<u>Peer evaluation when choosing a group paper</u>

To ensure balance of participation, your group will use peer evaluation. As a group, you will determine the percentage of the group grade each member receives. No group member can receive less than 80% (unless they did not contribute to the project) or more than 120%. For example, in the table below, the group agrees that Joe and Alice did the same amount of work but Sally did more than Joe and Alice. Joe and Alice give away 2% points to Sally in recognition of her contributions to the project:

	The group assigns a **peer grade** of		I assign a **project grade** of		**Actual Grade** in instructor's grade book
Joe	98%	×	85%	=	83.3%
Alice	98%	×	85%	=	83.3%
Sally	104%	×	85%	=	88.4%

I've found that I get excellent participation from students because they are aware from the beginning that they are being judged by their group, not just me. Encourage students to discuss their evaluation criteria frequently. If a student does not participate, then the group removes that person completely from the list (this means that they cannot use his or her points to boost their own grade. It's as if he or she were never in the group).

<u>Scheduling</u>
<u>How long does the entire assignment take?</u> I have frequently had students do this assignment in a seven-week, half-semester course. Of course, it works well during longer terms, such as quarter or semester. Here is my seven-week schedule.

Table 1: Suggested schedule for due dates and grading time

	Student	**Professor**
Week 1	Turn in notes to get you started. Professor evaluates concept and gives feedback before students go home.	This can be written in class or outside of class. I like to give them comments on the first night, so they can begin writing their narrative right away. With a small class, you can go around the room and have each student describe his or her critical incident (allow students 5 to 10 minutes to write it down first). The advantage of this method is they get to hear the others describe their ideas and your response.
Week 2		Professor returns grades and comments from Step 1: Notes to get you started. Allow 5 to 10 minutes to grade each "Notes to Get You Started." Alternatively, you cannot grade this assignment and just give them feedback on the first night of class.
Week 3	Turn in narrative	Ask students not to put their work in special binders. A paper clip or staple works best for faster grading.
Week 4		You grade narrative. Allow about 30 to 60 minutes to grade each case narrative.
Week 5	Turn in analysis.	
Week 6		You grade analysis. Allow about 45 minutes to 1½ hours to grade each case analysis.

Week 7	Turn in final edited version of narrative and analysis.	
Grades due!		You grade final versions. Allow about 15 to 30 minutes to grade the final edited version.

Grading Hints

Teach students how to separate fact from opinion. This is one of the hardest things for them to do. Fact is like a reporter, being careful of adjectives. If he or she wants to express an opinion, then recognize it as opinion by attributing it to the person holding the opinion (usually in quotes). Hold opinions until the analysis.

Teach students to write better. Teach students that writing is a skill that needs to be developed. I tell them that the narrative and analysis use very different writing styles. The narrative is like presenting a written history or report. You must learn to present the report factually, but with flair, so that the report gets read. The analysis usually follows the report or is written as an executive summary. It is also like a research paper. The idea is to back your opinion up with facts (from the case) and theory (from experts, including yourself). In business, we need both kinds of writing.

What are some good criteria for grading the narrative? I find it hardest to grade the narrative because it is about someone's experience, and how do you judge that? There are some key items that I look for, however, and I've put them in a grading template. Following that are some sample narrative grade sheets that I have used.

What are some good criteria for grading the analysis? One way to guide your thinking for grading is to use Bloom's taxonomy and evaluate the level of the students' cognitive ability. Some cases lend themselves more naturally to application or analysis and not to synthesis and evaluation. I'd use my judgment and give a higher grade if they've done a very good job at the application or analysis level. While it is a mistake to assume that Bloom's taxonomy is in a hierarchical order, excellent graduate work should demonstrate analysis and synthesis skills. The table below assumes good answers to these types of questions.

Table 2: Suggestions for grading by using Bloom's taxonomy

Bloom's taxonomy level (The chart assumes good answers to these type of questions. Grade lowers if poorly written answer to question type. Grade higher if excellent answer to question type).	Undergraduate	Graduate
All knowledge and comprehension questions	D to C	F to D
One Knowledge, Comprehension, and Application question	C+ to B	C- to C+
One Comprehension, Application, Analysis question	B to B+	C+ to B-
One Application question, two Analysis questions	B+ to A-	B- to B+
One Analysis, Synthesis, Evaluation question	A- to A	B+ to A

Use the question-type labels to evaluate their work, but there is a caution. Many students do not correctly label their questions. You must re-label the question types to use the chart above. I think it is only fair to tell the students ahead of time that you want them to move beyond knowledge, comprehension, and exploratory type questions. Many students want to use a knowledge question first to demonstrate that they know the theory. Tell them you already know the theory and that all they have to do is reference it and you'll figure it out. I try to teach my students to briefly (one-half sentence to 2 sentences) describe the concept and then build on the concept to apply, analyze, create, and evaluate.

What are some good grading criteria for the final edited version of Narrative and Analysis (Step 4)?

Have student mark one copy of their final paper. If you have the students "track their changes" or mark their copies on their final paper so that you can see where they made changes from the first graded narrative and analysis, then grading can be very easy. This is a real advantage at the end of a term. Make sure they compare the New document to the Old document, and not vice versa, otherwise you'll get a lot of strikeouts and red ink! I always have my students submit their previously graded work as well (in a large self-addressed stamped envelope), so I can look at my "margin notes" in my first grading.

If they substantially changed their document, have them submit a clean copy of the document. (It's too hard to read the "track-changes" document when there are significant changes.) They should hand-mark the sections that stayed the same!

The chart below might guide you in how to evaluate the final version.

Table 3: Suggestions for grading Final Edited Version

Did the student ignore suggestions made in margins and grading template?	Lower grade one full grade (e.g., if they got an 84 on narrative (step 2) and 82 on analysis (step 3), then they would get a 73 on their final version (step 4).
Did the student respond to some of the suggestions, mostly copy edit, but not substantive requests?	Lower grade a half grade (e.g., if they got an 84 on narrative (step 2) and 82 on analysis (step 3), then they would get a 78 on their final version (step 4).
Did the student respond to all suggestions, but you didn't have many substantive suggestions on their first two papers?	Give them the average between the two grades (e.g., if they got an 95 on narrative (step 2) and 89 on analysis (step 3), then they would get a 92 on their final version (step 4).
Did the student significantly improve his or her paper either because they responded well to your suggestions for substantive change or because they added their own ideas?	I give significantly higher grades on the final version, if it was poorly done in the first place and then brought up to standard, e.g., from 75 (step 2) and 65 (step 3) to 88 (step 4). If it was brought up to excellence, then I give them 95 to 100 on the final version.

In the next few pages, I provide examples of grading forms and feedback to students. Good luck!

Grading Template for Narrative[2]

Length and Straightforwardness
❑ Selection of Facts. Need to know which facts to keep and which ones to let go.
  - ❑ Some of the facts are extraneous (see marked case).
  - ❑ Develop better (see marked case).
  - ❑ Appropriate Length (6 to 13 pages). too short too long just right!
  - ❑ Missing Information. See back (if circled). Facts I'd like to know:

The Story
❑ The "Hook." Should help me know what the case is about and make me want to read on.
  - ❑ Doesn't reflect the nature of the case.
  - ❑ Lifeless/boring.
  - ❑ Really got me/excellent!
  - ❑ Other:

❑ The Body. Needs to be like a good story so that I can't stop reading it.
  - ❑ Not very interesting. Add:

  - ❑ Needs better description of:

  - ❑ It was compelling!
  - ❑ Other:

❑ The Conclusion. The conclusion in a decision case leaves us wondering what to do.
  - ❑ Told too much, put the ending in the epilogue.
  - ❑ Left me confused.
  - ❑ You're ready to analyze!
  - ❑ Other:

Case Organization
❑ Appropriate Style. Style depends on the case facts. I've checked the style(s) I think might fit.
  - ❑ Better if time-sequenced.
  - ❑ Tell it like a story.
  - ❑ Provide an overview/context first.
  - ❑ Tell the critical incident story (circle appropriate one) first middle last in the story.

Tone and Tense
❑ Objectivity. Point of view should be neutral observer or reporter.
  - ❑ Describe more; tell less.
  - ❑ Tell both sides of the story. More from the perspective of:
  - ❑ Did you leave out any information? Seems biased toward:
  - ❑ Well done.
❑ Past tense. Write in past tense.
  - ❑ The company information needs to be in past tense.
  - ❑ The people need to be in past tense.
❑ Third Person. Write in third person.

Potential topics or questions for analysis: See back of page for more.

---

[2] Adapted from Naumes, W. and Naumes, M. J. (1999). *The Art and Craft of Case Writing*. Thousand Oaks, CA: Sage, pp. 9–102.

Samples of grading of critical incident narrative

Diane
11/11/1997

The subject in this case is important to groups and leadership (and organizational behavior in general). You have chosen an incident that obviously had an impact for you. You write well and have the beginnings of a good case for analysis. To sufficiently analyze the case, however, I feel that the case needs further development and information.

I urge you to provide the reader (me and some of your classmates) with more details about the groupware process. I think it is very interesting to read about the theory of groupware and the actual outcomes your group experienced. Primary organizational behavior theory as I see it: Group-decision making

Include information that will help you evaluate the electronic meeting decision-making style: e.g., criteria for group effectiveness: 1) number of ideas, 2) quality of ideas, 3) social pressure, 4) money costs, 5) speed, 6) task orientation, 7) potential for interpersonal conflict, 8) feelings of accomplishment, 9) commitment to solution, 10) develops groups cohesiveness. (Source: Murnighan, "Group decision making: What strategies should you use?" *Management Review*, Feb 1981, p. 61.)
Questions I have for additional information to analyze your case:

You implied that there was a lot of conflict among the support staff. Did it revolve entirely around Sally? Was it divided by where one was located or the type of administrators/faculty served? I'm thinking that a secondary analysis might include interpersonal conflict or communications. (Reminder, your analysis requires you to examine at least two areas of organizational behavior).

You write, "needless to say the remaining weeks of the project were not as successful as the first. Walls had been built and sides had been taken…" What was the point of the project? Who was leading it? Could you write a section in the case about that person's hoped-for goals? Were they doing it as an experiment/research project? To solve interpersonal communication problems (as you imply with your comments) or to solve technical problems in the office work processes? Perhaps it is all of this… perhaps you had hoped for more interpersonal communication and were personally saddened that that wasn't accomplished. The organizational behavior theories that might apply would be goals and perceptions issues. Another interesting secondary or tertiary analysis.

The gender issue is interesting, and it does the trick of demonstrating some of the problems with the groupware style of meeting. I think you have given us sufficient information in the case to guide the reader. In the epilogue, could you let us know if a man was selected to replace the dean?

Your final paragraph in the case is very interesting. Keep it, but divide into two sections. First, include what happened to the report in the case, and develop it further as it demonstrates what happens to the material generated by groupware. In that section, address the gender issue just as you did in the case. In the epilogue, describe what eventually happened… "Eventually, the report and its contents faded…tensions over the sessions eventually cooled and were even laughed about later…"

In summary, for your final case, I suggest several subheadings added to this case with information organized around them. 1. Introduction: The work of the people (as you have already done). 2. Problems and conflicts. Describe more fully the problems that were surfacing that led someone to believe that groupware was the solution to these problems. If there was more than one type of problem (e.g., I imagine there were work-process problems and interpersonal conflict problems), then describe them both. Use quotes to describe your personal feelings and frustrations to add color and interest. 3. Groupware project. Describe what groupware is. Who was leading the project and information about him or her. Describe the room (or rooms) in which the meeting took place. 4) Groupware fiasco. Keep this section. Add any details that you feel you might need to do your case analysis. 5) Outcome of groupware meetings.

Describe what happened to the report including the ignoring of the gender issue and **how you felt about it.** I think it must have felt terrible to know that your comments were not anonymous and that some people pointed fingers at you for standing up to a sexist comment. Describe (throughout the case) your feelings about what was happening to you. Use quotes when you are talking. 6) On a separate page, include an epilogue.

Grade on Step 1B: **B+ (87%)** (I felt that more information on the electronic meeting and the reasons for using it would have strengthened this case—that is, it would have been more fully developed, and I would have fewer questions about what is the story behind the story). The writing and organization are good. I'm confident that you will have an excellent final case based on your understanding of organizational behavior theory that I saw demonstrated in class last week and your writing ability. If I can look at any drafts with you, please let me know. I look forward to working with you.

****

Jay

11/11/1997

At first reading of your case, I am not yet clear that it has the potential for an organizational behavioral (OB) analysis. However, after looking at the table of contents in several OB books, I think you could develop the case to look at several potential topics.

First possibility is the area of "work stress." If you were to give us some information about how the "impossible task" and the "constant rejections" affected you and your ability to work, you could examine work stress concepts more completely.

Another possibility might be in the area of "organizational culture" and/or "group norms." How do employees learn culture/norms...through rituals, stories, material symbols, language. If you could outline the ways that you were learning your organization's culture or the group norms, you might have a focus for your case.

Another angle might be in terms of "performance evaluation." What were you being evaluated on? How could your performance be measured; how did you know if you were doing well with all the rejections? How did the boss' interest in the final property impact your feelings of evaluation?

Regardless of the angle(s) that you decide to explore in your case, you will need to examine at least two organizational behavior concepts. I think your case has the making of a good case if you can add additional material to explain your feelings of approaching your boss one more time and the subsequent elation on both your parts.

I have some OB type cases in one of my textbooks that I'll bring to class for you to look at. It appears to me that you haven't been exposed to many cases before, so you would benefit from getting a "feel" of how cases are written. You do an excellent job describing your feelings and imagining your boss' feelings...so I'm not concerned with your writing ability. The case, however, lacks the necessary structure and information for you to do an adequate job in the analysis section. Imagine that you are first presenting the facts (in an engaging format) to me (as if you were a medical student presenting the history and physical information—the case) and then you present your diagnosis to the attending physician (the analysis).

If you want to show me a draft copy of your case before the final one is due, I'd be happy to give you verbal feedback.

Grade: C+/B- (79%). You did good work describing the depth of feelings you felt during the critical incident. I felt that I jumped into the middle of the story and there were a number of background items missing that would have helped clarify your feelings and position (although you did include some important ones, too, e.g., the type of property desired and the apparent difficulty in getting this type of property). In your final case, include a little background on the company and on the owner (and/or boss). Tell us a little about yourself, how you got the job, and what your job title was...were you there only to look at property or was this an additional assignment on top of your other work? What experience had you had looking at property in the past? How did the other employees feel about the boss? Did he always reject everyone's ideas? What did it feel like to be young and eager to please the boss? Why did you persevere when others had quit searching? If you can weave this type of information into your story, then we can analyze this case from a number of interesting organizational behavior angles. Good luck.

Grading Template for Analysis

Name:_____

The type of question were identified and written correctly? Yes No

    ____Please look at the critical incident assignment and label each question by type.

    ____Some or all of your questions are not in the form as described in the critical incident assignment.

    ____Your questions are not complex enough; they can be answered with a simple yes or no or by a single-word answer. See especially: Q1 Q2 Q3 Q4 Q5 Q6 Q7 Q8 Q9

Appropriate references were cited? Yes No Not needed.

    ____Please reference theory sections (e.g., knowledge type questions or definition sections).

    ____When referencing a primary source (e.g., Maslow) that was taken from another book (e.g., your textbook) follow this example: Maslow, year, p.# , as cited in textbook, year, p #)

Answers were edited, free from grammar, punctuation, and spelling errors?

    ____Minor errors (this did not affect your grade—please edit carefully for next round)

    ____More than minor, but less than significant, errors (this affected your grade somewhat)

    ____Significant errors (this affected your grade)

    ____Primarily editing problems

    ____Primarily clarity and sentence/paragraph structure problems

Content

    ____The most critical factors that influence the case were identified and discussed?

    ____Some or all of your answers were not thorough. See especially Q1 Q2 Q3 Q4 Q5 Q6 Q7 Q8 Q9

    ____Connect case facts more explicitly to the theory? (use words like: "For example" OR "because of" OR "due to."

Comments:

Continued on back page (if circled)

Suggestions for next round:

____Some new case facts are in the analysis: be sure to include them in the narrative in the final case narrative.

____You need a plan of action that considers the pros and cons of various options (including second-order consequences, that is, what might happen *if* you implement your idea).

____You need a refection of how you might have done things differently if you knew then what you know now.

____Add page numbers

Grade: _____% (Multiply the percentage by the total number of points possible to get your grade points.)

HOMEWORK ASSIGNMENT QUESTIONS

Some instructors prefer to give assignment questions in preparation for class discussion. On the following pages you will find a list of all the questions from the teaching notes. You may wish to photocopy this list and circle the questions that you want students to answer. Alternatively, if you design your entire course before the term begins, you may wish to type these questions into your syllabus.

A NEW MAGAZINE IN NIGERIA

1. For an enterprise that requires a measure of autonomy to be successful, how do you explain the actions of the publisher in terms of power? Did Charlotte possess any counterpower? Explain.

2. What if Ifeoma had let her professional commitment to *Excellence* override her instinct and moral commitment to Charlotte and her profession?

3. Using K. Thomas' conflict-handling modes, discuss what approach(es) could have been useful in resolving the conflict between George Mba and Charlotte Demuren?

4. What premises of the pioneering-innovating (PI) motive, and Maslow's self-actualization need are present in the founding of *Eminence*.

5. Explain why *Excellence* magazine was successful, and illustrate motivation theory (from your text) with case examples.

6. Describe how Richard Hackman and Greg Oldham's job characteristics model explains the success of *Eminence*?

A TEAM DIVIDED OR A TEAM UNITED?

1. What factors contributed to Madeleine's, Dan's, and Mark's job satisfaction before Mark's firing?

2. Contrast Dan's and Mark's interpersonal relationships with Claire. Why did Claire respond to each one differently when they both felt the same way about her? What conclusions do you draw from this analysis?

3. What were Claire's strengths and weaknesses as a leader?

4. Suppose you were a consultant to Claire, what advice would you give her to help her achieve the production goals set for her department?

5. Was termination the proper course of action for Mark? Assuming that termination was the proper action by Claire, how should she have terminated Mark to reduce Marketing Research Int'l's liability and to support Mark as a person?

COSTUME BANK

1. In the wake of Karen's resignation from The Costume Bank, whom should the board contact, and what should those people be told?

2. Over the eight-year history of The Costume Bank, what has the organization done well consistently and distinctively in its dealings with other organizations and persons?

3. What are some key connotations of operating a "bank," and how appropriate is "bank" as a guide for the future of The Costume Bank?

4. In view of what has transpired in the business environment in which The Costume Bank is located, how appropriate is it that The Costume Bank continue to operate under a nonprofit status?

5. What should be included in the job description that the board writes for the next executive director of The Costume Bank?

6. Why should The Costume Bank business continue after Karen Simon's resignation? (Or, what difference does it make that The Costume Bank continues in business for one more day?)

7. What message should Karen Simon communicate to the board, now that Karen and the board have met to discuss the board's decision to take greater control of Costume Bank operations?

8. In the wake of Karen's communication (Question 7) to the board, what kind of revised job description and compensation should the board be prepared to offer Karen in order for The Costume Bank to retain her services?

9. What do you expect will be Karen Simon's "next stop" in her career as an entrepreneur?

Student Instructions: Please answer the questions indicated.

DONOR SERVICES DEPARTMENT IN GUATEMALA

1. What was Joanna's diagnosis of the situation in the donor services department?
2. What should Joanna recommend to Sam? Note: Students should NOT read case B before answering this question, as the answer below is a summary of what happened in case B.
3. What are the cultural factors that influence this case? Would you expect any differences if it had taken place in the United States?

FIRED!

1. What type of compensation and rewards did Rycoff-Sexton offer its outside sales representatives?
2. What is the role of quotas and extrinsic rewards for people in sales jobs?
3. Did Tony seem motivated by meeting quotas?
4. What was Tony's greatest asset for developing his career?
5. Is the ability to network a useful tool in sales? If yes, why was Tony not successful at Rycoff-Sexton? How would open territories affect selling and sales representatives? What type of sales job would Tony be better at?
6. What stage is Tony at in his career development?

HANDLING DIFFERENCES AT JAPAN AUTO

1. What factors contributed to the problems between Barbara Smith and Chrys Haber?
2. Describe the noise barrier at LAPDC.
3. Using Tuckman's model of group development, at what stage is the administrative team?
4. Evaluate Chrys' communication with Barbara in terms of conflict management.
5. What recommendations do you have for Chrys and this team now?

HEART ATTACK

1. Using Hofstede's cultural dimensions, how could one understand Mr. Hamid as the boss?
2. Through the lens of western culture, how would one understand Shauna's reaction to the news of being fired?
3. Would the outcome for Shauna have been any different if she understood Mr. Hamid's management style?
4. How does the spillover model illustrate Mr. Hamid's behavior?
5. How does the spillover model illustrate Shauna's behavior?
6. Would the next employer's background be a major influence when Shauna applied for a job?
7. Was firing Shauna legal?
8. Could Shauna be eligible for any type of unemployment benefit?
9. Did Mr. Hamid misrepresent the truth about the job?

JENNA'S KITCHENS, INC.

1. What are the symptoms in the case that indicate that something isn't working the way it should or indicate that some managerial action is needed?
2. What are Judi Singleton's probable objectives as regional manager for her region and for herself?
3. What ideas, models, or theories seem most useful for understanding the situation Judi Singleton faces?
4. As of the end of the case, what appear to be the factors that constrain what Judi Singleton might do?
5. As of the end of the case, what specific action or series of actions do you recommend to Judi Singleton?

Student Instructions: Please answer the questions indicated.

JULIE'S CALL: EMPOWERMENT AT TACO BELL

1. Review what you know about your own experience with fast food outlets, i.e., the types of jobs, management style, and policies/rules that seem to prevail.

2. Based on your reading in the text, what have you learned about empowerment?

3. What is the purpose of empowerment supposed to be? Are there any difficulties such practices entail for managers and employees?

4. Put yourself in Marcie's shoes, and prepare yourself to respond to Julie's call. What will you say to Julie (and why)? How will you say it (and why)?

LA CABARET

1. Why didn't Betty and Bob defend Malcolm and Shelly?

2. What would you do if you were at a meeting at work and someone made a racial (or gender-based or sexual orientation-based) joke that you personally found offensive?

3. What are some examples of stereotypes from the comedy store incident?

4. What lessons might Shelly have gained from the situation at the comedy store?

5. Imagine that you are an African American in the audience. Why might you agree with Harry's judgment of Malcolm and Shelly? Why might you disagree?

MOON OVER E.R

1. Who is responsible for what happened to Katia Gore?

2. How has the move toward "managed care" impacted hospitals? What other environmental factors may be making work in hospital emergency rooms more demanding?

3. What should Hamilton Bronson do to safeguard the well-being of emergency room personnel? In addition, was there anything that Nurse Warner should or could have done to defuse the situation before it erupted into violence?

NO, SIR, SERGEANT!

1. How was stress a factor in what happened between Sergeant Mitre and Sergeant First Class Fenceroy? Could stress have been managed?

2. Using French and Raven's bases of power as a frame, describe the types of power evident in this case.

3. Of the six bases of power, which was the most important one to control Sergeant Mitre's actions?

4. How did Sergeant Mitre see empowerment in his role as section chief?

5. Why wasn't Sergeant First Class Fenceroy's authority accepted?

6. If Sergeant Mitre had followed Sergeant First Class Fenceroy's second order, what message might Sergeant Mitre have sent to the troops, and what might have been the reaction of the troops?

PEARL JAM'S DISPUTE WITH TICKETMASTER

1. Resource dependence theory argues that organizations strive to acquire control over resources in their external environments on which they are dependent for survival. On what external resources was Ticketmaster dependent? What strategies did Ticketmaster use to reduce its dependence? On what external resources was Pearl Jam dependent? What strategies did Pearl Jam use to reduce its dependence?

2. An organizational goal has been defined as a desired state of affairs that an organization attempts to realize. What were Ticketmaster's goals? What were Pearl Jam's goals? Were both organizations' goals internally

consistent? How effective were these two organizations in meeting their goals? Were the two organizations' goals compatible with one another's, wholly or in part?

3. Theorists have examined various sources of horizontal conflict between and among organizations and groups. Drawing on these theories, offer an explanation for why Pearl Jam and Ticketmaster became involved in a dispute.

4. Theorists differ on whether conflict is "good" or "bad" for organizations. In your view, what were this dispute's benefits—if any—for Pearl Jam and Ticketmaster? What were this dispute's costs—if any—to these organizations? With respect to the final outcome, do you think one organization gained more than the other? In general, was this conflict functional or dysfunctional?

5. What techniques did these two organizations use to resolve their dispute? Were these techniques effective, in whole or in part? What techniques of conflict resolution do you believe might have worked more effectively?

6. Was Ticketmaster guilty of antitrust violations?

PROBLEMS AT WUKMIER HOME ELECTRONICS WAREHOUSE

1. What is socialization theory?
2. Give some examples of socialization from the case.
3. Provide some examples as to how Jose and Christi could have helped the newcomer.
4. How do Hofstede's dimensions help explain the warehouse employees' perceptions and attributions in the case?
5. How would you resolve the music issue?
6. What factors explain the workers' attitudes toward Jim?
7. If you were Jim, what would you do to enter this group effectively?
8. If you were Christi, what decisions would you make at the end of the case?

QUESTIONS MATTER!

1. What type of behavioral control(s) did Julie use?
2. What type of behavioral control did Amanda use? Why?
3. What type of motivation did Cathy prefer?
4. Use Maslow's hierarchy of needs theory to explain which needs were met under each supervisor.
5. Define communication. Describe what was functional and dysfunctional in Cathy and Amanda's communication.
6. What could Amanda and Cathy have done to improve the communication process?
7. How could Amanda have positively motivated Cathy?
8. If you were Amanda, what would you have done to transform your leadership style?

SHAKING THE BIRD CAGE

1. After reading part A, what do you think Kathy, Jim, and members of the antenna team should do?
2. After reading part B, what do you think members of upper management should do?
3. What are possible ways to end this stalemate?
4. How would you characterize this team prior to the reorganization plans?
5. Why did the antenna team respond the way it did to the proposed reorganization?
6. How might power and influence theory explain case facts?

Student Instructions: Please answer the questions indicated.

SPLIT OPERATIONS AT SKY AND ARROW AIRLINES

1. What situational factors led to conflict between the operations employees of Arrow and Sky?
2. What were the effects of conflict on the Sky and Arrow employees?
3. How are organizational cultures characterized and managed? Compare and contrast the cultures of Sky and Arrow.
4. Could cultural issues have caused the failure of the split operations system? Explain
5. What situations cause stress? Are the components of a stressful situation present in Jack's situation?
6. Was Jack's reaction to Andrew at the end of the case a result of stress?

TEMPORARY EMPLOYEES: CAR SHOW TURNED UGLY

1. What are the basic issues in this case for both sides?
2. What can we learn about the factors that strengthen a group's position or power?
3. What would you do if you were Anita?
4. Who was probably at fault in this case?
5. Do you feel RC's intervention was appropriate? Why or why not?
6. What are the contextual factors that contributed to a win-lose result?

THE DAY THEY ANNOUNCED THE BUYOUT

1. How does Maslow's hierarchy of needs help explain the drop in productivity on the day of the announcement?
2. Do you agree with Diane Fox that the board of directors and president were greedy? Why would the board and president sell the bank?
3. Why did some employees stop trusting the president? Use communication theory to analyze this phenomenon.
4. Why did some people appear worried, but others, like Diane's dad, appeared calm?
5. Outline how you would improve the communication of the merger announcement. What are the positive and negative aspects of your plan?
6. Design a communication plan that the human resources department can use the day the possible buyout decision was announced.

UNMOVABLE TEAM

1. Given the case facts, how would you explain the behavior of the Analog management team members using the Homans' social system conceptual scheme (pedagogy in next section)?
2. Analyze the Analog management team members, in light of the theory on reward systems?
3. What should Paul Riley do to get his Analog management team members to meet the challenge of reaching the commercial market?

YOUR UNCLE WANTS YOU!

1. Describe the factors in the external environment that impact the recruiters' job.
2. How might the recruiters' job be changed to make it more satisfying?
3. What should Lt. Colonel Mason do now to improve next quarter's recruitment numbers?

PART IV

INDEX OF TOPICS

P

Participative management · 72
Perception · 142
Pioneering-innovations motive · 11
Planning
  strategic · 27
Positional bargaining · 95, 134
Power · 120
  basis of · 89, 134
  coalition · 11, 134
  conflicts · 11
  influence · 134
  sources · 11
  tactics · 11
Problem solving · 120
Productivity · 142

R

Racial diversity · *See* Diversity, racial
Racial oppression · 77
Racial reasoning · 77
Recruitment · 155
Resistance to change · 120, 149
Resource dependence · 95
Restructuring · 11, 72, 120, 142
Rewards · 46, 149

S

Sales context · 46
Satisfaction
  job · 21, 126, 155
Selection
  employee · 155
Skills
  management · 27
Small business context · 11, 59, 95, 134
Social reinforcement theory · 37
Social system conceptual scheme · 149
Socialization · 103
Specialization
  work · 37

Status · 67, 120
Strategic planning · 27
Stress
  job · 89, 126
Structure
  organizational · 37, 120, 126, 149
Styles
  management · 52
Synthesis case · 21

T

Task technology
  routines of · 72
Tasks
  work · *See* Work tasks
Teamwork · 52, 72
Termination · 21, 46
  legal issues of · 59
  procedures · 103
Total Quality Management · 72
Training · 134

U

Unions · 103
United States Military · 89, 155

V

Violence
  workplace · 85

W

Work design · 37
Work ethics · 59
Work specialization · 37
Work tasks,
  analyzing · 37
Workplace violence · 85
Workspace design · 37

90 0267668 6

WITHDRAWN
FROM
UNIVERSITY OF PLYMOUTH
LIBRARY SERVICES

A Guide to Publishing User Manuals

Charles Seale-Hayne Library
University of Plymouth
(01752) 588 588
LibraryandITenquiries@plymouth.ac.uk

KEN WHITAKER

WILEY TECHNICAL COMMUNICATION LIBRARY

DESIGN   EVALUATION   MANAGEMENT   RESEARCH   WRITING

SERIES ADVISERS:

JoAnn T. Hackos—Comtech Services, Inc., Denver, CO

William Horton—William Horton Consulting, Boulder, CO

Janice Redish—American Institutes for Research, Washington, DC

SERIES TITLES

JoAnn T. Hackos—Managing Your Documentation Projects

Larry S. Bonura—The Art of Indexing

Jeffrey Rubin—Handbook of Usability Testing: How to Plan, Design, and Conduct Effective Tests

Karen A. Schriver—Dynamics in Document Design: Creating Texts for Readers

Nancy L. Hoft—International Technical Communication

Ken Whitaker—A Guide to Publishing User Manuals

Jack DeLand—Mastering Win Help

OTHER TITLES OF INTEREST

William Horton—The Icon Book: Visual Symbols for Computer Systems and Documentation

Deborah Hix and H. Rex Hartson—Developing User Interfaces: Ensuring Usability Through Product & Process

William Horton—Illustrating Computer Documentation: The Art of Presenting Information on Paper and OnLine

William Horton—Designing & Writing Online Documentation, Help Files to Hypertext

R. John Brockmann—Writing Better Computer User Documentation, From Paper to Hypertext, Second Edition

Tom Badgett and Corey Sandler—Creating Multimedia on Your PC

Robert Virkus—Quark PrePress: A Guide to Desktop Production for Graphics Professionals

Helena Rojas-Fernandez and John Jerney—FrameMaker for UNIX Solutions

Jim Mischel—The Developer's Guide to WINHELP.EXE: Harnessing the Windows Help Engine